PLAY BALL!

A Keystone Book is so designated to distinguish it from the typical scholarly monograph that a university press publishes. It is a book intended to serve the citizens of Pennsylvania by educating them and others, in an entertaining way, about aspects of the history, culture, society, and environment of the state as part of the Middle Atlantic region.

PLAY BALL!

THE STORY OF
LITTLE LEAGUE®
BASEBALL

Lance and Robin Van Auken

A Keystone Book
The Pennsylvania State University Press
University Park, Pennsylvania

Library of Congress Cataloging-in-Publication Data

Van Auken, Lance.
    Play ball! : the story of Little League Baseball / Lance and Robin Van Auken.
        p.   cm.
    Includes index.
    ISBN 0-271-02118-7 (alk. paper)
    1. Little League Baseball, Inc. 2. Baseball for children. I. Van Auken, Robin. II. Title.

  GV880.5.V35   2001
  796.357'62—dc21

                                                          00-068819

Copyright © 2001 The Pennsylvania State University
All rights reserved
Printed in Canada
Published by The Pennsylvania State University Press,
University Park, PA 16802-1003

It is the policy of The Pennsylvania State University Press to use acid-free paper for the first printing of all clothbound books. Publications on uncoated stock satisfy the minimum requirements of American National Standard for Information Sciences—Permanence of Paper for Printed Library Materials, ANSI Z39.48–1992.

To Sarah, Lance, and Ruth

To Susan, a true Little Leaguer

To our families

To the millions of
good Little League volunteers

To Carl Stotz

And to the memory
of those we love and miss,
Mom and Dad

Contents

Preface and Acknowledgments

First-time visitors to Williamsport, Pennsylvania—the birthplace of Little League Baseball—may be surprised to find two shrines to Little League. There's a Carl E. Stotz Field in Williamsport and a Howard J. Lamade Stadium in South Williamsport. "Why two?" some might ask. "And which is the *real* home of Little League Baseball?"

At first glance, these are easy questions to answer. Carl E. Stotz Field is near the site of Little League's founding, but it is no longer Little League's home. Lamade Stadium, part of the Little League Baseball International Headquarters complex and home of Little League since 1959, is where the Little League Baseball World Series is played every year. For this reason it is the place most people think of when they think of Little League.

But behind these simple answers lies a much more fascinating and complicated story, one that still has deep reverberations in the Williamsport community, and one that will undoubtedly surprise many fans of Little League. That is the story we tell in this book.

It has been a challenge to digest six decades of history involving 30 million people, because the story of Little League Baseball also belongs to countless boys and girls, and to their moms and dads. Carl Stotz, Little League, Peter J. McGovern, Dr. Creighton J. Hale, Stephen D. Keener, and everyone who ever played in or volunteered for Little League are intertwined forever. We need to be respectful of the contributions of those who helped to shape the program, and of the fact that they have also, in a way, helped to shape the country and the world at the same time.

This story has many heroes. Carl Stotz, for instance, was the right man at the right place at the right time for Little League to thrive in its infancy. Dr. Creighton Hale is a hero as well, and his contributions to Little League Baseball (and to baseball in general) are well documented. Steve Keener too is a hero, for his fence-mending and his rock-solid love and devotion—first to his family, then to Little League.

We the authors are typical of Little League families worldwide. Our generation was lucky to have families involved in building the first Little Leagues, and we hope our children will carry on that tradition. Every spring, we gathered at our local Cross Bayou Little League field in Largo, Florida, to prepare for opening day. The final touch to the field has always been the planting of fresh flowers around the monument at Robert D. Van Auken Field. Robert Van Auken was a Little League pioneer, and today his children, their wives, and his grandchildren still manage teams, mow grass, umpire, clean concession stands, and raise children in that healthful environment.

Our branch of the Van Auken family came to Williamsport at the invitation of Steve

Keener, to become a part of the Little League Headquarters family. We moved because of our love for Little League and in the belief that, as an organization, Little League can do great things for the children of the world.

This is not to say that each of us has experienced Little League in the same way. One of us has fond memories of being coached by Dad, watching older brothers play ball, and growing up as a "ballfield rat." The other (guess who!) remembers watching her brothers play ball and *not* being allowed to play herself, because she was a girl, and recalls that she was a teenager by the time Little League admitted girls. Our recollections of Little League as adults have been very different as well. One of us had the thrill of coaching our son and umpiring in the World Series, and the other had the satisfaction (perhaps not quite as thrilling) of working in the concession stand, running bake sales, and cheering from the stands. Thus, it is fair to say that our different experiences have given us distinct views on Little League Baseball. This has been a real advantage in writing this book, because not all readers' experiences with Little League have been or will be the same. We've tried to be sensitive to that in telling Little League's story. When the opportunity arose to write this book, we eagerly took on the task. A comprehensive history of Little League has never been written, even though Little League has touched tens of millions of lives since 1938, when Carl Stotz made a promise to his nephews in his backyard. We were compelled to write, also, by our love and profound respect for baseball itself, and the realization that so much of life's highs and lows are reflected in the complexities—and simplicities—of a baseball game.

We are especially indebted to Little League Baseball, Incorporated, for the use of its archives, and to Steve Keener, Dr. Hale, Nancy Scudder, Jud Rogers, Mike Miller, Wilbert "Go Army" Wilson, Ron Scott, Joe Losch, Ted Trivigno, and the many dedicated employees of Little League who were invaluable to this effort. We also wish to thank Karen Stotz Myers, Grayce Stotz, and Monya Lee Adkins for the use of Carl Stotz's memorabilia, and Penny and Jim Vanderlin and all the Original League volunteers for their encouragement. We are grateful to Kenneth Loss for use of excerpts from the book *A Promise Kept: The Story of the Founding of Little League Baseball*, by Carl Stotz as told to Loss, and to *Miami Herald* columnist and Little League graduate Dave Barry, for his generosity and for making our lives brighter with his stories. Thanks are also due to Putsee Vannucci for many of the pictures from the Little League archives used in this book.

Many thanks to Sandra Rife, director of the Lycoming County Historical Society, and to Janice Trapp, Helen Yoas, and librarians of the James V. Brown Library. We appreciate the use of the *Williamsport Sun-Gazette* archives and the support of Jim Carpenter, Jim Barr, Dan White, Dave Troisi, and, in particular, Janice Ogurcak. Special thanks to Lou Hunsinger Jr. and David Voight for sharing their considerable knowledge of baseball.

Also, we cannot overlook the importance of three women, Margaret Gisolo, Katherine Massar, and Maria Pepe, whose courage and pioneer spirit helped to shape the future of Little League, of baseball, and of sports in general.

We are grateful to Scott and Kathie Rosenberg for their generosity and friendship. We are also grateful to Jeff Elijah for allowing us to reprint his essay on the first Little League program in Bosnia and Herzegovina.

We also wish to thank Peter J. Potter, editor-in-chief of Penn State University Press, for inviting us to write this book, and Peggy Hoover, copy editor, for her extraordinary patience and expertise. The entire staff has been professional, friendly, and thorough.

We will never forget Charlie and Vivian Brush, Cyle and Calvin Van Auken, Don and Carol Machen, Lynn Kasica, Larry Smith, Frank Dubee, John Boland, John Ambler, Bob Gibson, Chip Ford, Fred Andress, the Staffeld family, the Pauley family, Brian Adair, Kevin Smalley, Kenny Danielski, Bernie Futchko, Alan and Donna Godfrey, Gray Rutherford, and the countless volunteers we have worked beside in leagues in Florida and Pennsylvania.

And finally, thank you to our families for being so supportive. We love you all.

Dave Barry Recalls

I played Little League Baseball in the late 1950s and early 1960s when I was growing up in Armonk, New York. Just about all the boys in my class were in Little League; it dominated our lives in the late spring and early summer. We started around second grade, playing in what was called the "Farm Team" league; our uniforms were baseball hats, and T-shirts.

When we got older and more skillful, we got to go to the "big league," which was the Little League. We were issued real baseball uniforms (some of which had been worn by Armonk boys before us). I loved wearing my uniform; I thought it was the coolest article of clothing I owned.

The Armonk Little League teams were named after real Major League Baseball teams: the Dodgers, Giants, Yankees, Red Sox, etc. I was on the Indians. My uniform shirt said "Indians" across the front, but the shirt was a little too big for me (or I was a little too small for the shirt) such that the "I" and the "s" kind of got lost under my arms, so it looked like my team was called the "ndian."

It's funny, but after forty years I can't remember much else about a lot of the boys I grew up with, but if you give me one of their names, I can usually remember what Little League team he played on.

I was never a particularly good player. I threw left-handed, so I got to play first base, which I liked because I got to be involved in a lot of plays. I hated playing in the outfield, because I was never any good at judging where fly balls would land. They almost never landed in my glove.

I wasn't much of a power hitter, but I could usually make contact with the ball. Fortunately, the quality of fielding was such that if you put the ball into play—even only a few feet from home plate—there was always a chance you'd wind up with a triple.

Little League was my first, and best, exposure to organized sports. I learned a lot: what it feels like to have to perform under pressure; how to be part of, and have obligations to, a team; how to win; and how to lose. (We Indians got pretty good at losing.) I saw that hard competition could bring players on both teams closer together; I also saw that the desire to win, if uncontrolled, could turn some people—adults as well as kids—into jerks.

But most of my memories of Little League are positive. And I still like to play first base.

Pulitzer Prize–winning journalist Dave Barry played Little League Baseball as a boy in the 1950s and 1960s in Armonk, New York.

Early Series action finds a Roswell, New Mexico, batter swinging at a missed pitch in the 1956 Little League World Series. This photograph, like many in this book, was taken by Putsee Vannucci, who has documented every Little League World Series since 1947.

Introduction

On a typical spring evening, Little League Baseball is played on 12,000 fields in every U.S. state and 104 other countries by 360,000 children. The next day, a new group of 360,000 takes the fields.

With more than 4 million people playing and volunteering on Little League fields each year, the story of the world's largest organized youth-sports program is the story of everyone. Every conceivable human emotion is possible on a Little League Baseball field. From its tragedies to its triumphs, Little League is the story of every son, daughter, mother, father, neighbor, and friend. It's where everyone involved learns the lessons of character, courage, and loyalty, whether they become astronauts aboard the space shuttle, Pulitzer Prize–winning columnists, Olympic athletes, rock 'n' roll singers, professional baseball players, or just ordinary people. In turn, they teach their own children those same lessons.

Howard J. Lamade Stadium is filled with fans for a pre-championship game during the 1999 Little League Baseball World Series.

Each Little League season climaxes with the Little League Baseball World Series in Williamsport, Pennsylvania. It is truly a world championship, even though only eleven- and twelve-year-olds can play. More than 7,400 teams in 104 countries begin playoffs less than two months before the championship game. In fact, as many games are played in the fifty days leading up to the World Series as are played in six full seasons of Major League Baseball. ABC-TV has broadcast the final game on *Wide World of Sports* every year since 1963. Most of the preliminary Little League World Series games leading up to the championship are televised nationally on ESPN and ESPN2.

The games of the Little League World Series are played on the Kentucky bluegrass of Howard J. Lamade Stadium. Athletic-field experts lend their time year-round to help maintain the playing surface, which rivals most professional diamonds. With permanent seating for 10,000 spectators, the stadium includes terraced hills beyond the outfield fence that accommodate 30,000 more spectators on blankets, lawn chairs, and grass.

Little League World Series participants play on a global stage. Upon arrival in Williamsport, a Little League official reminds them that their actions—how they react to good fortune as well as to adversity—will help determine the world's opinion of their hometown. Twenty-two nations or territories have sent teams to the Little League World Series, and some have welcomed the young ambassadors home with ceremonies befitting war heroes—whether they won or lost in Williamsport. For most of the eleven- and twelve-year-olds, it will be their first time on television, and they will be watched by more than 10 million people.

After a Little League World Series game, the winning and losing teams make the long trek up the hill to dormitories. Swarming fans block the way, seeking autographs, and bold, flirtatious girls bestow kisses and hugs on blushing adolescent boys. A few players are asked to speak, along with their adult managers, at a news conference in a tent behind the stadium. Reporters range from part-time writers for weekly newspapers to award-winning "big guns" from *Sports Illustrated*.

About 120 miles north of Lamade Stadium is another town, sleeping at the headwaters of the Susquehanna, the west branch of which flows through Williamsport. That place, Cooperstown, New York, also is known for its legendary roots in baseball.

Four miles northwest of Lamade is Bowman Field, the second-oldest minor league baseball field still operated as such. About 200 feet beyond the outfield fence of Bowman Field is a monument to an event that occurred there in 1939, when the world was a very different place: Frozen in granite, three little boys in baggy baseball uniforms reach skyward with mitts for an unseen ball, at the site of the first Little League game.

Despite its apple-pie image, the story of Little League is not without controversy, even upheaval. During the decades since the first Little League was formed in 1939, Little League survived its own civil war of sorts, and has played a role in race relations, the cold war, gender equity, and easing ethnic tensions in Bosnia.

Little League has grown in scope far beyond anything its founder, Carl Stotz, or anyone else in 1939, could have imagined. In some ways, and in thousands of communi-

ties, it closely resembles the league Stotz and his followers had envisioned. But in many other ways it is far different.

It is not surprising that among the 30 million or so who have worn Little League uniforms, the ranks have included hundreds of eventual Major League players and a handful of Baseball Hall of Famers. National Hockey League players, National Basketball Association players, National Football League players, business tycoons, rock 'n' roll stars, one U.S. President and one vice president, actors, U.S. senators, Rhodes Scholars, astronauts, and Pulitzer Prize–winners have all played Little League baseball.

So this is the story of Little League Baseball, but it is more than a sports story. It is also the story of Little League's phenomenal growth, from thirty players and a few volunteers in a sleepy Pennsylvania town, to the largest organized children's sports program in the world; the story of detractors and benefactors; and the story of how Little League has reflected—and affected—American society.

Dwight D. Eisenhower, Thirty-Fourth President of the United States

"When I was a small boy in Kansas, a friend of mine

and I went fishing. I told him I wanted to

be a real Major League Baseball player, a genuine

professional like Honus Wagner. My friend said

that he'd like to be President of the United States.

Neither of us got our wish."

one

A MAN'S GAME, A BOY'S GAME

In a small stone building in Williamsport, Pennsylvania, are the gnarled remains of a lilac bush and its roots. This is certainly not the only artifact connecting Carl Edwin Stotz with the founding of Little League Baseball, yet its significance has the legendary quality of George Washington's cherry tree—at least in Williamsport, where the details of Little League's founding are still debated.

CREATING A LEGEND

For decades, many believed the roots of baseball itself could be traced to Abner Doubleday. In 1907, after two years of research, a committee of baseball's elder statesmen headed by sporting goods tycoon Albert G. Spalding decided that Doubleday had invented the game in Cooperstown, New York, in 1839. But there is no evidence that Doubleday invented baseball, save the early twentieth-century recollections of an elderly man named Abner Graves, who had lived in Cooperstown. Graves told Spalding's committee that Doubleday had drawn up rudimentary rules for a game he called "base ball" and divided a group of men into two teams to play.

Primarily interested in establishing that baseball was a thoroughly American game, Spalding's committee accepted the story and designated

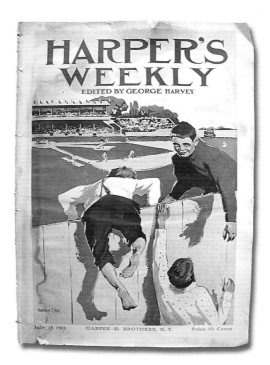

Doubleday as baseball's father. In fact, Spalding actually played a decisive role in the committee's decision, steering the committee to accept Graves's account. In Spalding's view, baseball *had* to be American.

That baseball could actually be traced to a union of two British games—cricket and rounders—was unacceptable to the committee. Cricket, a tedious game played by gentlemen on perfectly groomed lawns, certainly could not be a distant relative of America's national pastime, they believed. And rounders, a children's game in which runners could be put "out" by being pelted with the ball (the bases varied in number, usually from two to five), was similarly unpalatable.

Doubleday died on January 26, 1893, fourteen years before Spalding's committee designated him as baseball's inventor. But the bronze plaques on the obelisk over his tomb at Arlington National Cemetery make no mention of baseball. His obituary in the *New York Times* in January 1893 does not mention the game he supposedly founded, even though Americans already knew baseball as the "national pastime." Doubleday himself never claimed to have invented baseball. Yet even to the present day, and even though there is no evidence historians can find to support the legend, Doubleday is known most for being the father of baseball.

But the myth, which Doubleday never had a chance to refute, lives on, and in seeking a site for the National Baseball Hall of Fame and Museum, Cooperstown seemed a natural choice. After all, Spalding's committee had decided it was the birthplace of baseball, even though at the time and later the decision was seriously questioned. Doubleday Field in Cooperstown today is second only to the Hall of Fame itself as a baseball shrine. Even the United States Military Academy at West Point fell into step in 1939 on the

ABNER DOUBLEDAY

General Abner Doubleday was a military hero who served in the Mexican War and the Civil War, but he did not invent baseball.

The "Doubleday legend" is a quaint yarn about Abner Doubleday inventing the game of base-ball at Cooperstown, New York, in 1839. But Abner Doubleday is not the originator of the modern-day game. The legend came out of a committee formed in 1907 to investigate and establish baseball's origins. Unfortunately, a fire destroyed the committee's research, save for testimony offered by one Abner Graves, an elderly engineer who may have been a boy-hood friend of Doubleday.

In a letter to the committee, Graves wrote that "either in the spring prior to or following the 'Log Cabin and Hard Cider' campaign of General William H. Harrison for presidency" he had seen Doubleday organizing "20 to 50 boys" into a game of "town ball"—a form of "round-ers." Graves claimed that Doubleday placed the boys on teams with eleven players on each side and used four bases during the game, and thus that he had witnessed the invention of baseball.

The head of the committee, Albert G. Spalding, liked the tale, especially because he was eager to establish baseball as an Ameri-can game. The committee was glad to go along with Spalding and therefore declared Doubleday the father of baseball.

Although baseball historians have easily refuted the "Doubleday legend," baseball owners and players legitimated the claim by observing the game's "birth" with a season-long cente-nary celebration in 1939.

Many historians consider Spalding's collusion with the "Doubleday legend" spurious. Author David Quentin Voigt, in his *American Baseball: From the Gentleman's Sport to the Commissioner System* (Penn State Press, 1983), wrote: "In seeking a motive for Spalding's deliberate myth making, one finds him unscrupulous in his chauvinistic de-termination to 'prove' the American origin of the game."

Spalding disagreed with writers of his day, claiming baseball, like America, must be "free from the trammels of English traditions, customs, conventionalities."

But who is Abner Doubleday?

Born June 26, 1819, in Saratoga County, New York, Doubleday was part of the Class of 1842 at the United States Military Academy at West Point, a school not disposed to allowing plebes (freshmen) time to invent games. He was a veteran officer of the Mexican War (1846–48), and he fired the first Union gun from Fort Sumter, South Carolina, in 1861 in re-sponse to a Confederate attack at the begin-ning of the Civil War. In 1862 he was appointed brigadier general of volunteers and placed in command of the defenses of Washington, D.C., earning a promotion to major general later that year. He then went on to distinguish himself in battles at Bull Run, Antietam, Fredericksburg, Chan-cellorsville, and Gettysburg.

After General John Reynolds's battlefield death, he commanded the I Corps at Gettys-burg and held the Federal left during much of the first day of battle. Although his troops were eventually pushed back to Cemetery Hill in retreat, he held the Confederates off long enough to allow the Union Army to take strong defensive positions. He served in the army until retiring in 1873.

Abner Doubleday's war-hero status faded from memory, though, and—some would argue—he became known for something far more important. His name became forever linked with baseball.◆

centennial of baseball's "founding," naming its baseball venue for a distinguished graduate who had nothing to do with the game.

Actually, the origins of baseball predate anything Spalding or anyone on the committee considered. Children have played variations of stick-and-ball games for centuries. Villages and towns in America's colonies each had versions of the game, though it went by many names, including "town ball," "stick ball," "round ball," and sometimes "base ball." Over time, and as transportation improved, the games played in towns and villages eventually began to resemble one another more closely. The melting pot of the various baseball-like incarnations evolved in the mid-nineteenth century into something very close to today's game.

So, like the majority of Americans in 1907, when the committee did its work, baseball has a European pedigree, but it acquired its own identity on U.S. soil when the game coalesced, shaking off its aristocratic ancestry.

Baseball could not have been more American.

EVOLUTION OF A MANLY GAME

War, and those who make war, have played a big part in baseball's history. Soldiers played ball at Valley Forge during the Revolution, and both sides played it in the Civil War. Later, American soldiers introduced the game overseas, with an assist from missionaries. Athletics in general have long been connected with soldiering. Soldiers have always played team sports recreationally, but it was more than mere recreation. Outside the basketball/hockey facility at West Point, one of General Douglas MacArthur's favorite sayings is chiseled in polished black marble: "Upon the fields of friendly strife are sown the seeds that upon other fields on other days will bear the fruits of victory."

The link between war and sports goes back even further. The Duke of Wellington once said that the Battle of Waterloo, Napoleon's downfall, "was won on the playing fields of Eton." Hundreds of years earlier, English kings banned the playing of golf and football because it distracted men from archery—considered more important to the defense of the realm.

Centuries before Europeans arrived in North America, pre-Columbian Americans played games with balls as recreation. Ironically, one can argue that baseball really does have its earliest roots in America, further back in time than the arrival of European settlers. It is safe to assume, however, that if Spalding's committee had been aware of this evidence it still would have been rejected in favor of the Doubleday myth.

Baseball historian Harold Peterson, author of *The Man Who Invented Baseball,* set the record straight: "Abner Doubleday didn't invent baseball. Baseball invented Abner Doubleday." There is little argument now that the watershed moment for baseball came on June 19, 1846, when Alexander Cartwright's team, the New York Knickerbocker Baseball Club, met the New York Baseball Club for a scheduled game just across the river from Manhattan at Elysian Fields in Hoboken, New Jersey. But for several years, well-heeled

A drawing by Jacques Le Moyne depicts a sixteenth-century ball game in the New World.

AN AMERICAN INDIAN BALL GAME

There is archaeological evidence that people have played ball since the early days of civilization. Ancient cultures in Persia, Egypt, and Greece played the games for recreation and as part of certain ceremonies. Ball-and-stick games became popular throughout Europe by the Middle Ages as early as the fifth century, but they were widely considered children's games.

As they led expeditions into the territory of the Apalachee (now Florida's panhandle) in the New World, both Pánfilo de Narváez and Hernando De Soto discovered a more intense version of the game during the sixteenth and seventeenth centuries.

According to historian Robin C. Brown, author of *Florida's First People* (1994), "The most important athletic event was a ball game which was pursued with a ferocity that almost equaled warfare." Similar to a modern-day rugby match, two teams of up to fifty men each used a small, hard buckskin ball filled with dried mud. The players could use only hands and feet to move the ball toward the goal. The single goal was a tall post bearing an eagle's nest. The point was earned when the ball hit the post, and two points were awarded when it landed in the nest.

One of the first recorded histories of a ball game in North America is a Spanish missionary's eyewitness account written in 1677:

And they fall upon one another at full tilt. And the last to arrive climb up over their bodies, using them as stairs. And, to enter, others step on their faces, heads, or bellies, as they encounter them, taking no notice [of them] and aiming kicks without any concern whether it is to the face or body, while in other places still others pull at arms and legs with no concern as to whether they may be dislocated or not, while still others have their mouths filled with dirt. When this pileup begins to come untangled, they are accustomed to find four or five stretched out like tuna; over them are others gasping for breath, because, inasmuch as some are wont to swallow the ball, they are made to vomit it up by squeezing their windpipe or by kicks to the stomach. Over there lie others with an arm or leg broken.

Certainly, the Apalachee game does not resemble baseball, other than being an athletic competition involving men and a small, round ball. But there is another parallel: "Skilled players were prized," says Brown. "To keep them on the village team they were given a house, their crops were planted for them, and their misdeeds were overlooked—much like athletes today." ◆

New York gentlemen had been meeting in Manhattan for informal pickup games.

Cartwright and Daniel Lucius Adams, a New Hampshire physician, laid out the rules for this first scheduled baseball game between two organized teams. The rules established foul lines and the diamond shape of the infield, and allowed for runners to be put out only if they were tagged or thrown out in a "force play," not by being hit with the ball—the previous custom. The game lasted four innings, and Cartwright's team lost 23–1.

Sports in America changed forever after that day in 1846. The Industrial Revolution meant more leisure time, for men mostly, and the new game helped fill the gap. Baseball teams sprung up around New York, each usually affiliated with a particular trade. Organizers established the National Association of Base Ball Players in 1857, eleven years after the first game.

It is important to note that baseball evolved, and continued to evolve. Rules were refined. Originally, the first team to score twenty-one runs won, but games were too long and eventually the team with the most runs at the end of nine innings prevailed. No longer could players use their caps to catch the ball. In the 1850s, instead of the original forty-two paces between first base and third base, the distance between each base was set at 90 feet, where it remains today. Umpires were permitted to call strikes, but until 1887 a batter could still call for a high or low pitch. The "fly rule" was adopted in the 1860s, with much dissent, allowing a batter to continue running if a fair ball touched the ground. Before that time, any clean catch—even on a ground ball—resulted in an out. Proponents said the fly rule would make the game more "manly," as it demanded greater skill from the fielders. Gloves followed, but met resistance from traditionalists.

In the late 1850s Henry Chadwick, a newspaperman and shortstop on the Knicker-

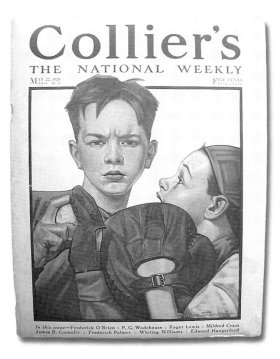

LEFT
Independent,
May 22, 1920.

RIGHT
Collier's,
May 22, 1920.

bockers, convinced the New York newspapers to devote space to the new game sweeping the city. Eventually he established the format for the box score. British-born and "proper," Chadwick gained fame as perhaps the most respected man in baseball's early days. He cast off cricket as his favorite sport, embracing the faster-paced baseball. (The same argument would be made against baseball more than 100 years later, in favor of such sports as football and basketball.)

Chadwick struggled, as many did, to keep the new game in the province of gentlemen. But as more people found baseball appealing, greed crept in. Team owners and ballpark operators began charging admission. Betting on games followed, and scandals after that. Professionalism crept in too, as club organizers created sham jobs for good players in return for their services on the baseball field.

By early 1861 there were sixty-two clubs in the National Association of Base Ball Players—most in the Northeast, where industrial jobs allowed men more time for baseball. In the cities of the largely agrarian South, though, it also took hold. Confederate forces attacked the Union garrison at Fort Sumter, South Carolina (with Abner Doubleday returning the fire!).

The Civil War raged for the next four years, but instead of curtailing baseball's march it helped it spread. Throughout the war, soldiers on both sides played baseball to pass the time between battles. Union soldiers confined to Confederate prisoner-of-war camps played baseball, introducing the game to Southern men. Guards at the Union camps also played, and Confederate prisoners picked the game up from them. Some brought the game home when the war ended, and before long many American towns had their own baseball teams.

GROWING PAINS

Baseball experienced growing pains. The rules were relatively simple, and players found ways to gain advantages. That did not sit well with those who wanted to keep baseball "genteel." At first, the pitcher merely served the ball to the batter so it could be hit. But pitchers experimented with deception by actually throwing the ball hard, in an attempt to retire batters on strikes. They found ways to make the trajectory of the balls curve as the pitch approached home plate. On the offense, enterprising players and coaches added bunts and base-stealing to the game. After all, the rules did not prohibit such shenanigans. Baseball players, managers, coaches, and team owners continued to seek ways to circumvent the rules, and still do.

Chicanery, to the dismay of those who considered such tactics ungentlemanly, became a permanent part of the game. With the sport still in its infancy, baseball purists were already yearning for the "good old days."

More outrage awaited baseball purists. Even though players supposedly were amateurs, under-the-table payments for services on the ballfield were common. In 1869, the Cincinnati Red Stockings shook off all pretense and took the field as the first openly professional baseball club. Harry Wright managed the team, salaries paid by a group of Ohio investors. The Red Stockings reeled off a long string of victories during two seasons before finally falling against the Brooklyn Atlantics in 1870.

The streak made Cincinnati the capital of the baseball world, temporarily wresting that title from New York. When the streak finally ended at New York's Capitoline Grounds with the 8–7 loss to the Atlantics, Wright said it was "the finest game ever played." Cincinnati's fans, however, were not so understanding. With the streak at an end, attendance fell and investors pulled out. The team disbanded, and some thought professional baseball would not recover.

Wright knew better. Undaunted, he took most of his players and the team name to Boston. After all, only two of his players were from Cincinnati, and to him baseball was a business. Many consider him to be baseball's first strategic genius, but his greatest contribution—openly paying his players—led to the formation of the first all-professional league, the National Association of Professional Baseball Players, in March 1871. Although the Association collapsed after the 1875 season, the National League of Professional Baseball Clubs followed in 1876 and endures today.

"THE ONLY PERFECT PLEASURE"

In 1850s New York, adult baseball teams became so plentiful that dozens of affiliated junior clubs for boys were formed. In many ways, baseball is a game well suited to boys, because great size and strength are not the key to success. Quick, sure-handed, and diminutive second basemen can be more valuable than hulking outfielders. Home runs, in fact, were a rarity in professional baseball until the "live ball" era of the twentieth cen-

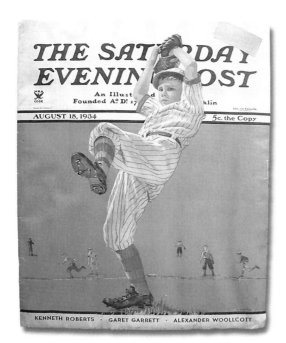

tury, so speed and finesse were the best qualities in a ballplayer. In the earliest days of professional baseball, the balls were more suited to the smaller parks and did not travel as far when hit. But as the game became more popular, more-lively balls were used, as seating capacity—and home run production—increased in the twentieth century.

Nevertheless, boys did not flock to the game. In the last few decades of the nineteenth century, child labor in America's cities did not allow time for such frivolities, and farm boys already worked long hours. Industrialization allowed more leisure time for men, though.

Boys were usually forced to play the game with substandard equipment. Homemade baseballs often consisted of a core of India rubber wound with wool and covered with hand-stitched leather. "Real" baseballs became so overused that the horsehide covers tore off when the stitching gave way. Friction tape became standard equipment for making mid-game repairs. Few boys' games featured real, intact baseball bats. Wooden bats break easily, or split along the grain, if not held just right when striking a ball. Small nails—along with the ubiquitous friction tape—repaired the salvageable ones. Lacking a proper bat, a handle from a broom or shovel would do.

Los Angeles Times columnist Jim Murray explained sandlot baseball for the readers of the 1967 Little League Western Regional Series program:

> What we had was a tarred road and 10 minutes between cars. First base was a rock, second base was a chalk square in the road and third base was a telephone pole. The biggest kid on the block was the pitcher, never mind whether he could get the ball over the plate or not. Usually, *he* called balls and strikes, too.

The ball was a taped spheroid about the size, density and weight of a small bowling ball. The bats were taped, too, because you broke them the first time you hit that miniature shot-put with them.

A few stores carried bats in boys' sizes, but they were usually made of unseasoned wood—not the better northern white ash used by early professionals. If these bats were not held right, a swing and contact could result in a two-foot splinter of wood pinwheeling into the infield. The problem endured in youth baseball until the early 1970s, when with help from Little League Baseball, sporting goods manufacturers introduced aluminum bats. As with most innovations in baseball, purists railed against the "ping" of aluminum, pining for the more satisfying "crack" of horsehide against wood. Eventually, nonwood bats would be used at almost every nonprofessional level of baseball.

Beanballs, purposeful or mistaken, became a problem too. Until the 1950s, even professional baseball players considered the use of helmets less than manly. Gloves for boys, introduced to the game in the late 1800s, became prized possessions. If a boy had a uniform it was probably homemade. Catchers' equipment exceeded unbroken bats in rarity for boys' baseball games. At best, the two catchers in a game could share a wire mask. Without chest protectors and shin guards, catchers stood far behind the plate to field their position.

Plenty of space to play the game existed outside the city, but manicured fields were almost nonexistent. Anything could be used as a base—a rock, a wooden post, or even a discarded newspaper. City boys either walked or took a trolley or ferry to open spaces. Sometimes the streets themselves became infields as players dodged wagons and horses.

Left to their own devices, boys found ways to emulate the adult heroes emerging from organized baseball. They met at appointed places at appointed times and chose sides. Usually the two best players, "captains," alternated picks until all the teams filled. Ability meant everything; social status meant nothing. The first pick's father could be a banker or a bum, but as long as he could hit, field, and throw, his caste on the baseball field reigned supreme.

Even a dearth of players could be overcome. One field (right or left) would simply be closed, depending on the propensity of the batter to hit one way or the other. A ball hit to the wrong field would be called foul. Other games allowed the players to rotate through several positions on the field, and the offense never had more than four players. When too many players showed up, the worst ones simply did not play. A hundred years later, psychologists decry such practices, which are still taking place on sandlots and school playgrounds today, as detrimental to a child's self-esteem.

Without umpires, the games sometimes dragged. Because there were no official balls and strikes, a batter could simply brush off pitches until he found one to his liking, prompting jeers from the defense as well as from his own teammates. Fistfights became common, the result of disagreements about what was foul or fair, safe or out.

Baseball, touted by some as a diversion to steer boys from idle pursuits, actually resulted in arrests. Some cities enacted ordinances prohibiting baseball games on Sunday. A well-hit ball resulting in a broken window could land a boy in children's court. Still, baseball became the game of choice for American boys. It was "the only perfect pleasure we ever knew," said famous attorney Clarence Darrow, who played baseball as a boy in the 1860s and 1870s.

Boys' baseball games in the nineteenth century and into the twentieth remained mostly of the sandlot variety, as the idea of fathers spending "quality time" with their sons had not taken hold. Only when fathers had more time to spend with their families—after the Great Depression—did organized boys' baseball take root and grow nationally.

BASEBALL BOOM

Meanwhile, organized baseball for men boomed as the century turned. More professional teams sprang up, most in the East and the Midwest. Baseball became quite competitive, far removed from the gentlemanly style of play Chadwick championed, though he remained involved in the sport. Fans and players alike mercilessly heckled the umpires, and sometimes attacked them.

Competition between leagues saw professional organizations rise and fall, with only two enduring. Wright's National Association lasted only four years and was supplanted by the National League in 1876. The American Association started in 1882 but died out in 1891. A year later, baseball's magnates formed "The National League and the American Association of Professional Base Ball Clubs," a twelve-team monopoly that wallowed in debt until its demise in 1901.

Along came another reformer, Byron Bancroft "Ban" Johnson. Born on January 6, 1864, the son of an Ohio professor, Johnson had covered the sport for the *Commercial Gazette* in Cincinnati, and then in 1893 took over the Western League, a struggling minor league operation—turning it into a financial success. While president of the Western League, Johnson grew to abhor the tactics of the monopoly league, so he founded the American League in 1901, primarily from the four least-profitable teams that had been cast off by the National League: Boston, Philadelphia, Washington, and Baltimore. Johnson, who weighed nearly 300 pounds, promised that the American League would bring families back into the ballpark by offering a more gentlemanly game, and specifically by pledging to stop umpire-baiting.

National League owners ignored Johnson at first, but not for long. The new league was making money and successfully luring some of the best players away from the "senior circuit." A two-year war ensued, with lawsuits, ticket-price battles, counter-raids of players, an offer to make Johnson president of the National League, and offers to the most successful American League cities to join the National fold. When the tactics failed, a truce—the National Agreement—ensued, and the present two-league system was formed. Johnson also is credited with proposing the end-of-season contest between the champions of the two leagues: the World Series. He retired in 1927 and died on March 28, 1931.

Baseball's popularity skyrocketed, fueled in part by the interest boys were showing in it. Boys lucky enough to live in or near cities with Major League Baseball teams witnessed some of the giants of the game playing in stadiums that were revered as temples. During the next fifty years, lifelong love affairs with baseball began in stadiums with names like Fenway Park, Ebbetts Field, Wrigley Field, and Yankee Stadium. For a boy, a trip to the ballpark developed into something akin to a religious experience.

Cities and social organizations launched fledgling attempts to establish boys' baseball as a way to solve social ills. School alone was not enough of an outlet. Baseball, many believed, could maintain health and keep boys out of trouble, while at the same time developing character and good morals. Schools began organizing athletic programs as early as the 1850s, with baseball a major part of the curriculum. By the start of the next century, when millions of children began attending public school regularly, most American boys had at least some exposure to playing baseball.

In the cities, the Young Men's Christian Association (YMCA) also helped to advance baseball. Hundreds of YMCAs offered athletics as a healthy outlet, and most offered baseball. The New York City YMCA sponsored a thirty-team baseball league for adolescent boys in 1889, a forerunner to Little League, and furnished the trainers. Local businesses, churches, public schools, and colleges sponsored the teams. The difference between the YMCA and later Little League Baseball was parental participation—or rather, lack of it. YMCA personnel, not parents, operated the Y-league games. Parents remained in the background there and in other pre–Little League programs organized around factories, churches, schools, or service clubs.

Other cities took notice, building playgrounds that included baseball fields. "The Playground Movement," part of the larger Progressive Movement, aimed to enhance the lives of Americans in general and children in particular. By 1911, hundreds of cities set aside public land for recreation, ignoring the cries of some—heard even today—that dedicating land to a baseball diamond was a waste of space benefiting only a few at the expense of many. But baseball had taken permanent root in American society, and diamonds became plentiful across the nation.

Meanwhile, professional baseball continued to grow, despite the scandals in the first three decades of the twentieth century. Worst of them was the Black Sox Scandal, in which several Chicago White Sox players were accused of throwing the 1919 World Series to Cincinnati. The players were acquitted for lack of evidence in court in 1920 but were banned forever from baseball by Kenesaw "Mountain" Landis, baseball's commissioner. Though the decision brought some credibility back to baseball, some thought its reputation had been irreparably damaged.

Then came George Herman "Babe" Ruth, who is credited with rescuing baseball, making it more popular than ever. Boys' baseball waited a bit longer for its savior, however. A few programs started here and there, but none could assemble a following much beyond a city's limit—until 1938.

That's when a man in Williamsport, Pennsylvania, stepped on a lilac bush in his backyard.

Nolan Ryan, baseball's all-time strikeout king

"Little League was a great period in my life.

We never won a championship,

but we tried real hard.

I guess that's what Little League

is all about—trying."

two

FROM A LILAC BUSH

The year 1939 was a pivotal year in baseball history as well as in world history. Nazi Germany crushed Poland, igniting World War II. The specter of Adolf Hitler controlling all of Europe led the American government to assist England with the Lend-Lease Act, while Americans remained blissfully isolated from the horrors of war. The Great Depression slowly abated, but it would soon be in full retreat as the manufacture of war materiel turned the U.S. economy around.

In baseball, 1939 developed into a year of beginnings and a particularly poignant conclusion: Lou Gehrig at once established one of baseball's most important records and brought it to a profound, tragic halt. Baseball's "Iron Horse" played his last game on May 2, ending an incredible string of 2,130 consecutive games played. On June 21, it was revealed that the Yankee captain had amyotrophic lateral sclerosis, a fatal disease. On July 4, the man who personified the word "hero" only solidified that title when he announced to a sold-out Yankee Stadium crowd that he considered himself "the luckiest man on the face of the earth."

Gehrig died in June 1941. His mother, Christina, outlived her son and later served on the board of directors of the Milford (Connecticut) Little League. More than a half-century later a former Little Leaguer named Cal Ripken Jr. broke Lou Gehrig's streak of consecutive games played.

Ted Williams, announcer for ABC's *Wide World of Sports,* interviews a player during the 1967 Little League World Series.

Also in 1939, a Boston Red Sox left fielder named Ted Williams batted .458 in the last three weeks of June, finishing with a batting average of .327 with 31 homers and 145 runs batted in — in his *rookie* season. Joe DiMaggio overcame an early-season injury, returning to the Yankees lineup on June 7, 1939, and going on to his greatest season, batting .381. Following his playing days, Ted Williams dispensed hitting advice to twenty-one-year-old Boston Red Sox outfielder Carl Yastrzemski, a former Little Leaguer inducted into the Baseball Hall of Fame in 1989. He also provided color commentary for ABC Sports at the Little League World Series. Joe DiMaggio, the kind of player for whom the Hall of Fame was built, gave batting tips to eleven- and twelve-year-old players at the Little League World Series in 1976.

On June 12, 1939, ignoring history, baseball celebrated the centennial of its founding by dedicating the National Baseball Hall of Fame in sleepy Cooperstown, New York. Cooperstown is a burg of 2,500 on the shore of Otsego Lake, the headwater of the Susquehanna River. At its origin, the Susquehanna is little more than a trickle as it winds southward, past Binghamton and into Pennsylvania. The West Branch of the Susquehanna flows through another sleepy town, Williamsport, Pennsylvania, on a course to its terminus in Chesapeake Bay.

A city of about 44,000 today, Williamsport is still known as the *former* "Lumber

Capital of the World," for the West Branch was a natural highway for moving lumber to sawmills. Rich soil in the old mountains along the river produced huge amounts of lumber, which in turn made many people wealthy. Before the turn of the century, Williamsport claimed more millionaires per capita than any other city of its size in the world.

But Williamsport's heyday ended long before 1939. A series of devastating floods and overcutting doomed the industry, and lumber barons left town. Williamsport waited nearly a half-century for a new identity. Still, some of the finest homes in the world, built in the late 1800s and early 1900s, contain decorative wood from the trees of North Central Pennsylvania.

On June 6, 1939, nobody could have predicted that the little river town would acquire a new identity and become a permanent part of baseball lore. June 6 was fifteen days before Lou Gehrig's illness was revealed; two weeks before Ted Williams destroyed American League pitching; one day before Joe DiMaggio's storied return to the Yankee lineup; and six days before Cooperstown became the site of baseball's holiest shrine. And June 6 was the day two teams met, for the first time, in a Little League game.

The true roots of the momentous events of 1939 are much deeper though. The first Little League game didn't *just happen.*

LILAC BUSH ROOTS

As a boy, Carl Edwin Stotz (1910–1992) loved baseball, and his experiences were typical. In an interview recorded on video shortly before his death, he led a reporter through some of the mementos and memories he had amassed from the early days of Little League. He picked up a ball covered in friction tape and described the sub-par equipment, handed down from older players, that boys were forced to use in his day: "This is the kind of ball we had—that's the tape ball. Bats? [We used] one that had been broken and nailed together, and tape put around it. And when you choked up on it, the end of it was in your stomach."

LEFT

As a teenager, Carl Stotz played for St. John's Lutheran in the Sunday School League in Williamsport. In this photo from 1923, Carl is kneeling, fourth from the left.

RIGHT

"Major" Gehron and Jimmy Gehron, baseball-loving nephews of Carl Stotz, were the impetus for Stotz creating the Little League program in 1938. The brothers played on Stotz's Lycoming Dairy team.

Jimmy and Harold "Major" Gehron were typical of American boys too. They lived in Williamsport, and they loved baseball. The boys frequented the Williamsport Grays Eastern League games at Bowman Field in town. When they could not attend, they listened to play-by-play coverage of the games on radio station WRAK. In their backyard games of catch, Jimmy and Major imitated sportscaster Sol Wolf's commentary as they mimicked their heroes. Jimmy, age six, and Major, age eight, along with their Uncle Tuck, helped give Williamsport its new identity.

"Uncle Tuck"—Carl Stotz—was the kind of uncle a boy loves to have. Even though he rarely attended games at Bowman Field, Carl never quite got baseball, or childhood, out of his system. As a teenager, he once said, he "lived and breathed baseball." By the time he reached his late twenties, the Great Depression, marriage to Grayce Ake of Hollidaysburg, and a two-year-old daughter, Monya Lee, drove Carl's intense love of baseball into temporary dormancy. But when his nephews came around, Carl indulged them. A clerk at the Pure Oil Company, Carl relived his boyhood days through Jimmy

WILLIAMSPORT: GATEWAY TO THE MAJORS

Williamsport, Pennsylvania, is not just "The Birthplace of Little League Baseball." It also has a rich minor-league legacy. Early in its history, baseball clubs scheduled matches on the city's common grounds and sandlot fields, and locals gathered to watch the games. On July 29, 1865, some 200 miles west of the center of the baseball universe, New York City, the Williamsport Athletic Club battled Philadelphia & Erie Railroad in the first recorded baseball game in Williamsport. The game tied at 27–27.

By the 1870s, professional teams formed and baseball became a business. Club investors and local lumber barons anticipated larger ballparks with grandstand seating for paying crowds, like Williamsport's upriver neighbor, Lock Haven, which had just constructed its Oak (Herdic) Park racetrack. In 1926, Williamsport entered the modern era of professional minor-league baseball when it constructed a new ballpark, Memorial Field, at the northwest corner of the Max M. Brown Memorial Park. In 1932 the name was changed to Bowman Field.

The ballpark was a multipurpose stadium, long before the concept came into fashion, also hosting boxing matches and even high school football games. Its original dimensions—400 feet to left field, 450 feet to center, and 367 feet to right field—were cavernous compared with the field's current measurements. Only ten home runs were hit out of the ballpark from 1926 to 1933, prompting officials to shorten the distance.

Al Bellandi, an Italian immigrant hired to dig posts for Bowman Field's inner fence in 1935, so impressed his employers that he was appointed head groundskeeper. Although the Detroit Tigers and the Baltimore Orioles tried to lure Bellandi away, he devoted his life to maintaining the ballpark until he retired in 1961.

The city's minor-league team, the Williamsport Grays, a franchise in the Eastern League, earned Williamsport the right to brag that it was the "Gateway to the Majors," as nearly 400 former Williamsport Grays players have graduated to the major leagues. The list includes Jim Bunning, Nolan Ryan, Bill Mazeroski, Ron Swoboda, Jim Rice, and Tino Martinez; managers "School Boy" Rowe, Glen Killinger, Spence Abbott, and Harry Hinchman; and Williamsport natives Don Manno (Boston Braves), Dick Welteroth (Washington Senators), and Bill Witmer, among others. Some of the National Baseball Hall of Fame players and personalities also visiting the field were Connie Mack, Branch Rickey, and Casey Stengel.

Thanks to Carl Stotz's close ties to the Grays and subsequent affiliates, minor-league baseball in Williamsport played a critical role in nurturing Little League Baseball during its early years. Little Leaguers were often invited to play exhibition games at Bowman Field, and during the Little League World Series the teams were allowed to use Bowman's lockers and shower facilities, which was convenient because the two fields were only yards from each other. In August 1940, Little Leaguers were included in the Grays' weeklong seventy-fifth anniversary celebration of baseball in Williamsport. Undoubtedly these ties helped Little League gain exposure it would not have otherwise enjoyed, as hopefuls spread the word about the fledgling youth baseball organization beyond the borders of Pennsylvania.

Bowman Field, once considered the gem of the Eastern League, remains the second-oldest operating minor-league ballpark in the nation. Spending a warm June evening in its stands still is considered a treat, as fans, tossing shucked peanut shells on the concrete, shout, "Strike him out!" ◆

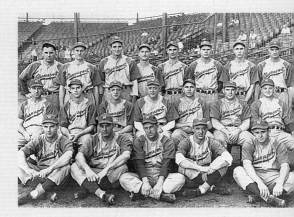

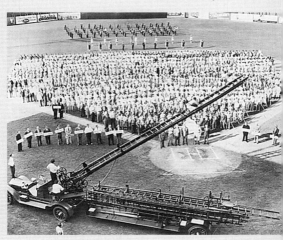

TOP
The 1941 Williamsport Grays at Dunn Field in Elmira, New York, just before a playoff game against the Pioneers. The fifteen members of the 1941 Grays who reached the Major Leagues included Roger Wolff, Irv Hall, and Don Richmond.

MIDDLE
Williamsport celebrates baseball in 1947. All the city's youth leagues take part in the festivities in this photo, which originally appeared in *Life* magazine.

BOTTOM
Bowman Field, remodeled for the 2000 season, under the lights.

and Major and the hundreds of boys in Williamsport who thought of him as a father.

Carl credited a nasty scratch caused by a lilac bush with being the impetus for Little League. The withered remains of that bush are part of a collection of hundreds of artifacts maintained by the Stotz family and displayed during the week of the Little League World Series in the Original League Clubhouse. Carl kept nearly all the things connecting him to the origins of Little League: the whistle he used to get the boys' attention at the very first tryout, the home plate he carved out of a piece of rubber, the first Little League emblem he drew—and the lilac bush.

He retold the story hundreds—if not thousands—of times to anyone who would listen. He welcomed strangers into his home for decades, his memory encouraged by the artifacts he saved. Reporters—many visited over the years—began interviews with "How did it all start?" Hours later, they had their answer.

"WHO WOULD WE PLAY?"

Carl Stotz delighted in describing an August day in 1938 when, as usual, his nephews Jimmy and Major came over to play. On that day, they ran from their home on Anne Street to the Stotz home on Isabella Street, a "half-double" shared with the Jake

The Repasz Band, a community band founded in 1831 in Williamsport, has performed at every Little League World Series. Renowned worldwide, the band always performs "The Repasz Band March."

Flickinger family in Williamsport. In an interview Carl said: "You know about sibling rivalry? These boys were from a large family—six children—but still they were so much together that the parents just referred to them as 'the boys.' Whenever they said 'the boys' everyone knew they meant Major and Jimmy. They would come to my house. They always liked to come and work with me."

As usual, they wanted to play catch. Carl agreed enthusiastically—as usual.

Like many boys around that time, Jimmy and Major were in love with baseball. Part of the credit for that, Carl said in an interview, went to Sol Wolf, radio announcer for the Williamsport Grays, then a Class A Eastern League team.

> Sol's broadcasts of the games up at Bowman Field were so exciting, so interesting to those little boys. After they heard him announce a game, they would go in their backyard and play catch and make the same statements he did. To Sol, the bases were never loaded—the ducks were on the pond. The batter never walked—he drew an Annie Oakley. Because of Sol, [the Gehron brothers] had such high feelings for the game that they would come to my house and ask me to play catch with them in the backyard.

On that summer day in 1938, one of Major's throws went astray, toward the Flickingers' half of the backyard. Carl ran to catch the ball, but scraped his ankle when he stepped on the sharp stems of a lilac bush that recently had been trimmed. He limped to the Flickingers' back porch and sat on the steps. In an interview, Carl recounted what happened next:

> Now this next thing is hard to explain unless you have experienced it yourself sometime in your life, where all at once something comes to you that they call a flashback. … There it is in one scene. And that's what happened when they come there … and they start talking baseball to me, then immediately passed before me the conditions under which I played baseball.

And that's when I said to them, "How would you like to play on a regular team, with uniforms, a new ball for every game and bats you could really swing?"

And they said, "Who would we play? Will people come to watch us? Do you think a band would ever come to play?"

The first question, Carl thought, did not present a problem. He knew plenty of boys in the neighborhood would want to play on the teams.

Later he instructed his nephews to spread the word among friends about an idea taking shape in his mind. He set a time and date for the first experimental training session. People didn't start watching until the next year, and the bands came a bit later—but they came.

Playing space, at least initially, was plentiful. Carl picked the boys up in his 1934 Plymouth two-door sedan and brought them to a place near the Susquehanna River, just west of Williamsport's downtown. The roster in that very first Little League practice (even though the moniker had not been dreamed up) consisted of the Gehron brothers, Charles "Pete" Fortner, George Fortner, Ray Best, Stan Keys, George Keys, Charles "Noonie" Smith, James "Pete" Smith, and Bobbie Smith.

Carl recalled the very first practice: "I took a whole carload of boys up to [Memorial Park], the place where I used old newspapers to indicate where the diamond is, and the boys positioned themselves accordingly. Tossing the ball so the kids could hit it, I was trying to see how far back first base should be, so that when a boy was throwing from third or shortstop it would be a good close play—not out by a mile or safe by a mile. And that's where the sixty-foot dimension was determined."

During the rest of the summer, Carl took the boys to the field and kept experimenting. As it turned out, the distance between bases was exactly two-thirds the distance on a standard field. The distance between bases on a Little League field has been 60 feet ever since. Carl initially set the pitching at 38 feet, later lengthened to 44 feet and eventually to 46 feet after Carl severed his ties with Little League. Other rules needed revisions, and Carl pondered them as summer ended. He decided to focus his attention on boys between the ages of nine and twelve, but he would not turn away "precocious" eight-year-olds. Meanwhile, the boys were enthusiastically looking forward to the next spring, when Uncle Tuck would start taking them back to the field.

Then Carl Stotz lost his job.

UNCERTAINTY STRIKES

Pure Oil Company, Carl's employer, shut down its plant in Williamsport late in 1938 after the construction of an oil pipeline across the mountains. Even though his wife, Grayce, remained employed, and Carl's unemployment checks helped, forming a new baseball league for boys took a back seat to making a living.

As the Depression drew to a close, job openings became more plentiful, but good

WHO WAS CARL EDWIN STOTZ?

Carl E. Stotz

"Where it all began . . ."

Carl Stotz is immortalized on a baseball trading card.

Depending on who is asked, the reply to "What kind of a person was Carl Stotz?" brings similar answers. Honest, sincere, loyal, down-to-earth, all those seem to have applied, but nobody sang his praises higher than the boys who played Little League in the early days of the program.

One was Art Kline, whose father wanted his son to play for the Maynard Midgets so he could leave work during lunch to watch his son play. The elder Kline worked at Bethlehem Steel inside Maynard's boundaries, but the family lived within the boundaries of the original Little League. So in 1946 ten-year-old Art tried out for and won a spot at Original, the program founded by Carl seven years earlier. Kline, retired personnel director for Little League, recalled the first time he met Carl Stotz:

Carl probably was as good with young children as anyone you could meet. I recall that when I first tried out, I went over alone, since my dad was working night shift. I tried out and had to go out to catch fly balls. And all I had was my first baseman's mitt.

One of the [other players] said, "You can't go out there and catch those balls with a first baseman's mitt. You need a fielder's mitt."

I said, "Well, this is all I have. It's all my family can afford."

I was getting ready to leave when someone tapped me on the shoulder and asked, "What's the problem?"

Art explained, and the man replied: "Well, I don't see that as a major problem. I don't want you to leave. I have a fielder's mitt right here that I don't use. I want you to have it."

Art refused at first, knowing his family would disapprove of accepting such a gift. The man had a solution to that too. "I'll tell you what, I know your dad. How about I sell it to you for $5?"

Art explained that he didn't have the money, so the man struck a deal. Art could give him 25 cents a week until it was paid off. "You go on out and use that fielder's mitt," he said. "And that fielder's mitt was Carl Stotz's. And that's a true story of the type of person Carl Stotz was."

Kline says Carl's kindness extended beyond merely providing baseball for boys. "Carl was involved also from the standpoint of his own values and morals, as a person who believed in the Christian faith and did a lot to bring troubled boys into the various churches in the area. In his own way, he paid special attention to those boys."

Praise comes easily from those who knew Carl Stotz. People who might have been strangers became instant friends. In 1953, Sylvia Sutherland was volunteering at a league in Chicago when she took a winter trip to New York City and decided to make a side trip to Williamsport:

I called Carl. There was some snow. I told him I was at the train station and I just wanted to say hello. He said, "You

wait there. I'll be there in 20 minutes."

I was quite embarrassed. I said, "Please, I just wanted to look, then I'm going."

"No," he said, and he took me to six fields and to his home, where he and his wife lived. "You see, we have no mementos of Little League Baseball. It's all at the office," he explained. Which is quite interesting because that's not how it turned out. [His office *was* his home.] That was very memorable for me. He took me to the original field and then returned me to the depot, and I went back to New York. That was probably the most memorable visit I've had there.

Even after Carl and Little League parted ways, he continued to be a quiet hero in Williamsport, regaling visitors with stories and granting interviews whenever asked. He also continued to volunteer his time at Original League, even when his body rebelled with age. He never spoke in public of the split with Little League, and had no harsh words for anyone in the program. And he kept volunteering.

"Right up to his eighties, he was still dragging the field, doing things," Kline said. "That's Carl Stotz personified." ◆

jobs were still scarce. Carl tried many jobs during the next two months.

He worked for one night shift at a Venetian blind factory, dip-painting the blinds into foul-smelling paint, but he could take only one shift like that. Then he earned $40 for designing the landscaping for an ice cream plant, using the plants he cultivated in a vacant lot near his home. The money helped, but the experience in horticulture came in handy when the need arose to cultivate the grass on a baseball field. He applied at a hardware and lumber company—no luck there. He applied at Lundy Construction Company and showed the owner, Richard Lundy, some drawings of a compact home he designed. That didn't pan out either—yet.

Finally, a former boss from Pure Oil called and offered him a job with a company in Bellefonte, about 50 miles from Williamsport. If that job had worked out, and the Stotz family had moved, Little League might never have been born—or Bellefonte, Pennsylvania, could have been the home of the Little League World Series!

Carl stayed in Bellefonte for only a week, earning $121. Returning home for good, he called on Lundy Construction again, this time finding success. The drawings he left with Lundy had paid off, and he began work there on November 1, 1938, making scale drawings of brick homes being remodeled. Although he soon lost this job—Lundy needed someone with more experience in drafting—the Lundys offered a fallback position.

Richard Lundy suggested that Carl apply at Lundy Lumber Company, another family business. He landed the job, which proved fortunate beyond the mere fact that it meant steady pay. If landscaping design and scouring Lycoming County for a job prepared and tempered Carl Stotz, working as a bill collector for Lundy Lumber completed his education. Besides dunning delinquent customers, he filled in at the sales counter and helped the bookkeeper.

In years hence, Little League would benefit immeasurably because of its relationship with the Lundy family.

"FOR THE BOYS"

Once employed, Carl turned his thoughts back to his boys. He wanted to start a real baseball program for the younger boys, but all across America the game seemed geared only to older boys and adults. Besides the obvious physical differences, such as the size of the field and equipment, certain rules were not suited to younger boys.

For instance, the rule allowing a batter to try for first base on a dropped third strike was out of place in the boys' game. Carl figured catchers of that age did not have the skills to ensure a clean catch on most third strikes, and were not likely able to throw a runner out when a ball trickled away.

Leading off base was another problem. Eighty years after renegade players in the nineteenth century introduced the "stolen base," Carl decided to all but eliminate it from Little League play—but not in order to bring the game back to its genteel roots. Both catcher and pitcher were the reasons: Generally, neither could keep runners from stealing

Carl Stotz's 1939 Lycoming Dairy team. Lundy Lumber, Jumbo Pretzel, and Lycoming Dairy were the first three Little League teams in history.

second and third bases at will if the runners were permitted to lead off. He created a rule permitting runners to leave base only when the ball had passed the plate. (Little League later refined the rule, allowing the runner to leave the base after the ball reached the batter.) And six innings, instead of the standard nine, seemed just about right for boys this age.

What about the baseballs? By the end of the nineteenth century they had become more or less standard at nine inches in circumference and about five ounces in weight. Smaller, youth-sized balls were available, but Carl found them inferior. His boys didn't seem to have any problem handling the standard ball anyway, as long as it was not as "lively" as a professional model.

Funding presented an even larger problem. Carl realized that a new program required local sponsorship—at least at the beginning—and he thought big, hoping to interest a large company in sponsoring his program. That's when the skills acquired while collecting bills for Lundy, particularly persistence, came in handy.

By his own admission, Carl Stotz was stubbornly persistent. Dozens of businesses turned him down, so he doggedly pursued others. For two and a half months, "No" was the only answer he received. Undaunted, he ordered a dozen baseballs and a catcher's mask, paying $3.67, plus 82 cents postage, from his personal funds. Owing perhaps to the thriftiness forced on all but the most affluent families by the Depression, Carl kept meticulous records of every event in the early history of Little League, including all purchases. Those receipts are among the artifacts kept at the home of his daughter Karen Stotz Myers except during Little League World Series week, when the mementos are displayed at the Original League Clubhouse.

BUILDING A PROGRAM

Spring 1939 arrived. The first season was at hand, and time ran short. Fifty-six businesses declined the opportunity to be a sponsor. Finally, on the fifty-seventh try, in a meeting with Floyd Mutchler at Lycoming Dairy Farms, Carl received a positive response to his request for $30, the amount he estimated he would need to outfit one team. Mutchler's answer made Lycoming Dairy the very first sponsor of a Little League Baseball team: "We'll go along—for the boys."

Eight years after Carl's death, Karen spoke of her father's search: "You've heard that story about Father going to fifty-six businesses? Have you ever heard the names of those people or businesses? Nobody ever did. He didn't even tell his own family who they were. I think that speaks about the kind of man he was."

In the January 2, 1949, issue of the weekly newspaper *Grit*, Stotz is described as having "a strange admixture of temperamental elements. He is at one and the same time a combination of impetuosity and placidity. Carl Stotz is amiable and well spoken. There is a certain crispness in his voice that makes you want to listen, but perhaps his salient attribute is persistence—his dogged persistence. Without it he could never have built the magnificent organization that now flies the flag of the Little League of Williamsport."

LITTLE LEAGUE FINDS A NAME

Carl wasted no time putting the sponsor money to use. He bought two bats, a catcher's mitt, a pair of catcher's shin guards, and four more baseballs. Then the search began for uniforms. He bought ten sets from Kresge's (which later became K-Mart) and ordered more from Harder's Sporting Goods Store—the start of another long association between Little League and a Williamsport business. When companies first began manufacturing equipment stamped with "Little League," in 1948, Harder's took a financial risk by accepting much of the stock and banking on mail orders. To this day, Harder's supplies Little League teams in the Williamsport area.

Buoyed by the response from Lycoming Dairy, Carl used personal funds to keep the movement going. In *A Promise Kept: The Story of the Founding of Little League Baseball,* by Carl Stotz as told to Kenneth Loss, he recalls: "Although I had only one sponsor and one manager, me, I saw no turning back. It was time to begin calling boys together for team tryouts." Not wanting to attract so many boys that he would have to turn them away, Carl put out a modest call to the boys at St. John's Lutheran Sunday School, where

LEFT
**Bert Bebble's 1939
Jumbo Pretzel Little
League team.**

RIGHT
**George Bebble's
1939 Lundy Lumber
team.**

he was a member, to try out for the still-unnamed league. At 6:00 P.M. on May 8, 1939, the first true Little League gathering commenced.

Another nephew helped. Carl Gehron, Jimmy and Major's fourteen-year-old brother, brought a whistle attached to a braided lanyard and gave it to his uncle. They separated the boys into groups of four and played catch. But with only one manager, Stotz, the tryout was more like a mass practice.

Carl Stotz had talked to several men during the previous week, but none accepted the other two managing positions. Without managers, the league would not survive, and Carl needed two more men to take over the other teams in the three-team league he envisioned.

Grayce Stotz helped out this time. In an interview, Carl cited George and Bert Bebble as the very first adult volunteers recruited in Little League history: "It was the spring of 1939 when we were having the boys try out up at the field. My wife worked at the hosiery mill alongside a machine operated by Annabelle Bebble, George's wife. My wife was telling her what I was doing there with the boys and that I didn't have any men helping me. And she says, 'Well why don't you ask George. He likes baseball. Maybe he'd like to manage a team.'"

Carl needed not only managers but also help with other phases of the program. Heavy rains one day washed cinders from some old trolley tracks onto the field, and Carl had to remove them himself. So he invited George and Annabelle Bebble to dinner and used the davenport to display some of the uniforms and equipment he had purchased. After listening to Carl's plans for the league, George Bebble agreed to manage.

Then he recommended his brother, Bert, to manage the other team. As Carl described in an interview, the rainstorm played a big part in Little League's birth: "That was a very, very important thing. That incident caused me to call George and Bert Bebble

together. When they accepted the managership of the team, it was with the condition that I wouldn't schedule any games on Wednesdays and Saturdays because they were still playing in the County League as players."

The tryouts progressed, and the managers picked the first three teams through a cooperative arrangement to divide the talent equally. With players, equipment, uniforms, and managers in place, they needed a place to play.

The city council refused to allow Carl and the Bebbles to build a field at the park where they conducted tryouts. They fretted that Carl's experiment involved "hardball" and that stray balls might hit people in the park outside the field. Instead, the city offered an alternative site at nearby Park Point, where the Sunday School League had played years earlier. After some improvements, Carl and the Bebbles readied the field.

With only one team sponsor, money remained short, even with scrimping wherever possible—like sharing a single set of catcher's equipment for all three teams. Just before the season began, Carl convinced Jesse "Buckeye" Smith at Penn Pretzel Company, a Williamsport business, to sponsor a team named Jumbo Pretzel in two installments. Next, Carl turned—reluctantly—to his employer. Confident of his new league's success, but mindful of his place as a new hire, Carl sold the idea on speculation. He explained: "I went to Jack [Lundy] and told him what I was planning to do, and he says, 'You should talk to my brother. He's the baseball fan.' So I told Dick [Jack's brother] what I was planning to do, but I didn't ask him for a sponsorship. Instead, I asked if he had any objection if I call the team 'Lundy Lumber.' Then, after he sees what we're doing, if he would like to make a contribution, that would be good."

Jack Lundy made the contribution in September 1939, and never stopped giving. To this day Lundy Construction sponsors youth sports teams in the Williamsport area. John W. "Jack" Lundy, who was a member of the Little League Baseball International board

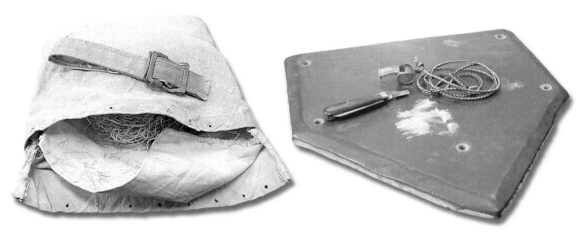

of directors until he retired in November 2000, speaks of Carl's reluctance: "He didn't want to ask his employer—which was me. Finally he ran out of steam, and economically he needed three sponsors. So he asked us, and we went along with him. We didn't know he was looking for sponsors. He needed money because he promised the kids he would buy them uniforms like the big league players."

Lundy recalls Carl's early days organizing Little League and how Little League sometimes took precedence, even over his job:

I recall very distinctly he used to say to me, "Jack, I have to take off early this afternoon because I'm meeting with the boys to play ball. I'll make up the time," says he, being always very sincere and very conscious of his responsibilities. And I said, "What boys?" And he would say, "Well, I'm starting a [baseball league] for my nephews. I'll make up the time. I work Saturdays and anytime you want me. But I've really got to get off this afternoon and get with the boys at the ballfield."

The 50th anniversary commemorative team gathers at the dedication of a statue at the site of the first Little League game. From left are: Bill Bair, George Spooner, George Meck, Frank Sipe, James "Pete" Smith, Carl Stotz, Luther Snyder, David Hinaman, Al Yearick, Tom "Tuck" Frazier, Ralph Hornberger, Ray Best, Maurice Reeder, and, in chair, Fred Sander.

He would take off at 4:30 in the afternoon, and of course we worked until six o'clock. … We were a very small company, and if you take one of four people out of the organization, you lose twenty-five percent. And he would be off teaching kids how to play ball. But there was never a problem because he was conscientious.

Still, the $30-per-team estimate for sponsorship proved too low, forcing Carl to fabricate some of the equipment himself. He decided home plate should be a little over 14 inches wide, compared with the standard 17 inches to which the Little League plate eventually reverted in 1959. Having a custom home plate manufactured was prohibitively expensive, so Carl fashioned his own from some rubber he found in his father's basement. Later, he made a pitcher's plate 18 inches long and 4 inches wide. (A standard pitcher's plate is 24 inches by 6 inches.) The Little League pitcher's plate is still the same size. Carl solved another problem by enlisting help from his sister Laurabelle. She made the bases from scratch using white canvas duck filled with Excelsior, a wood shaving.

Carl was solving the equipment problems, but the fledgling organization still had no name. On a visit to *Williamsport Sun* sports editor Bob Steinhipler, Carl sought advice from his boyhood chum and recalled the meeting in the 1992 interview:

> I thought about calling it Junior League, but I found out there was a woman's organization called the Junior League. I wanted it to be just like the big leagues, but for the little boys. So I was thinking maybe "Little League." So [Steinhipler] says, "As soon as you know it for sure, if you let me know it by noon, I can get it in tonight's paper." So I went from there over to the *Grit* [newspaper] and talked to [sports editor] Bill Kehoe, and gave him the same presentation. When I said "Little League," I saw something in his face, and that was it.

Carl called his friend with the name. That evening "Little League" appeared for the first time in a newspaper. Until then, word-of-mouth provided the only spread of information about the experiment being conducted by Carl Stotz, George and Bert Bebble, three sponsors, and thirty boys.

The biggest thrill of all belonged to the boys on the field. One of them in that first game was Allen "Sonny" Yearick, a ten-year-old chosen to play on Carl's Lycoming Dairy team. Yearick went on to become the first Little League graduate to play professional baseball, in the Boston Braves organization, before returning to Williamsport. Yearick vividly recalls the excitement of receiving his first baseball uniform:

> The uniforms. I can remember that. It was something that nobody had ever seen. We were all so excited, we were elated—we had socks, we had shirts, we had pants. The cost of them was almost nil, but at that time that was a lot of money. We were just unbelievably excited. One cannot tell how a little boy can be so happy over getting something and becoming a part of something.
>
> I remember they were kind of crinkly, kind of itchy. The material wasn't real good material at that time—twenty-five cents a uniform, but we were the envy of every kid in the whole area. Other kids were coming around now saying, "How can we get on?"

Gary Carter, former catcher for the Montreal Expos and the New York Mets

"I could still recite the Little League

pledge today if you asked.

It says win or lose, always do your best.

That's what I learned most

from Little League Baseball."

three

CARL STOTZ KEEPS HIS PROMISE

The acknowledged founders of both baseball and Little League Baseball had inauspicious debuts as managers. In the first scheduled baseball game in 1846, Alexander Cartwright managed the losing team, the New York Knickerbocker Baseball Club. Ninety-three years later, in 1939, Carl was at the helm of Lycoming Dairy for a loss in the first Little League game.

Both games were lopsided. In each, the winning team scored twenty-three runs. Both games also had a lasting impact. Cartwright's experiment led to the Black Sox Scandal, Babe Ruth, Jackie Robinson, free agency, and George Steinbrenner. Carl's experiment led to batting helmets, a federal charter, aluminum bats, and crowds of 40,000 watching eleven- and twelve-year-olds play a baseball game.

FIRSTS FOR LITTLE LEAGUE

Just ten months from the time Carl Stotz scraped his ankle on the lilac bush, he kept his promise to Jimmy and Major Gehron. Considering what would follow, little in the way of fanfare accompanied the first Little League pitch thrown. With no place to sit, only a few people showed up to watch. Both squads sat on a single park bench.

Firsts ruled the day. Louie Brown umpired the first Little League game. From his position behind the pitcher, Brown called "Play ball!" and Frank Sipe delivered the first pitch. Carl's team, Lycoming Dairy, scored the first run in the top of the first inning. The lead evaporated in the bottom half of the first inning when George Bebble's Lundy Lumber team scored seven runs, then added eight more in the second inning for a 15–1 lead. Major Gehron became the first relief pitcher, giving up four more runs.

Not all the firsts were game-related. In the middle of the contest, Carl went to the pitcher's mound and announced to the small crowd the need for more funds. Sponsorships, he said, were a big help, but they needed additional support. He held out a hollow rubber ball, about the size of a baseball but with a third cut away, and placed it on the ground near the backstop for contributions: $1.42 for the first game.

John Lundy remembers the first game: "It was the first time they had been in uniform for a game. Our whole family was there to see it, but it was not a large crowd." Lycoming Dairy outscored Lundy Lumber 7–4 in a much closer second half of the first Little League game. The final score, 23–8, did not set the tone for the rest of the season, however. Lycoming Dairy finished with an 8–8 record. Lundy Lumber was 9–7, and Jumbo Pretzel was 7–9. Thirteen of the twenty-four games were decided by two runs or less.

As the season progressed, Carl and his volunteers discovered what many local Little League volunteers discover: the sport gets under your skin. With ten or so children counting on a few adults, it becomes difficult for the adults to say no. When problems come up, and they do, the responsibility for dealing with them most often falls to a small cadre of volunteers.

In *A Promise Kept,* Carl recalled the second date on the Little League schedule, a typical summer evening when the weather refused to cooperate:

During the late-afternoon downpour on June 8, for example, big cinder clinkers washed onto the infield from the slightly higher abandoned trolley-car roadbed nearby. Looking at the field on my way home from work, I decided if we worked quickly we would still be able to play that night. So instead of sitting down to supper, I hurried to the field with equipment and bushel basket in hand. Borrowing a rake, we removed the cinders and smoothed the area around third base where the rain had formed a shallow ditch that drained into the outfield. Bert put down the bases and I got the pitcher's rubber and home plate in place in time for play.

Their efforts went for naught. Another heavy shower hit the area just before the game, postponing it for a week.

Carl arrived early to prepare the field on June 15. A group of young men also arrived, intending to use the field for a softball game, unimpressed that the Department of Parks had reserved the field for Little League use. As Carl recalled, in *A Promise Kept*, the cavalry arrived in the form of Little Leaguers in uniform: "Their presence made a stronger impression than anything I said, and one of the cooler heads among the softball players suggested that perhaps they should find a field elsewhere. It was clearly because of the Little Leaguers that they left in good humor."

Lundy Lumber defeated Jumbo Pretzel 11–5 in the ensuing game, but rain postponed the next contest too. It became imperative to find a better site, a site dedicated only to Little League and close enough for the boys to reach easily.

FIRST SEASON CHALLENGES

Each time he went to the site of the 1939 games, Carl passed an unused, overgrown lot at the corner of Memorial Avenue and Demorest Street. Ideally located, the property, owned by Williamsport Textile Company, needed extensive improvements. It included a wooded section and a weed-filled tennis court. The Bebbles agreed to help once Williamsport Textile agreed to let Little League develop the site for a ballfield. In scenes that would send shivers down the spines of today's risk-management experts, adults and children of the fledgling organization pitched in to clear the land.

VISION FOR AN EXPANDED LITTLE LEAGUE

Even though he wanted to keep the program grounded and simple, Carl Stotz had big ideas for Little League's future. In fact, his original ideas did not limit Little League to baseball, as he explained in an interview in which he recalled the winter of 1938–39: "Thinking about this over the winter, I got carried away with the possibilities. I realized that maybe some kids don't want to play baseball, maybe some kids can't play baseball. Couldn't we have track meets? Couldn't we have basketball games on the school playgrounds? The name is Little League. It could have been Little League track for boys, basketball, anything."

Little League did add another sport, softball, to its repertoire in 1974. Some have suggested that Little League extend its organization and infrastructure into other sports for which there are no large national programs, such as basketball.◆

Demorest Field, an overgrown lot owned by the Williamsport Textile Company at the corner of Memorial Avenue and Demorest Street, became the first baseball diamond created and used by Carl Stotz and his Little League volunteers.

OPPOSITE PAGE
Demorest Field in use by Stotz's Little League. Later, the youth sports program moved to Memorial Park.

On a visit from Connecticut, Ralph Stotz, Carl's brother, lent his automobile to the effort, using the Hudson to uproot stumps. They hauled away trash and brought in topsoil to improve drainage. The infield grass area was plowed and seeded. A maintenance crew from Williamsport Textile helped, and development of the site continued through the summer, even as the first season progressed at Demorest Field.

Newspaper competition greatly benefited Little League in the first year. Williamsport's three newspapers—*Grit* (a weekly), the *Evening Sun,* and the *Williamsport Gazette & Bulletin*—each endeavored to scoop the others on local stories. And Carl's experiment provided plenty of stories. Nearly every game in the first season received extensive coverage, with descriptive narratives and box scores.

A problem that still plagues Little League and other organized youth sports programs arose in the very first season. At a game in late June, a fan berated the umpire for a call. In this case, the umpire simply walked off the field. Carl went to the mound to address the crowd, explaining that the umpires were volunteers and that while Little League tried to emulate Major League Baseball, loud criticism of the officials was undesirable. Carl coaxed another volunteer from the stands to continue officiating, and the game continued.

Finding qualified volunteer umpires became difficult for some leagues, and remains so today. Normally, plenty of fathers or mothers come forward to manage or coach their sons and daughters, with the chance to share in the glory of triumph, but umpiring often is thankless and demanding. While Little League's regulations do not prohibit paying umpires, some programs turn to quasi-professionals as a way to ensure that an umpire is at each game. Even pay does not guarantee the best officiating, though.

At the end of the first season in 1939, work at the new site halted for the five-game championship series—Little League's first—with Lycoming Dairy, the first-half champ, versus Lundy Lumber, the second-half champ. (Carl arranged the schedule in halves, allowing for a slow-starting team to come on strong at the end of the season and have a chance at the title. That formula is used by most Little League programs today.) Lycoming Dairy, with Carl managing, defeated Lundy Lumber three games to two. The loser of the first Little League game, by a score of 23–8 in June, came back to win the first Little League championship in August.

TRYOUTS, ROSTERS, SPONSORS, STAFF

Work on the new field continued throughout the fall and the spring of 1940, and meanwhile the concept of Little League was catching on. More boys wanted to play. Carl re-

Early Little League World Series action.

ceived inquiries from fathers in other parts of the city who wanted their sons to be Little Leaguers.

This meant that limits had to be set on the rosters. One field and a small corps of volunteers could not accommodate everyone, as Carl explained in *A Promise Kept:*

> I believed the fairest system would be one that provided an opportunity for boys who played together at school or in the same neighborhood to play together on the baseball diamond. That's why, when the final plans were drawn up, we settled on school-attendance boundaries to set residency requirements. Parochial-school pupils who attended schools outside these boundaries but lived within them were eligible, too. Initially, until more leagues were formed, boys in adjacent districts could only look, and wish adults in their districts would form teams for them.

That philosophy continues in Little League today and is the basis for some controversy. Parents asking for waivers argue that one child who wants to play outside the established boundaries can't make a difference. But Little League's position on boundaries remains unchanged and few exceptions are granted. Carl said in *A Promise Kept:* "Clearly established league boundaries and strict enforcement are as important now as they were then. By limiting the number of boys eligible to try out for teams, Little League expands the possibility that a given candidate will qualify for a position. If a league territory has twice as many eligible candidates as it can use, then the desirable procedure is to set more-restrictive boundaries and form a second league, making it possible for all the boys to play."

In the 1950s, Little League established a maximum population limit of 15,000 for the area from which a single league could draw its players, later increasing the limit to 20,000.

Playing ability also was a factor. In the first season, tryouts merely determined the team to which players would be assigned, to ensure a competitive balance in the league. A fourth team was added in 1940, but with more boys coming forward it became evident that not every boy could be selected. From these ranks a farm league was established, later known as the Morning League. Some of the youngest players in the "major division" also played in the farm league, because they did not get as much playing time on the more competitive teams.

For Carl's first experimental workouts in 1938, the players ranged from age six to eleven. As the league coalesced, however, it required strict age guidelines. The league rules adopted for 1940 required that teams have no more than five players who were twelve years old, and not less than three players age ten and under. Tee Ball, where batters hit off a batting tee rather than live pitching, did not make its first appearance in Little League until the 1970s.

The second year of Little League proved more secure financially, although Carl continued to provide personal funds to carry the program until 1943, when he could finally be reimbursed. Income for the inaugural season totaled $174.63. (Sixty years later, in 1999, Little League Baseball's annual budget was more than $13 million.) The board ambitiously budgeted $260 for 1940, despite a deficit of $36.72 remaining from the previous year.

Adding a fourth team required another team sponsor, and Penn Pretzel Company folded early in 1940, leaving the program short by two sponsors. This time, Carl found the search a bit easier, thanks to the publicity created by the first season. Harry Stein, owner of a local service station, came through. Stein paid $25 toward a full sponsorship, with the balance to be paid later, to replace Penn Pretzel. Richardson Buick became the fourth team's sponsor. Owner Tommy Richardson, master of ceremonies when the three Little League teams met at Bowman Field in 1939, had publicly invited Carl to see him about sponsoring a team the following season.

The program essentially administered by Carl and the Bebbles in the first season needed more adults involved if it was going to survive. The second season brought several key volunteers, who provided a solid foundation for the future of the program. To fill the position of manager for the fourth team, Carl at first asked Howard Gair, a

JOHN LINDEMUTH

When organizing Little League's first board of directors, Carl Stotz approached John Lindemuth, a track star in his youth, about being a manager for the fourth team, before the second season began in 1940. He accepted, and became a member of the board as well, with his wife. The board, then, consisted of Carl and Grayce Stotz, George and Annabelle Bebble, Bert and Eloise Bebble, and John and Peggy Lindemuth.

The Stotzes and the Bebbles created and signed a constitution designating their small group as "Little League" at a March 7, 1940, meeting. The Lindemuths, however, did not attend, and signed it at their next meeting, March 22. Carl presented the season's first budget—$260—and his first task was to order four dozen uniforms.

Lindemuth continued to work with Carl and eventually became a full-time employee with Little League, with the support of the U.S. Rubber Company. After Carl's separation from the corporation Little League had become, Lindemuth remained as commissioner.◆

John Lindemuth, an early manager and member of the first Little League Baseball board of directors, became a full-time Little League employee and eventually commissioner.

HOWARD GAIR

Howard Gair, umpire consultant for Little League Baseball, was seventy-eight years old when he died on October 17, 1973. He had spent forty-two years umpiring, first with the Sunday School Leagues popular in Williamsport, then with Little League Baseball. He also umpired sandlot ball, semi-professional and collegiate baseball, and Little League World Series games.

When Little League needed his assistance in 1940, Gair had already committed to umpire at Penn State University, so during the first season he only managed to work four games. But over the next fifteen years, he racked up an incredible 495 games in the original Little League.

Gair trained his son, Vance, to umpire too. Vance umpired for three years—a total of fifty-two games—before he left for a stint in the U.S. Navy. Upon his return in 1946 and throughout 1967, Vance officiated in 637 games.◆

Early World Series action shot with Howard Gair umpiring. During his tenure, he umpired a staggering 495 games.

Williamsport resident who umpired college ball at Penn State home games. Gair could not commit to the time needed to be an effective manager, but his future contributions proved far more valuable to Little League.

Howard Gair became perhaps the best-known amateur umpire in baseball history. He officiated in only four games in 1940 (including the championship), but in 495 games over the next fifteen years. Gair's son, Vance, also umpired in the early years, except for a three-year stint in the U.S. Navy during World War II. Vance had umpired in 637 games by the time he retired in 1967.

That left the managerial position still open. Carl turned to John Lindemuth, whom he had known from their high school days, when Lindemuth was a gifted track athlete. Lindemuth accepted.

CONTROVERSY IN THE SECOND SEASON

Carl Stotz—not only Little League's first president but also its first purchasing agent—found it difficult to find uniforms, despite the program's increasing popularity. With war heating up in Europe, material for baseball uniforms became scarcer and scarcer.

Such shortages, perhaps more than any other reason, prevented Little League from expanding dramatically during the first seven years of its existence. Nevertheless, the small core of volunteers pressed ahead with preparations for the 1940 season. The new site was ready for opening day of the 1940 season on June 3.

The draft system devised by Carl for 1940 became the standard for many years in Little League, and a variation is in use today by a handful of teams. Most have adopted the system advocated by Little League, in which the first pick is made by the last-place team from the previous season; the second pick is by the second-to-last place team; and so on.

Carl's system allotted 20,000 points to each manager. The returning players to a team from the previous season were assigned a point value that was deducted from the 20,000. Each manager then bid for the newcomers with their remaining points. A player agent was selected to oversee the process and maintain the records confidentially—still a key position in local Little Leagues. The first player agent was Edwin "Ned" Grove, who remained at that post until 1945, when he moved out of the area. Carl, no longer managing by then, became player agent.

On the field, Lundy Lumber won the 1940 season's first half, and Lycoming Dairy won the second, setting up a repeat for the championship series. This time, however, it ended in controversy and forfeit—another lesson resulting in new rules.

George Bebble's Lundy Lumber team was batting in the third inning of the final game when a Lundy batter, Bill Pflegor, hit an apparent inside-the-park home run. (Any home run in the first few years was inside the park because there was no outfield fence.) Pflegor came in to score, but the defense appealed to the umpires that Pflegor had missed third base. The third-base umpire called Pflegor out, but the plate umpire overruled the

Players from a 1963 Little League World Series team visit the Lincoln Memorial in Washington, D.C.

call and the run counted. Carl continued the game under protest—standard procedure for such events in baseball—and the final score was 3–0.

The league's board of arbitration took up the issue. (For regular-season play, this later became the protest committee; for postseason playoffs, it became the Little League International Tournament Committee.) The board agreed with Carl's protest and ordered the game replayed, but Lundy Lumber's parents refused to allow their children to take the field. That left Carl with no choice but to declare his own team, Lycoming Dairy, the champion by forfeit. Later Carl regretted not having dropped the protest: "My actions were not conducive to a harmonious resolution of the dispute."

A half-century passed before another forfeit ended the Little League season, when the Far East champion team from Zamboanga City, in the Philippines—a 15–4 winner against Long Beach, California, in the 1992 Little League World Series final—used ineligible players. Little League's International Tournament Committee stripped the Zamboanga City team from the former U.S. Territory of its title.

Two major rules grew from the 1940 experience. They continue today. First, protests of playing rules in International Tournament games must be resolved before another pitch or play takes place. It is known informally as the "manager's right rule" and allows a manager to refuse to continue play until the issue is addressed at a higher level, all the way to the International Tournament Committee in Williamsport if necessary. If the manager agrees to continue playing, however, the protest is automatically dropped.

Second, league presidents were prohibited from managing teams. As Carl explained in *A Promise Kept,* such dual roles created conflicts, but the work in progress kept improving: "League presidents should not be managers! … This incident provided lessons which were well learned. We were covering new ground and learning as we went through each unplanned experience. Fortunately, what I was learning would prove to be beneficial to Little League in the future."

EARLY AMBASSADORS

Despite controversy on the field, people began to notice Little League, and Carl found himself in demand as a public speaker in the Williamsport area. The experience was good training for extensive travels to future speaking engagements as Little League's ambassador.

Little Leaguers took a train to the 1940 New York World's Fair in their Little League uniforms. At each exhibit, public-address announcers welcomed the "Little Leaguers from Williamsport, Pennsylvania" and gave a brief description of the organization's activities. One of the exhibits—on a new form of media, television—would transform America and Little League in the coming decades.

A year later, the Little Leaguers traveled to Philadelphia for a game at Shibe Park between the Philadelphia Athletics and the New York Yankees. At the game, Yankee Joe DiMaggio continued his still-standing record of fifty-six consecutive games with at least one hit. The teams also toured Independence Hall.

Similar trips became common not only for the first few Little League teams in Williamsport but also in subsequent years for local Little League programs around the

This 1944 photo of the Original Little League field, now Carl E. Stotz Field, is taken from the dike along the Susquehanna River. Note the backstop, moved in 1942 from Demorest and Memorial to its new home here.

nation. And in many years the winning Little League World Series team traveled to Washington, D.C., to be congratulated by the President of the United States in person. In the spring of 1999, President Bill Clinton invited the 1998 Little League World Series champs, the Toms River (New Jersey) East American Little League team, to visit. It disappointed the team that Clinton had to attend the funeral of Jordan's King Hussein, but Vice President Al Gore honored the team in an East Room ceremony.

CAPITAL IMPROVEMENTS

The 1941 season began, thankfully, with no worries about lack of a playing field. No playoff was needed for the third season either, as Carl's Lycoming Dairy team won both halves of the season for its third consecutive championship. While it may have seemed as though a dynasty had begun, it would be six more years before Lycoming won another league title.

Partway through the season, Carl recruited a new manager for the Richardson Buick team: Martin L. "Marty" Miller. A dedicated volunteer, Miller managed for eighteen years. He embodied many Little League volunteers that followed in thousands of communities around America and the world, willing to do just about any job that needed to be done.

The future looked bright for Little League Baseball, as the board halved the budget deficit by the end of the 1941 season, but unfortunately events on the local and national scene intervened. Lycoming Motors, which manufactured aircraft engines, needed to expand its plant near the Little League field because of increasing government-contract work. Little League would have to vacate the land by the end of the summer. Less than four months later, the United States would dive headlong into the most widespread, cost-

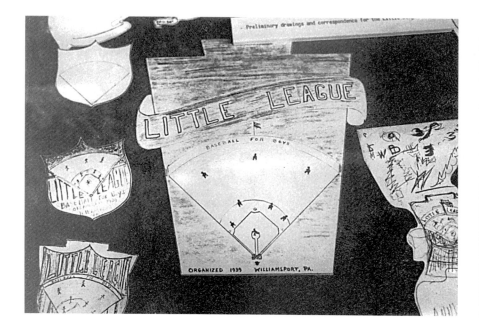

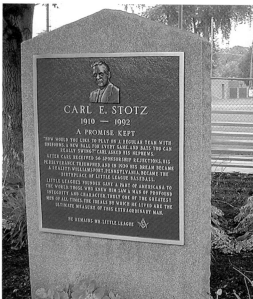

LEFT
Early drawings of the official Little League emblem sketched by Carl Stotz are on display at the birthplace of Little League Baseball.

RIGHT
The Pennsylvania Masons erected this monument at Carl E. Stotz Field to honor Stotz, who was a Mason, for his "promise kept."

liest, bloodiest war the world has ever experienced. The nation's collective mind, and Williamsport's, turned from ballfields to battlefields.

When Carl first approached Williamsport city fathers about building a field at Max M. Brown Memorial Park in 1939, they turned him down. After all, who was Carl Stotz? At the time, Little League didn't even have a name, much less a growing reputation. By late 1941, few in Williamsport did *not* know about Carl and Little League, and City Hall liked his ideas. Besides, with Little League's popularity growing, anything but approval might mean political suicide.

The U.S. Army Corps of Engineers, having built a dike along the Susquehanna River adjacent to the park where Carl reapplied for use, had jurisdiction over a portion of the area. Resident engineer E. J. Luetje agreed to the project as long as the corps could maintain access to the area. Along a busy road, the spot—now known as the Carl E. Stotz Field, Original League, in the Max M. Brown Memorial Park—became the site of the first twelve Little League Baseball World Series tournaments. Said John Lundy, "My recollection is that it didn't become real popular until they moved into Memorial Park, into the public eye where more people could see it."

ENSHRINING YOUTH BASEBALL

The 1942 season began with the Little Leaguers marching in a Memorial Day parade. A friend mentioned the "Little Eagles" to Carl because two boys had led the procession with a large cutout of an eagle, created by Carl with "Little League" lettered on the wings. Carl then designed several new logos and settled on one that combined a baseball diamond, a U.S. flag, and a keystone shape (representing Pennsylvania, the "Keystone State").

With a few changes, the emblem is today Little League's most recognized symbol. "At a Memorial Day parade, I had the boys marching in the parade and I made one of those eagles. After it was over, at least one of my friends said, 'Gee I sure like those little eagles.' That was the thing that made me think we need a different seal than that."

Stein's Service Station won the first half of the season. More fans came to the games. Crowds of 500 or more were common, and the local papers gave the games more ink. Ed Yonkin, a pitcher for Lundy's, provided Little League another "first," late in the season. He pitched the first no-hitter in the four-year history of Little League, tying his team with Stein's for the second-half title. The ball used in the game is on display in the Peter J. McGovern Little League Museum in South Williamsport. Lundy's won the second half in a one-game playoff, and then won the league title in five games, breaking the string of three consecutive championships by the Lycoming Dairy team.

For the first four seasons, all home runs were of the inside-the-park variety, so an outfield fence became the next addition. Initially, the Department of Parks turned down Carl's request because a fence might violate the conditions of the use of land at Max M. Brown Memorial Park. But after checking into the deed, he found that the city had never erected a marker honoring Brown, as required. Seizing the opportunity, Carl offered to build a fence with removable sections that would include a panel identifying the park. Although the sign on the outfield fence still identifies the park, the field itself is now named Carl E. Stotz Field.

Carl's last season as a manager was the 1942 season, because of a change in his work schedule. Bill Bair, a teen who volunteered as Carl's assistant, took over as manager. He later pitched for Penn State University's baseball team. Carl, his role more administrative, devoted time to improving the new field.

Through the war years, additions to the field at Max M. Brown Memorial Park turned the place into a shrine to youth baseball. Jacob Lehn, a parent of one of the players, built a portable electronic scoreboard. Bob Stout, a Williamsport Technical Institute student, set up an amplifier system so he could announce the names of players as they came to bat. Stout later joined the Merchant Marine, and William F. "Mac" McCloskey took on the announcing chores as well as scorekeeping. Volunteers built a clubhouse behind the backstop, as well as dugouts and more seating areas to accommodate larger crowds.

Carl reserved special fondness for a volunteer who usually receives even less recognition than the umpires: the scorekeeper. Though scorekeeping is something of a lost art in baseball, McCloskey's career as a scorekeeper spanned twenty-seven years and an incredible 1,327 *consecutive* games at the program Carl founded. McCloskey, Carl once said, was "the most faithful and loyal person I have ever known."

McCloskey's streak began on August 20, 1940, when the regular scorekeeper was absent. A father of one of the players on the expansion team, McCloskey filled the vacancy. Not unlike Lou Gehrig's replacing Wally Pipp at first base for the New York Yankees, resulting in Gehrig's famous "Iron Horse" moniker, from that day in 1940 until the 1967 season McCloskey kept the scorebook at every game played. McCloskey's significant improvements for the 1945 season included a real innovation. At his own expense, he built the world's first remote-control electronic baseball scoreboard—another of the treasures saved by Carl's family.

THE END OF ONE GAME

As the war raged on two fronts, Little League felt the effects. Besides the shortages of equipment and cloth for uniforms, Uncle Sam did not hesitate to call away some of Little League's most dedicated volunteers, including George Bebble and Vance Gair. In 1944, even Carl Stotz received an invitation, but the government revised draft regulations soon after the notice and he was exempted from service. In August 1943, Little League published its "Armed Services Honor Roll" listing the names of the Little League volunteers who had been called to serve their country.

Little League continued to lurch ahead, in spite of the war. The end of the war, however, brought about the first Little League game suspended by anything other than weather. In the third inning of the Stein's Service vs. Richardson Buick game on August 14, 1945, Mac McCloskey noted the attendance (350) and the fact that the weather was fair and hot. The other note he scribbled explained why there was pure joy even though the game was stopped. "At 7:15 P.M. game called as President Truman broadcast the proclamation that the Japs had accepted our surrender terms and that World War II had come to an end."

Although the end of the war caused the termination of one Little League game, peace meant the organization would soon spread far beyond anything Carl could have imagined six years earlier when World War II—and Little League—began.

Bill Bradley, Rhodes Scholar, former U.S. Senator, former New York Knicks star, and member of the National Basketball Hall of Fame

"I used to think I couldn't live without baseball.

Probably the most important lessons

I learned in Little League were to be a good loser

and a graceful winner; to put the team effort ahead

of personal goals; and to put 100 percent of myself

into every game and practice."

four

THE WORLD DISCOVERS LITTLE LEAGUE

During its early years—the war years—only twelve programs were patterned after Little League, but baseball fever was catching. The program offered men the chance not only to manage and coach miniature baseball teams but also to help young boys become better sports. The first league outside Pennsylvania formed in 1947, the year of the first national tournament. By 1948, seventy-seven leagues had formed and Little League became the media's darling. U.S. Rubber became Little League's first corporate sponsor, alleviating financial worries. Little League moved from small town to the big time. Soon, it would become an international program.

LITTLE LEAGUE FLOURISHES

Until Little League came along, parents' involvement in youth sports consisted almost entirely of watching the games. Hundreds of boys' baseball teams flourished in the late nineteenth and early twentieth centuries, but professional managers and coaches led them. Carl Stotz's youth baseball league was not the first one, but his experiment was different from earlier tries in that Carl's endured and involved parents.

Timing played a big part in Little League's unprecedented success. While World War II slowed Little League's spread, the end of that war

AUTOGRAPH HEAVEN

One of the strangest sights at the Little League Baseball World Series is a twelve-year-old signing autographs for middle-aged men, women, boys—and lots of girls. The tradition began early, with the very first Series. Art Kline, who played first base in the first Series in 1947, remembers signing, but it was no big deal for him at the time. "It was like that every night you played," he says.

Autograph-seeking caught on and has been a Series staple ever since, though it eventually wears thin, even on twelve-year-olds. The August 29, 1959, *New York Times* explained how the Hamtramck, Michigan, team played jokes when a pretty girl passed an autograph book among the players: "Some of the Hamtramck boys confided that besides signing their own names, they invariably inserted a 'love' over the signature of the previous player to sign."

While fame was fleeting for most Little Leaguers at the Series, the event has attracted some of the most famous ballplayers to don a baseball uniform. Most have visited to receive awards or honors, or to provide commentary on radio or television. In such a setting, visiting current or former major-leaguers have for the most part been happy to comply with requests for autographs. Jackie Robinson, for instance, visited the Series in 1962 for television commentary on WPIX, out of New York City. He signed hundreds of autographs and took time to soothe the pain of losing for the runner-up from Kankakee, Illinois, as described in the August 26, 1962, *New York Times*:

> Robinson, after the awarding of the trophies, went to the Kankakee dugout, where there was still much consoling to be done.
>
> "You can't win 'em all," the former Dodger star told the losers. "I know, I've been in losing series too."
>
> Dan Brewster [a black Little Leaguer] barely managed to dry his eyes.
>
> "You did fine," Robinson continued, "and remember, you're still champs." ◆

TOP
Paul Crawley of Texas signs autographs for girls at the 1952 World Series.

BOTTOM
"May we have your autograph?" Howard Silverman, pitcher for the 1952 Hackensack World Series team, obliges.

led to a boom. Fathers returned from the battlefields of Europe and the Pacific to families whom they may not have seen for several years. Having played the game as boys, many American men knew enough about baseball to teach it to their sons. So Little League provided a way for families to become reacquainted. Mothers, also, were needed at Little League fields: they painted fences, corralled boys, worked in concession stands, and formed ladies' auxiliaries. Daughters, if dutiful, helped their mothers in the stands, but often girls stood near the dugouts with autograph books, admiring the little baseball stars.

Each season brought more media exposure. The *Williamsport Sun* reported on December 31, 1946: "Throughout the United States, leagues patterned after Carl's brainchild are springing up like weeds in a flower bed." Nearby communities copied Little League's model, prompting its board of directors to consider forming an umbrella organization to oversee all the leagues patterned after Carl Stotz's. But Carl himself nixed the idea after the 1946 season, and turned down an offer to become president of a citywide Little League. He believed each local league should be independent and self-governing. Still, new league organizers begged for Carl's ideas and advice. In the months leading up to

Little League personnel in 1947. Front, from left: Oliver Fawcett, Howard Gair, Clyde Clark, Bert Haag, Vance Gair. Back, from left: Martin Miller, Carl Stotz, John Lindemuth, Mac McCloskey.

the 1947 season, he visited or mailed information to dozens of communities on how to start and operate a league.

A LITTLE LEAGUE WORLD SERIES

The future of youth baseball changed forever following a visit by Carl, his wife, Grayce, Little League board member Oliver Fawcett, and his wife, Helen, to a nearby field where the Brandon Boys League played. Until then, Carl had not viewed a baseball game outside of the league he had founded eight years earlier. While they watched, Fawcett suggested arranging a game between teams in the two leagues as a "new and worthwhile experience for the boys."

Carl Stotz presented the idea to the board of directors, and after some discussion the idea of a tournament for *all* known Little Leaguers at the end of the regular season emerged. The board agreed to act as host for such a tournament, if it could be accomplished.

Familiar with most of the organizers of the boys' baseball programs patterned after his in the region, Carl and Grayce assumed the task of organizing the tournament. Although Carl espoused local autonomy, he believed that all the teams entering the tournament needed to follow the same rules, so he drew some up.

The set of rules he devised for the event became the first document relating the organizations under Little League. The competing leagues would be permitted to send either their regular-season championship squad or a team of all-stars chosen from all eleven- or twelve-year-old players in the league. The rules required each boy to have played in at least 75 percent of his team's regular-season games, and the league must have been in operation for two full regular seasons before gaining eligibility for the tournament.

The board of directors named the event the "Little League National Tournament," even though of the twelve teams participating only one team—the Hammonton, New Jersey, All Stars—was from outside Central Pennsylvania.

The 1947 tournament was a community-wide event. The Williamsport Tigers allowed the teams to use locker and shower facilities at Bowman Field. Calvary Methodist Episcopal Church, a few blocks away, provided meals. Other supporters included the YMCA, Confair Bottling, Capitol Bakers, and Grit Publishing. Stotz borrowed the concept of team hosts—local volunteers assigned to specific teams to make them feel welcome—from the national Soapbox Derby in Akron, Ohio. Known as "team uncles," these volunteers remain a fixture of the Little League World Series experience in Williamsport.

The players were not aware, of course, that they were playing in the first tournament of a program that would eventually become the world's largest organized youth sports program. For Art Kline, who played in the first Little League World Series in 1947 (then called the National Tournament), playing in the city tournament (a series of games between the regular-season champions from all the leagues in Williamsport) took precedence:

THE FIRST LITTLE LEAGUE WORLD SERIES

Although Little League did not use the term "World Series" until 1949, the 1947 tournament is considered the first Little League World Series. Twelve teams took part in the 1947 tournament, and all but one hailed from within twenty miles of Williamsport. The twelve teams were the Williamsport (Original) Little League; the Williamsport Sunday School League; the Maynard Midget League; the Lincoln League Stars; the Brandon Boys League; the Milton Midget League; the Montour Little League; the Montgomery Little League; the Jersey Shore All Stars; the Lock Haven All Stars; the Perry Lions; and the Hammonton, New Jersey, All Stars.

during tournament play, Stover's record—most strikeouts in ten innings—will likely stand forever.

One of the stars of the tournament was Jack Losch, who played center field for Maynard. Says Losch, "I can't explain how excited we, our parents, and our friends were to see us win that first Little League World Series. We all gathered around home plate and received our trophy, and each of us got a gold medal."

The fleet-footed Losch progressed to more athletic glory. After high school, he won a football scholarship to the University of Miami (Florida) and set several rushing records

LEFT
The Maynard Midgets were the winners of the first Little League National Tournament in 1947. The tournament featured only one team from outside Pennsylvania.

CENTER
Jack Losch, former Little League player and member of the 1947 Maynard Midgets, was drafted by the Green Bay Packers after a successful college football career with the University of Miami.

RIGHT
Posing for a photo are members of the Lock Haven team, runners-up in the 1947 Little League Baseball National Tournament.

Only one team—Hammonton, New Jersey—traveled from outside Pennsylvania. In subsequent World Series tournaments, through the year 2000, eight teams made up the field, eliminating the need for byes. In 2001, for the first time in Little League's history, the World Series field expanded to sixteen teams.

The 1947 championship game was won by Maynard Midget League, which defeated Lock Haven 16–7. But the best game of the tournament came in the semifinal round as Maynard defeated the Lincoln League Stars 2–1. In that game, Don Stover struck out nineteen batters in ten innings (four extra innings for a Little League game). Because Little League pitchers are now limited to nine innings in a game

there that endured for decades. The National Football League's Green Bay Packers drafted Losch in the first round in 1956 (future Hall of Fame quarterback Bart Starr was the Packers' seventeenth-round choice that year), but an injury prevented Losch from playing football beyond the 1957 season. He became a businessman, retiring as a General Motors executive in 1996. Today he lives in Williamsport.

Jack's brother, Joe Losch, is still with Little League, serving as Little League Baseball's vice president of operations and corporate secretary. It was Joe Losch who traveled to the Philippines in 1992 to investigate allegations of the use of ineligible players by the Philippines team.◆

TOP
Charms were given to all Little League National Tournament participants during the 1940s.

BOTTOM
This uniform patch belongs to the 1947 Maynard Midgets.

A view from the dike shows a Little League game during the 1947 National Tournament held at Memorial Park.

Probably the most important thing was getting a suit. Getting picked on an all-star team—we didn't know what it was all about.

I think what really surprised us is how many people showed up to watch these games. I guess the concern on my team was, "Gee, this isn't going to replace the city championship, is it? We're still going to get to play on that?"

You know how incubation is when you first start something? You're hoping the teams will show up on time—kinda reminded me of the district [tournament] and you hope two teams show up. And poor old Mac McCloskey, who was the score-keeper forever. Mac was just trying to figure out who was going to arrive and play what base.

National Tournament results made it to the Associated Press wires. One newspaper prophesied that the tournament would grow so large it would have to be moved to a larger stadium, where admission could be charged. Half this prediction was right. In 1959, after twelve tournaments at the small field at Brown Memorial Park, the tournament (and the headquarters of Little League) moved to South Williamsport, where Howard J. Lamade Memorial Field could handle crowds of 40,000 and more. However, admission to the Little League World Series remains free.

THE FIRST NATIONAL SPONSOR

More Little League programs sprang up as a result of the 1947 tournament and the attention lavished on the event by the media. The organizers of Original Little League knew they needed financial help, as teams from hundreds of miles away would be invited to the end-of-season tournament. Having abandoned the notion of a large-company sponsorship nine years earlier, Carl revived the idea, setting up a meeting in New York City with U.S. Rubber. He paved the way with letters, then traveled all night by bus for a meeting on December 3, 1947—another day that changed Little League forever.

Carl Stotz met with Charles Durban, assistant advertising director for U.S. Rubber. A pioneer in the early years of television, Durban had written magazine articles and produced plays before joining U.S. Rubber in 1937. Satisfied about Carl's intentions, Durban promised that the company would help out. The following winter, U.S. Rubber became Little League's first national sponsor with a one-year commitment of $5,000.

Sponsorship money allowed Original Little League to operate the National Tournament; it was not for regular-season operations of local leagues. Carl concurred, believing individual leagues should have autonomy to operate as they saw fit, with little connection to a national authority—and certainly no financial obligation to a central authority. Carl's new group would assume authority only when a team assembled for tournament play.

Carl suggested to U.S. Rubber that perhaps they could come up with an athletic shoe that would be appropriate for Little Leaguers. The next year, U.S. Rubber, under its Keds trademark, marketed the first rubber-cleated athletic shoe—the first of many products created specifically with Little Leaguers in mind.

Baseballs and bats for the players came next, at Carl's insistence. The Spalding company, sports equipment manufacturer, agreed to manufacture a ball for Little League stamped with the words "Official Little League," provided a market for the balls could be guaranteed. Through the mid-1950s, the baseballs carried Carl Stotz's facsimile signature. Hillerich & Bradsby agreed to a similar arrangement for its line of youth-sized Louisville Slugger bats.

The 1948 Little League Baseball World Series, sponsored by U.S. Rubber, was called the Keds National Little League Tournament. Stotz placed the sponsor's name on the uniforms, but U.S. Rubber feared it would be criticized for exploiting children. Ever since, uniforms for the Series have carried only the team's state, country, or region name.

LEFT
The May 14, 1949, issue of the *Saturday Evening Post* featured a story on Little League. Because of the national exposure, it seemed that everyone wanted a Little League program, and Carl Stotz was happy to oblige.

RIGHT
A film crew for Emerson Yorke captures footage of Little League Baseball officials in a group shot in 1948 at the field at Memorial Park.

Harder's Sporting Goods in Williamsport accepted the entire production of Spalding's Little League balls and Hillerich & Bradsby's Little League bats, selling them by mail order. Before the 1948 season, Carl wrote to all the leagues to explain the new lines of shoes, bats, and balls and how they could be ordered. At the time, Little League did not receive royalties on the sale of merchandise bearing the Little League name. The symbiotic relationship benefited Little League by increasing public awareness and by increasing revenue for sporting goods manufacturers.

NATIONAL EXPOSURE

Carl accelerated his promotion of Little League too. Scores of new leagues popped up, each hungry for information from Little League's now-famous founder, which he enthusiastically provided. When he could, he traveled to nearby towns to make personal presentations. In short, Little League consumed his life.

With solid financial backing, Carl and the Tournament Association made big plans for the 1948 Keds National Little League Tournament. He made hotel reservations for the eight teams, hoping eight states would qualify teams for the tournament. The association codified new rules limiting the size of bats and the number of players on a roster. They decreed that no player could reach his thirteenth birthday before August 1 of the year in question—a regulation that is still in force.

One of Carl's actions met with disapproval from U.S. Rubber. For the first national tournament in 1947, players simply wore regular-season uniforms. But with extra funding for the 1948 tournament, Carl quite naturally continued the tradition of placing the sponsor's name on uniforms. In each game, one team wore uniforms bearing "U.S. Keds" and the other wore "U.S. Royals." To its credit, U.S. Rubber balked, fearing the company might be accused of exploiting children. For every subsequent World Series tournament, uniforms bore the team's state, country, or region name. Says John Lundy, "It was a low-key event. The U.S. Rubber Company did not want to make it appear they were taking over the youth sports area."

Carl took a trip in the spring of 1948 that resulted in a most important event in Little League's history. In the town of Dushore, Pennsylvania, about twenty-five miles northeast of Williamsport, Carl spoke to a group that was interested in starting a league made up of teams from several small communities in rural Sullivan County. A few weeks later, Guy Baldwin, an organizer of the new league, convinced Carl to bring a team from Williamsport to play an exhibition game, to spur interest locally.

One particularly impressed spectator attended the exhibition game. E. H. Brandt, a senior editor at the *Saturday Evening Post,* vacationing at nearby Lake Macoma, accepted an invitation from Baldwin's wife, Peg, to attend the game. Impressed, Brandt assigned a writer and a photographer to attend the national tournament and tell the Little League story. Writer Harry Paxton and photographer Bill Strout gave Little League national exposure in the May 14, 1949, issue of the *Post* ("Small Boy's Dream Come True"). In it, Paxton observed: "Already the idea had captivated thousands of boys and men in hundreds of communities. This is probably only the beginning."

Carl later said that no other promotional influence was as important in Little

Williamsport's WRAK radio announcer Irving "Bud" Berndt, who announced the first Little League Baseball National Tournament, interviews Solita Palmer, author of the song "Little Leaguer," in 1949.

LITTLE LEAGUE'S "ARTFUL DODGER"

Irving "Bud" Berndt became the voice of Little League Baseball to thousands of listeners during the youth organization's first World Series. A radio broadcaster with WRAK in Williamsport, his play-by-play of the championship game in 1948 wafted across the nation, attracting parents to the program from places as far away as Chicago and New Mexico. Western Union telegrams and letters addressed to Berndt, mistakenly associating him with the program's leaders, begged for more information about the budding boys' baseball league.

With WRAK from 1936 to 1974, Berndt recalled his days with Little League in a 1972 article: "I broadcast that Series seated underneath a shade umbrella behind home plate. No radio booth in those days. There was a low screen in front of us, and I had to depend on my ability as an 'artful dodger' to keep from being beheaded by foul balls. The first time I did the World Series it was a little confusing. The rules were different from the [Eastern League] baseball I broadcast from Bowman Field [the Williamsport Grays]. Shorter distances, wild ball handling, and even wilder base running. Even with the umbrella, I got sunburned. But not too many years later we were doing the Series from well-protected broadcast booths."

Little League fever caught on, and in 1951 the National Broadcasting Company decided that the championship game might make good listening on a Friday afternoon. The company invited Berndt to provide color commentary with the NBC host. "It was my privilege then to share the microphone with Ted Husing, recognized as the best in the business. Ted was genuinely interested in the Series. He spared no effort to acquaint himself with its fine points. Later he became a member of Little League's board of directors. From that time on, Little League became a prized goal for all kinds of broadcasts—local, network, and foreign." ◆

League's history. The story exposed more than 4 million subscribers to Little League and resulted in a deluge of inquiries. From 1949, when the *Post* article was published, until 1953, the number of leagues or players in Little League doubled each year.

The exhibition game in Sullivan County produced more promotional fruit. Writer Peg Baldwin authored an article about Little League for the *Reader's Digest* August 1951 edition, appearing in the United States, Canada, and Japan. She also wrote a book with Carl, *At Bat with the Little League,* a guide for starting and operating a Little League program.

Little League publicity extended to other media. Film editor Emerson Yorke, who specialized in newsreels, was so impressed by Little League that he produced a short movie on the 1948 Keds National Little League Tournament. Yorke later became a member of the first Little League board of directors. Carl provided commentary in the film, shown as a trailer in thousands of movie theaters, further boosting Little League's popularity. During a three-week period in 1949, about 80 million Americans saw newsreels from the Little League National Tournament. The 1948 National Tournament also received television exposure. Little League occupied three minutes of the fifteen-minute *Camel* program on CBS-TV. On radio, New York's Ted Husing, another future member of the Little League board of directors, broadcast a play-by-play account of the final game over 106 NBC stations.

At the 1949 Little League Baseball National Tournament, held at Memorial Park, cameramen and radio and newspaper reporters prepare their equipment in the newly constructed press box.

This photo of an action play at first base during the 1952 Little League World Series became a publicity still distributed by filmmaker Emerson Yorke in his quest to promote Little League.

CARL STOTZ HITS THE ROAD

Carl Stotz teetered between performing mighty and minor tasks as his baseball league demanded more of his volunteer time. Confair Bottling was an understanding employer, allowing him to make up the time and use company equipment for certain projects. But demands at the park were varied and endless.

In the wee hours one May morning, the league's uniforms had still not arrived, so Carl and another volunteer poked around a railroad car with flashlights looking for the shipment. He also produced a twenty-five-page booklet on the ten-year history of Little League and assisted in various construction projects at the field. The Little League Tournament Association demanded his time as well, putting the $5,000 from U.S. Rubber to work. Carl handled most of the details, including travel arrangements, hotel reservations, and meals for teams.

After the 1948 tournament, more requests about league formation poured in. Carl struggled to juggle the ever-increasing requirements of Little League with his "real" job at Confair Bottling, where he received a promotion to plant and office manager. When he could, he traveled throughout Pennsylvania and nearby states, delivering his sales pitch, which consisted of a short movie (produced by Yorke), a speech, and a question-and-answer session. Hundreds of communities wanted their own Little League programs, and they wanted Carl Stotz to show them how.

U.S. Rubber offered relief by asking Stotz to become Little League's national director and first employee. The sole corporate sponsor until 1959, the company was in a position to provide funding for a full-time administrator and public relations person. The company proposed just that, and the Little League board and Carl Stotz accepted. This made it possible for Little League to grow to its fullest potential. If there was no one to spend the time sowing the seeds for Little League, other programs might have stepped in and filled the void, and possibly stepped into Little League's shoes.

So Carl resigned from Confair, accepting a ten-year contract to promote Little League nationally for $100,000 plus expenses from U.S. Rubber. He became more of a media celebrity, and he finally had the time to dedicate to the media. His first of many television appearances came on May 10, 1949, in New York City in a live fifteen-minute interview. A story in *Life* magazine later in the year boosted Little League even more.

The avalanche of publicity made Carl's travels mostly positive affairs, but occasionally he came up against detractors who questioned the benefits of organized baseball for children. On a visit to Penn State University to speak to physical education classes in 1949, Carl was peppered with students' questions about Little League's usefulness and whether it might be detrimental to children. The students charged that Little League left the teaching of athletics in the hands of mere volunteers and not, as it should, trained professionals. Professionals leveled the same charges later in the year at the national convention of the American Association for Health, Physical Education, and Recreation in Boston, Massachusetts.

In both cases, however, Carl had experience on his side. Having been the sole witness to Little League's ten-year history, he knew that the direst predictions had not come true, and believed they were not likely to happen. He reasoned that activities like drinking and smoking, proven to be dangerous, were being condoned. He argued that boys played baseball whether Little League was there to provide it or not, and that Little League offered a far safer alternative to sandlot games. Carl also refused to accept the idea that boys were emotionally scarred when not selected for a team. He said that if the selection process was fair, children accepted their not making a team, an issue that Little League has had to defend ever since.

Carl visited seven states in early 1949 to promote Little League. Places he could not visit received a copy of Yorke's 1948 National Tournament highlights film. He mailed an average of one film a day to interested communities requesting them.

Carl Stotz's extensive travels were largely responsible for the fact that Little League was becoming a household term in America.

A pocket-size schedule, with roster for each Little League team competing in the National Tournament, soon to become the Little League Baseball World Series, was published each year by Little League volunteers.

Although he didn't encourage foreign teams playing in the Little League World Series, Carl Stotz would promote Little League abroad. Here he visits with teams in Nova Scotia in 1953.

LITTLE LEAGUE'S ROYALTY

Wherever Carl Stotz went he was well received. Auditoriums were filled with men and women hungry for Little League presentations, and Carl was happy to oblige. He, and sometimes his wife, Grayce, traveled all over North America preaching Little League, and sometimes there were parades in Carl's honor. People gave Grayce bouquets of flowers. In short, they were considered royalty.

But their daughter Karen Stotz Myers recalls a different couple who began a program for youth with a simple purpose: "Mom and Dad weren't the dignitaries. They were the workers. And Dad's dream was not a World Series. He believed that the benefit of the Series was to showcase Little League and to excite men all over the country so that they would have a desire to start leagues in their own towns. This would make it possible for Little League to expand, so more boys could play. He wasn't necessarily interested in expanding for expanding's sake—just so that the boys could play."

INTERNATIONAL GROWTH

The Little League program so impressed the Reverend Ray Hanrahan, a former Maryknoll missionary in China who spent a few days in Williamsport in 1949, that he brought the concept of franchising to Hawaii—a U.S. territorial possession at the time. Baseball was already a popular game in the Islands, having been imported there nearly 100 years earlier by Alexander Cartwright and enhanced by U.S. military personnel before, during, and after World War II.

LEFT
Little League action attracts heavy hitters to the 1951 Little League World Series. In the front row, from left, are Notre Dame's football coach, Frank Leahy, and National Baseball Hall of Famer Cy Young.

ABOVE
In a real Little League World Series, Latin America and Canada earned berths in the 1958 tournament and paraded their regional banners proudly at the pre-game ceremony.

LITTLE LEAGUE PUBLICATIONS DURING THE COLD WAR

Little League publications promoted both democracy and Americanism throughout the cold war. Retired Army Colonel W. H. "Cappy" Wells produced *Little League Hits* from New York City from 1950 until 1952, mixing news from the headquarters in Williamsport with anecdotes from leagues around the nation. He spiced the four-to-eight-page newsletter, sent to every local Little League president, with advice on curing social ills and with patriotic prose reflecting the era of the Red Scare.

Wells's relationship with Little League began in 1949 when U.S. Rubber hired him on a temporary basis to handle media relations for the Little League World Series. Dozens of U.S. newspapers sent reporters to the event, as the American public sought more news about the national championship for boys. By the third Little League World Series, volunteers alone could not handle the flood of journalists.

Publication dates of his newsletter were determined by the need to get news to the volunteers and by the volume of information provided from the field. Throughout the 1960s, Little League also used its World Series program and later publications to promote Americanism, and as a platform for political or economic commentary. Here are a few excerpts from those publications:

> We congratulate the individuals who have been instrumental in launching the movement in their communities. You men and women are part of a dynamic force—the promotion of Americanism. (February 1951 *Hits*)

> [Regarding the idea of managers organizing their own teams instead of the Little League auction system.] That system, while it fosters athletics, does not promote Americanism. It tends to nourish unwholesome clashiness in every walk of life. This is particularly dangerous for boys in our age group—the formative period of their lives. Little League is one medium which, through the Auction System, takes definite action to insure that our players are not subjected to detrimental "isms." … We know of one town where residential areas could be quartered into sections of the well-to-do, the foreign born, the workers and the slums. It was not unusual for gangs of boys from these various areas to roam the town, engaging in hoodlumism and all too frequently gang fights. Those youngsters were not developing into the type of citizens we need and many of them were well on the road to juvenile delinquency. Then, Little League was introduced. The Auction System was adopted. Youngsters from all walks of life found themselves on the same ball teams. Every boyish gang and clique in the community disappeared. The juvenile delinquency rate fell. (March 1951 *Hits*)

> Little League Baseball is providing a splendid way for young people to fit themselves for the rigorous competition of life. … A clean, healthy body begets a clean, healthy mind, and the two are absolute essentials to good Americanism. (From a letter to Little League management from F.B.I. Director J. Edgar Hoover published in the Summer 1950 *Hits*)

> The young Americans who compose the Little League will prove a hitless target for the peddlers of godless ideology. (Herbert Brownell Jr., Attorney General of the United States, quoted in the 1954 *Little League World Series Official Program*)

> A new group of comparatively very young men take over reins of government. There is bound to be a surging, pushing, experimenting, upheaving change—surely a period of great activity. In broad retrospect, the campaigns of both candidates were remarkably alike. Nixon lacked Kennedy's personal appeal and lost. His biggest mistake was to become embroiled in the TV debates. Second guesses. (November 17, 1960, *Headquarters Newsletter to Presidents of Local Leagues*)

> On the national scene, many people are saying this is not a recession—merely one of the lowest booms we've had in some time. Things are so bad on the home front in Russia and in the critical food shortage in Red China there is possibility the brush fire wars and push button riots have to be suspended while we feed them again. Sputniks to Venus do not help empty stomachs. (March 10, 1961, *Headquarters Newsletter to Presidents of Local Leagues*)

Little League Hits became *The Little Leaguer* in 1953, when all administrative aspects of the program were transferred back to Williamsport. For 1955–56, it was a magazine available for subscription, but it reverted back to a newsletter format thereafter. The *Little Leaguer* newsletter is now printed four times a year, with a circulation to 13,000 district administrators and league presidents. ◆

J. Edgar Hoover, director of the Federal Bureau of Investigation, also was a member of the Little League Baseball Board of Trustees.

The first chartered Little Leagues outside the United States in 1950 were on each end of the Panama Canal, according to Little League newsletters that year. In 1949, Carl provided the potential new franchises with information on how to start a league. Because of annual spring monsoons, the first regular season of Little League play in Panama began in January 1950 and ended in April. A mixture of U.S. military dependents and children of Panamanian workers at U.S. military bases in the Canal Zone made up the teams, so it was not truly a "native" league. The same year, Canada, Cuba, Puerto Rico, Hawaii, and Alaska followed Canal Zone with the local Little Leagues established outside the borders of the forty-eight states.

Carl opposed allowing non-U.S. teams to participate in the Little League World Series, but he found their formation for regular-season play elsewhere acceptable. It could not have been stopped, in any event. Soon foreign teams were prepared to enter tournament play.

Canada's Little Leagues grew most rapidly. By 1951, Quebec, Manitoba, and British Columbia boasted programs. A year later, Prince Edward Island and Nova Scotia joined. Canada and Canal Zone, having played their first season on probation in 1950, became the first two countries to enter postseason tournament play the following year.

At that time, however, the board of directors required non-U.S. teams—even though they were national champions—to play through a U.S. regional tournament in order to qualify for one of eight Little League World Series berths. Canal Zone, welcomed royally to the United States, played through Region IV in Trenton, New Jersey. The champs from the Pacific side of the Canal toured New York City when they arrived on July 25, including Radio City Music Hall. Francis Cardinal Spellman, bishop of the Catholic Diocese of New York, received the team after celebrating Mass at St. Patrick's Cathedral.

Canal Zone and Canadian teams failed to win their respective regional tournaments, and thus a spot in the 1951 Little League World Series. The next year, however, the champs from Montreal, Quebec, shocked observers by winning a regional tournament against U.S. teams, becoming the second nation to be represented at the Little League World Series. During the next forty-eight years, Canada earned a berth among the final eight teams forty-three times, although the Canadian champion received an automatic bid in 1958 and nearly every year thereafter. A Canadian team reached the final game only once: in 1965, Stoney Creek, Ontario, fell to Windsor Locks, Connecticut, 3–1 in the championship.

The U.S. military helped spread baseball, as it did eighty-five years earlier during the Civil War. The Army Signal Corps converted the sound track of Yorke's promotional Little League featurette from English to Japanese and distributed the film throughout Japan in 1950—a component of Douglas MacArthur's plan to at least partially westernize Japanese culture. Within a decade, Japan introduced baseball into its elementary school curriculum. Today, Japan boasts the greatest number of Little League programs in any country outside North America.

Dr. Robert Sloan, president of Baylor University (Waco, Texas)

"In a way, all the basic elements of life are in baseball

and Little League. You have to show up at a certain time.

If you're late, you let the team down. And just like life, there

are isolated individual performances that stand out.

But in the end, it's what the team did that really matters.

How you contributed to the cause is important."

five

LITTLE LEAGUE'S CIVIL WAR

In 1949, Carl Stotz was making all the big decisions for an organization that quickly became national, even international, in scope. During the next few years, Stotz began to resent that Little League had become what he called "a commercial enterprise" and that New York–based businessmen—not volunteers from Little Leagues—were part of the board of directors as it became "Little League Baseball, Incorporated." In 1955, Little League founder Carl Stotz—and the program he created—parted ways after a heartbreaking, well-publicized court battle.

HONEST DIFFERENCES

Carl Stotz was busier than ever in 1949 as he sought to balance his new job as Little League Baseball's president with his volunteer duties with his original baseball program. He met with national executives of baseball-manufacturing companies on specifications for a new ball, solicited local companies regarding team sponsorships, traveled thousands of miles to start new leagues, helped with tryouts at home at the field at Memorial Park, worked on plans for an exhibition game at the end of the 1949 Little League season—a tournament called the "Little League Baseball World Series"—and then, if needed, filled in as a manager for teams at his Little League. While he dealt with matters affecting thousands of

Carl Stotz, busy with paperwork at his office in the late 1940s. He worked tirelessly on behalf of Little League, all the while fearing that it was becoming too commercial.

children around the nation, he also worked to improve the local league and volunteered during its regular season.

Charles Durban of the U.S. Rubber Company decided Carl needed help. In June 1949, Durban sent a company employee, Jack Kuhn, to brainstorm with Carl on Little League's future. Carl later said Kuhn's plan called for a strong, centralized Little League administration, including ownership of the fields around the United States, with every Little Leaguer a paying member of the organization.

But Carl's vision was "almost exactly opposite" he said in *A Promise Kept:* "Our discussion ended amicably. In retrospect, though, I can see that it was the beginning of a deep philosophical conflict. At the time, I didn't dwell on it, but sadly, such honest differences continued and grew."

LITTLE LEAGUE BASEBALL, INCORPORATED

Carl had little choice in the matter. The Little League program had become so popular that protection of the name "Little League" was imperative. The next step was for Little League to become "Little League Baseball, Incorporated." The *1949 Little League World Series Official Program* (cost: 15 cents) noted the board's intention to make this change, and the first national newsletter for all Little League franchises, *Little League Hits,* announced the news in the spring of 1950: "Little League is now a corporation organized under the laws of the state of New York. This was deemed desirable by a group of public-

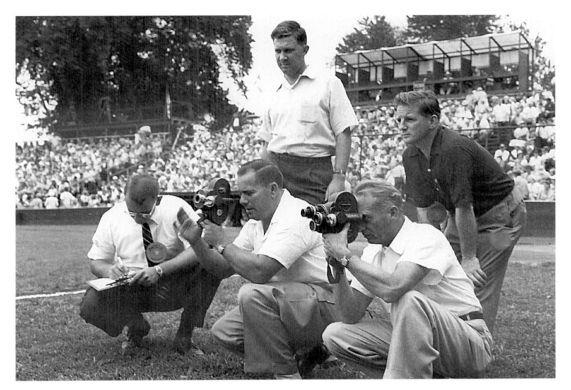

spirited citizens who were aware of the necessity of having legal protection for the name, objectives and activities of the League."

The first formal meeting of the Little League board of directors took place at the New York Athletic Club on January 6, 1950, and elected Carl Stotz board president and Little League commissioner, Charles Durban as chairman of the board, and John Lindemuth as treasurer. The balance of the board, seven men, consisted of Ford Frick, president of the National League of Professional Baseball Clubs in New York City; Paul Kerr, vice president of the National Baseball Hall of Fame and Museum in Cooperstown, New York; Emerson Yorke, owner of Emerson Yorke Studios in New York City; Bernie O'Rourke, treasurer for the city of Middletown, Connecticut; Howard J. Lamade, secretary of Grit Publishing Company, Williamsport; and Ted Husing of radio station WMGM in New York City.

J. Walter Kennedy of Stamford, Connecticut, was elected secretary of the board, a nonvoting position. Kennedy had previously worked in public relations for Notre Dame University and for the National Basketball Association. Kerr became chairman of the board, an unpaid position to this day. Another new director, Dr. Arthur A. Esslinger, added academic flair. Esslinger served in physical education leadership positions at Bradley Polytechnic Institute, Stanford University, and Springfield College. In 1943, he received a commission as a major in the U.S. Army and took charge of physical training for the Office of the Surgeon General.

According to Karen Stotz Myers, Carl was never comfortable with some of the people selected for that board of directors and was "a little put out that Mr. Durban had appointed some people to a board of directors without talking to Dad about it. This disturbed my dad, because he really felt that people on the board of directors should be people who worked with the league, not these prestigious names."

Anticipating trouble, Carl worried that U.S. Rubber would pull its sponsorship of Little League. According to Karen, "Durban checked with the legal department of U.S. Rubber and assured all that 'it would revert to Carl,' which of course didn't happen. But Dad didn't contact an attorney. This wasn't his thing."

Illness prevented Charles Durban from attending the 1952 Little League World Series, and he never returned. Peter J. McGovern, a U.S. Rubber executive from Detroit and 1926 graduate of the University of Pennsylvania, replaced Durban as Little League president in 1952. However, McGovern did not remain in New York, as Durban had. Little League had grown so large that an absentee business manager became impractical. So McGovern moved to Williamsport to become Little League Baseball's full-time president, and that further eroded Carl's influence. Carl and Durban had seen eye-to-eye on most matters, but Little League's new directors clashed with the old guard. Carl retained the title of commissioner, giving him sweeping powers at first, similar to those of bygone commissioners of Major League Baseball, but his operational responsibilities dwindled.

THE GULF WIDENS

Peter J. McGovern, a U.S. Rubber executive from Detroit and a 1926 graduate of the University of Pennsylvania, became Little League Baseball's business leader in 1952.

McGovern, a strong-willed businessman, disagreed with Carl Stotz on many issues, and the gulf between the Little League's board of directors and its founder widened as philosophical differences increased. Karen acknowledged: "There was trouble from Day One. Mother's perception of the men that were brought in here from the bigger cities was that they really didn't feel that [my father], from Williamsport, could know what he was doing. But he wanted Little League to expand, and he wanted boys to play ball. It was his life."

Physically, McGovern and Stotz could hardly have been more different. Peter McGovern was tall and robust, an athletic man who was accustomed to having things his way. John W. Lundy noted: "McGovern [was a] fine gentleman, the finest gentleman I ever met, very imposing, very soft-spoken, [but] domineering in his appearance, and when he spoke he was domineering. The man was not forceful, but [he was] commanding. Can I say this as affirmatively as I can? Mr. McGovern was an autocrat. He ran the thing as he pleased, and the board of directors went along with him. Whatever he wanted, we did. Whatever he *suggested,* we did. Nobody ever took exception to what he did."

Carl Stotz was slight, not much taller than the boys on his baseball team were, and he was humble, always giving credit to fellow volunteers. "He didn't have an ego," said Lundy.

Few in Williamsport's history earned the love and respect Carl Stotz commanded. Art Kline summed up the feelings of many: "Carl was, in a sense, if I can use this term,

The 1954 Little League World Series remains the tournament that produced the most major-league baseball players.

The biggest name among the graduates to make the big leagues was John "Boog" Powell, who went on to star at first base for the Baltimore Orioles. Powell was a pitcher for the Lakeland, Florida, Little League team.

Another future major-leaguer was Jim Barbieri, a center fielder for the Schenectady, New York, Little League. Barbieri played in the major leagues only one year, but his path crossed Powell's twelve years after their first meeting. Lakeland and Schenectady met in the finals of the Little League World Series, with Schenectady winning. Twelve years later, Barbieri was a relief pitcher for the Los Angeles Dodgers in their Major League World Series loss against Powell's Orioles.

One of Barbieri's teammates was Bill Connors, who went on to play for the Chicago Cubs and the New York Mets. One of Powell's teammates was Carl Taylor, who later played with Pittsburgh, St. Louis, and Kansas City. ◆

LEFT
Major League (and former Little League) Baseball players Bill Connors, left, and Jim Barbieri blow bubbles in their milk at lunch one afternoon during the 1954 Little League World Series.

CENTER
Bill Connors, a member of the Chicago Cubs Major League Baseball team, also was on the 1954

Schenectady, New York, team. He played in both the Little League World Series and the Major League Baseball World Series.

RIGHT
Members of the 1954 Little League World Series championship team, Schenectady, New York, board their bus for home after winning the series in Williamsport.

an evangelist. He was so sincere. He could get up in front of a group and convince you that there was nothing better than Little League Baseball. He was simply outstanding. … He was always surrounded by people. Carl was a celebrity, although he was a very humble man and he didn't like to think of himself as a celebrity. He loved people."

Yet, with all the differences, there were similarities. "Mr. McGovern would say, 'Don't forget that Little League is for the kids,'" said Jack Lundy. "And that's the way Carl Stotz always looked at it. Stotz—he did everything for the kids."

Carl too was an autocrat, Lundy added. Though he remained unassuming and constantly sang the praises of others, he was accustomed to having his way. For instance, Carl argued that a representative of the *Williamsport Sun-Gazette* (the *Evening Sun* and the *Gazette-Bulletin,* Williamsport's daily newspapers, merged in 1955) should be on the initial board if Howard Lamade—secretary of the company that owned the rival *Grit* newspaper—was elected. The board sided against him. He argued against including non-U.S. teams in the Little League World Series, believing the tournament should be national only. The board sided against him on that issue as well.

One by one, philosophical differences mounted, and Carl, his daughter confessed, became "the great dissenter." She continued: "He was always the dissenting vote. He did not suddenly, in 1955, decide he didn't like what was going on. This started very early. People would say, 'Carl, you were there for the vote.' Yes, and he was always outvoted."

LITTLE LEAGUE SLIPS AWAY

Watching Little League slip away as his influence and prestige waned was torture for Carl. Oral understandings between Carl Stotz and Charles Durban (Durban died in 1952) had no legal weight as powers were distributed to others. No longer could Carl veto an idea, even if he thought it might be detrimental to the program.

Now the board had the legal power to make decisions, and Peter McGovern headed the board. While Carl traveled throughout the United States in the spring of 1955, Little League was issuing franchises to new leagues clamoring to get started, and staff members made rule interpretations without consulting their commissioner. A *Grit* story on November 27, 1955, reported: "Stotz said that under the original contractual agreement he was to have the right to make the rules and regulations of play and to authorize regional directors to grant franchises and to rule on the eligibility of those leagues." Little League countered by saying that the procedures had been changed in previous board meetings, with Carl present and voting, and that there were leagues growing impatient for the go-ahead to play ball.

Carl Stotz, founder of Little League, left, congratulates the team from Morrisville, Pennsylvania, winners of the 1955 Little League World Series. It was his final Series as commissioner of the program.

Complicating matters for Carl was the death of his friend Cy Young at age eighty-nine on November 4, 1955. On a visit to Canton, Ohio, in 1951, Carl had struck up a friendship with Cy, one of baseball's most hallowed figures and the all-time winningest pitcher in major-league history. Young lived in Peoli, Ohio, and came to Canton to throw out the ceremonial first pitch in that league's opening ceremonies. Starting in 1951, Young traveled to Williamsport at Carl's invitation, attending every Little League World Series until his death. The two became close friends, and a tearful Carl Stotz was a pallbearer at Young's funeral.

The final straw came in June 1955, when Stotz returned from a promotional tour in Europe to find that his secretary had been dismissed and that mail intended for him as commissioner had been opened. In Carl's absence of many weeks, Little League officials had been granting charters, a privilege that had previously been Carl's alone.

CARL LOCKS THE DOORS

Dissension had been mounting for years, and Carl Stotz fired the first shot of Little League's civil war on November 21, 1955. On that day, the Little League board of directors was meeting in special session at The Lycoming, a stately hotel in downtown Williamsport, purportedly to approve a new budget. Peter McGovern called the meeting because U.S. Rubber had announced its intention to end sole sponsorship of Little League on December 31, 1955.

Carl, however, had a different agenda. Accompanied by his attorney, Daniel F. Knittle, Carl presented two resolutions: one called for McGovern's immediate resignation, and the other called for the organization to revert to the 1950 bylaws in which the commissioner—Carl Stotz—held most of the power. Carl not only saw Little League slipping away from him but also believed that it had grown top-heavy and far removed from the grassroots level. He wanted more representatives on the board—specifically "field personnel," or volunteers actually involved in local Little League activities.

According to newspaper reports, McGovern said Stotz threatened to sue for breach of contract unless both resolutions passed, but the motion failed for lack of a second, and Carl left the meeting with Knittle. While the meeting continued and the directors considered the new budget, Knittle visited the office of the prothonotary at the county courthouse to file a writ of foreign attachment against Little League, preventing the New York–based corporation from moving its assets from the state.

A deputy sheriff carried the document to the Little League headquarters, then at 120 West Fourth Street in downtown Williamsport. He served the writ on Robert H. Stirrat, Little League's public relations director and at the time the highest-ranking Little League official in the office, because Little League's board of directors was still in session a block away. The deputy notified Little League employees about the writ and advised them to vacate the offices. Once the offices were emptied, the deputy padlocked the two swinging doors.

While the doors were being locked, the board voted to remove Carl Stotz from his position as commissioner and named John Lindemuth, Carl's assistant and friend, as acting commissioner. Carl, and many of his loyal followers, never spoke to Lindemuth again.

Immediately after the padlocking, the directors took action to reopen the offices by posting a bond. A local attorney retained by Little League telephoned the courthouse to set up a hearing before Lycoming County judges Charles S. Williams and Charles F. Greevy. In the hearing at 4:00 P.M. that day were Carl's attorney (Knittle), Little League's counsel S. Dale Furst Jr. (a local lawyer) and Alfred Lee (a New York attorney representing Little League Baseball), and Peter McGovern. The court set the bond at $130,000, double the amount of property and assets seized in Stotz's writ.

John Lundy remembers it as a dark day: "Carl got excited. He went down with that padlock, so they had to get a court order to remove the lock. I think he got caught up in an argument and he didn't know how to back down. And he had poor advice."

Little League posted the bond, and at 10:45 the next morning, November 22, 1955, a deputy removed the padlock. The business of Little League continued, though hardly as usual.

Statements issued through attorneys to the media gave each side's view of the dispute. Carl's statement, reprinted in the *Williamsport Sun-Gazette,* reads:

> My original contract with Little League Baseball, Inc. included provisions, which would enable me to safeguard the original concepts of the Little League program. This contract vested in me and representative volunteer field personnel certain powers which were intended to maintain a sound Little League program.
>
> Over a period of time this contract has been breached to the point of endangering Little League in that the commissioner and volunteer field personnel no longer have a representative voice in Little League policy decisions.
>
> Accordingly, to end this intolerable situation and to compel a return to the original principles of Little League Baseball, I am suing Little League Baseball, Inc., for $300,000 for breach of contract.
>
> I would like to emphasize that I have not brought this suit with any thought of personal gain. All monies recovered as a result of this suit will be used solely for the purpose of perpetuating Little League Baseball as originally conceived.
>
> Also, I have called a meeting of volunteer field personnel to meet with me at an early date to discuss the manner in which a sound Little League program might be continued.
>
> I have taken this action after the gravest consideration and after all other means have failed. I am firmly of the opinion that this action is essential to the survival of Little League Baseball as it was originally conceived.

Little League Baseball issued the following statement later in the day, also reprinted in the *Sun-Gazette:*

At noontime today, Lycoming County's sheriff's office, by order of a writ obtained by Carl E. Stotz, attempted to close the offices of national headquarters of Little League Baseball, Inc., 120 West Fourth Street, Williamsport.

This action, seemingly calculated to disrupt the operation of headquarters, came during a meeting of the board of directors of Little League Baseball, Inc., which was being held at the Lycoming Hotel. The writ was served on Robert H. Stirrat, Little League's public relations director, in the absence of officers of the corporation who were attending the board meeting. All employees of headquarters were ordered from the premises.

Peter J. McGovern, chairman of the board and president of Little League Baseball, said action had been taken to dissolve the writ. According to McGovern, Stotz attended the meeting this morning in company with his attorney. A proposal submitted by him to the board was not accepted, whereupon Stotz and his attorney left the meeting. McGovern pointed out that the action taken by Stotz did not include an offer to resign his annual $14,000 position.

Within the hour … a representative of the sheriff's office appeared at national headquarters and ordered the staff to leave preparatory to padlocking the premises.

Mr. Stotz' action was termed by Mr. McGovern as "unnecessarily dramatic" and an unbelievable act.

Speaking on behalf of the Board, Mr. McGovern said that the directors genuinely regretted that for quite some time, culminating in his walk-out today, Mr. Stotz had been unwilling to accept decisions which the board had felt were in the best interests of the boys who play Little League Baseball.

Rumors flew around Williamsport as residents took sides in the dispute. Many sided with Carl, whose life had gained local legendary qualities. Some thought McGovern had fired Carl. In an effort to control the rumors, Little League released statements like this one in the first few days following the lockout:

Despite reported rumors to the contrary, Carl Stotz has not been dismissed by Little League Baseball.

Action instituted by the board does not change contractual obligations of Stotz to Little League Baseball, Inc., nor does it affect his status and responsibility as a board member.

The resolution passed by the board in relieving Stotz of all duties and conduct of the office of commissioner, and rescinding any and all authority previously vested in him to act for or represent Little League Baseball, is based on his refusal to abide by and carry out decisions of the board.

It is further emphasized that the law suit is a personal action instituted by Stotz against Little League Baseball, Inc.

Little League Baseball for boys will be carried on with the wholehearted determination that always has characterized the program.

The only ambition of the national office is to give more boys each year a chance to enjoy benefits of the program.

Another statement to the media explained Little League's attempt at damage control outside of Williamsport:

Safeguarding the interests and benefits of the thousands of boys across the country who play the game is the substance of Little League Baseball, according to President Peter J. McGovern.

In a statement prepared as a report to more than 4,000 affiliated local leagues, McGovern re-affirmed the position of national headquarters in relation to developments of the past week which culminated in a law suit instituted by former Commissioner Carl E. Stotz against Little League Baseball, Inc.

We believe the only thing of real importance in Little League is whether or not the youngsters for whom the program is designed are getting a chance in a safe and beneficial program, and that their parents and adult leaders have the opportunity to work along with them in better relationships.

In his report to officers and other personnel of the leagues, McGovern emphasized that the suit, reportedly for $300,000, would have no effect on the normal function of the national headquarters' office. He said the staff was engaged, as is customary at this time of year, in the processing of franchises for the 1956 season. He pointed to the fact that more franchises had been issued up to this point than in a comparable period last year.

We regret, he declared, that Carl Stotz, who has been given every kindness and consideration in the past, has seen fit to reject decisions of the board of directors. These men, all of them competent, honorable and outstanding leaders in their respective fields, have given invaluable time as volunteers to support and safeguard the fundamental aims of Little League.

McGovern also informed the leagues that Stotz had been relieved of all duties and responsibilities of his $14,000 a year position. John M. Lindemuth, former assistant to the commissioner and a veteran of 16 years association with Little League, has been appointed acting commissioner.

The people of Williamsport were not the only ones choosing sides. Sam Porter of California, one of the four board members not present at the meeting earlier in the week, wired his resignation to headquarters. The Associated Press noted that Porter intended to assist Carl "in his effort to return the Little League program to the basic principles, pattern and policies on which it was founded in 1939."

On November 26, 1955, Carl filed a lawsuit against Little League claiming that the original bylaws of the corporation had guaranteed Carl a job as head of Little League Baseball, for the rest of his life, and that the bylaws had subsequently been changed to give other people his duties. It also claimed Carl had been told that the bylaws would never be changed from their original method of electing directors.

McGovern's answer: "Stotz omits to state that he was present and voted for the changes in the bylaws to which he now objects. … It is evident that the complaint is one of dissatisfaction alone."

SECEDING FROM LITTLE LEAGUE

Carl Stotz and Sam Porter were not the only ones to secede in Little League's civil war. At first, entire leagues followed Carl out of the program, agreeing with his position calling for more autonomy for local leagues and less central authority. Letters poured in from the field to Little League National Headquarters and to Stotz's home, asking for clarification about the dispute.

Four Little League employees—Howard Gair, Allen Yearick, Richard Snauffer, and Ralph Hoyt—resigned and joined Carl's team, along with Irma Gehrig, who had been Carl's secretary at Little League. Gair was Little League's umpire consultant. Yearick, Snauffer, and Hoyt were coordinators, employees who helped local leagues in specific geographic regions in administrative matters.

Yearick, who played for Carl's Lycoming Dairy team in 1939, said he never regretted his decision to work with Carl at Little League, and then to leave with him: "It was a great thing in my life to be asked to come with an organization as one of the first-year players. The man who was heading the organization was Carl Stotz. Nobody had a better fatherly image, more of a Christian approach. Nobody had more concern about each and every kid. I mean, I'm saying this from the heart because this is how I felt. When I made the decision to go with him, it wasn't hard because I was in the right program."

The new organization, named "Original Little League" (a reference to Carl's first league), opened an office in downtown Williamsport at 318 Government Place. Carl announced that three leagues in Lycoming County, including his original Little League at Memorial Park, had committed to joining the new organization. A few more followed, though not in the numbers he expected. A report in the *Williamsport Sun-Gazette* quoted Carl as saying he was receiving support from volunteer workers throughout the nation, "even though they have not yet received the letter I sent, which explains my differences with Little League, Inc." He added that each of the nearly 4,000 franchised Little Leagues would be offered membership in the new league and that "steps are being taken to make it abundantly clear that I will not permit my name to be associated with the corporation."

These developments did not sit well with Peter McGovern, who insisted that Carl Stotz was still under contract to Little League Baseball. McGovern's reply in a *Sun-Gazette* story said Little League's attorneys "will undoubtedly look into the question of a Little League employee opening another headquarters."

Carl, in a November 28, 1955, interview, maintained that his association with Little League had ended at the board meeting a week earlier, so he charged ahead with plans

NORTH VS. SOUTH

Ninety-four years after the Confederate Army ignited the Civil War in 1861 by firing on the U.S. Army garrison at Fort Sumter, South Carolina, a few Little League volunteers in South Carolina rebelled against Little League, only a few miles from Fort Sumter. In both cases, secessions resulted. Hundreds of Little League franchises in the South severed ties with the Pennsylvania-based organization. The difference is that South Carolina returned to the Union soon after the Confederate Army's defeat in the Civil War. Most of the franchises that left Little League in 1955 never came back.

The reason South Carolinians gave, both in 1861 and in 1955, was that they needed to protect the right of individual states to govern their own internal affairs and continue their own customs, however odious they might be to others in the nation. So while Little League grew in other areas of the country and overseas, domestic racial problems in the mid-1950s stifled growth of the program in some Southern states for decades.

Little League has been integrated from the start. Although no African Americans participated on the first three teams in 1939, Williamsport's black community became a part of the program the next year and every year thereafter. By the time "Little League" became a household word, the organization proudly trumpeted the fact that boys could play regardless of background or race. States in the Deep South embraced Little League as soon as it became available. Although the first Little League

World Series featured only teams from Pennsylvania and New Jersey, the program expanded quickly, and in 1948 Florida sent a team all the way to the final game.

But the leadership of Little League continued to be solidly Northern. When Little League spread beyond Pennsylvania's borders and non-Williamsport residents were brought in to serve on Little League's board of directors, no member of the board was from the Deep South. And the Little League chain of command ran directly from the headquarters in Williamsport to local leagues, with no official organization between. As the program grew, Little League Baseball Headquarters had less direct contact with local leagues, so loosely defined state organizations sprang up to help with administra-

OPPOSITE PAGE
The 1955 Cannon Street YMCA (South Carolina) Little League team visits the 1955 Little League World Series as guests. The team failed to make the playoffs after all-white teams refused to play them. After clashing with Little League Baseball headquarters, the all-white teams left the program.

LEFT
"Lights out!" Coach says. The 1955 Cannon Street YMCA team prepares for bed.

tive affairs of local leagues, and to help spread the movement to more towns. Such was the case in South Carolina.

Little League programs first appeared in South Carolina in 1949, and by the 1955 season there were sixty-two leagues in the state. But in sixty-one of those leagues, every player was white. One all-black league, Cannon Street YMCA Little League of Charleston, had broken the barrier, receiving a franchise for 1955.

The all-white leagues in the Charleston area, with the support of Danny Jones, state director for Little League, refused to play against the all-black team, and all the other leagues in the state followed suit, planning instead to hold their own unsanctioned state tournament. They contended that Little League officials in

Pennsylvania should not be able to control the internal affairs of local Little League programs in South Carolina.

Little League refused to budge. If the white leagues refused to play a duly franchised league, regardless of race, they would not be permitted to participate in the tournament. This resulted in a mass exodus of teams from Little League, leaving only one "legal" team in South Carolina. The Cannon Street YMCA Little League played a full season of Little League ball and chose an all-star team to represent it, but Little League policy prevented Cannon Street from entering the playoffs because it had not played in district and state tournaments (which was impossible because all the state's teams had bowed out). Nevertheless,

Little League invited the team to Williamsport for the World Series. The Cannon Street All Stars, guests of Little League, experienced everything any other Little League World Series team would, except they could not play a game.

Amid the turmoil in Little League in 1955, the program took a stand against racism in a time and place where racism was in vogue. Little League ended up losing franchises over the controversy, but the strong stand Little League took remains one of the organization's shining moments.◆

for the new league. Armed with a mailing list of all local Little League presidents, Carl wrote to the leagues, inviting them to a general meeting in Pittsburgh, December 10–11, 1955. At that meeting, as he had in the past, Carl intended to capitalize on his veneration as Little League's founder and persuade leagues to support his original Little League program.

Little League Baseball did not just sit back and watch its franchises secede. In a statement to league presidents, Little League said, "Carl Stotz has not been 'ousted,' 'fired,' or 'dismissed.' He is still bound by his contract." The statement added that the board of directors "would use every resource at its command to prevent a further split of Little League through the formation of a nonsanctioned program patterned directly after Little League and using the name or any semblance of the name." Little League urged its member leagues "not to succumb to impulse nor jump to any conclusion until the smoke screen clears and all the facts are known." Little League officials—including McGovern and Lindemuth—were dispatched to various parts of the country for damage control.

Carl's side remained busy as well. Knittle obtained permission from the Lycoming County Court for the Original Little League (the new organization Carl started—not to be confused with the local league of the same name) to enter the offices of Little League Baseball, Incorporated, to inspect documents on file there. The order granted permission to enter at 10:00 A.M. on November 29, 1955. But at 8:45 that morning, Little League filed a petition to transfer the case to the local federal district court. McGovern told the *Sun-Gazette* that, because Little League was incorporated in New York and federal trademarks were involved, the case more properly belonged in the higher court. Inspection by Carl's attorney then required an order from the U.S. District Court, as the case no longer resided in the Lycoming County Court, but the order was never issued. It also meant that proceedings in the county court ceased—a clear setback for Carl because local popularity worked in his favor.

Little League sought an injunction against Carl to prevent him from establishing a rival league. The court scheduled a hearing before Middle District Court Judge Frederick V. Follmer for December 5, 1955, to consider Little League's injunction request.

Judge Follmer held out hope that a settlement could be reached. "I don't know of anything that would thrill me more than to have some part in disposing and settling the matter satisfactorily," he said. "I am trusting and hoping an amicable adjustment can be made. All I am interested in is saving Little League Baseball for the youths of America." Follmer dealt Carl another setback when he issued an oral restraining order after the first day of the hearing, temporarily preventing Carl from creating a rival organization to Little League. Follmer said, based on papers and affidavits he had seen, that "immeasurable damage" might result if a restraining order was not decreed while the issue received a hearing.

Chances for arbitration ended on December 7, 1955. In the first day of proceedings, one of Little League's attorneys suggested arbitration: "I am firmly convinced there is a way. I am convinced there is a place for Carl Stotz and that there is a job for him to do."

Knittle suggested that a special board of arbitration might be convened, if it was composed of U.N. Secretary Dr. Ralph Bunche, nationally noted clergyman Dr. Norman Vincent Peale, and U.S. Olympic Committee Chairman Kenneth L. Wilson. Judge Follmer responded, "No one is ever allowed to choose his own jury," and went ahead with the hearing.

The first witness, Little League Secretary-Treasurer Albert F. Houghton, echoed the sentiments of many at the time, and the sentiments of many even today, in his testimony: "I always considered the name of Stotz and Little League Baseball as synonymous."

Judge Follmer may have tipped his hand when he asked Knittle, "What is going to happen to the kids of America with two leagues? They are not interested in a Stotz league but a Little League—this may prove to be very harmful to set up a competitive league." He continued: "Are not these examples of poor internal management? Can't something be done without setting up a new and competitive organization?" Later, when he remarked, "I believe many people that have heard of Little League have never heard of Carl Stotz," several in the courtroom booed.

Even in 1956, there were protesters. Here, a fan walks through the crowd during a Little League World Series game carrying a sign calling for Carl Stotz to return to the Little League program. Stotz left the organization in December 1955.

LOSING THE BATTLE

Knittle tried to convince Judge Follmer to dissolve the oral restraining order, knowing that Carl Stotz had planned a meeting with defecting local Little League volunteers. The general meeting planned in Pittsburgh that weekend, December 10–11, loomed, and Carl needed to be able to speak freely. But on December 8, 1955, Judge Follmer placed written restraints into the record, specifically prohibiting Stotz from taking any action that could damage Little League and from making any effort to set up a new league by convincing others to join his cause.

Testimony resumed on December 9, 1955, with Peter McGovern taking the stand. The *Sun-Gazette* reported that McGovern termed the recent events "devastating and demoralizing beyond any description I can give," and added, "The damage is very serious." He also testified that Stotz and the four who resigned from Little League to cast their lots together were still in possession of confidential Little League matter, such as membership lists.

Perhaps as a strategy, Carl seemed to "soften" at the prospect of negotiations. The attorneys met at The Lycoming Hotel, and Judge Follmer gladly held the court's proceedings in abeyance. Both sides agreed to refrain from making public statements while talks continued.

The Pittsburgh meeting took place on December 10 and 11 with representatives of about 150 local Little Leagues, mostly from the Northeast, attending and with John Stevenson of Haddon Heights, New Jersey, as its chairman, to support Carl. Stevenson had resigned as Little League's director in the Southern New Jersey area. The December 12, 1955, issue of the *Sun-Gazette* reported that Stotz did not attend.

Although he had verbal commitments from hundreds of regional directors, Carl lost just about every battle he waged. Negotiations broke off on December 29, 1955, and the case returned to court. Judge Follmer put more teeth into the restrictions concerning forming a new league, issuing an injunction on January 6, 1956. A jury trial in Lycoming County Court to settle the issue of Stotz's $300,000 lawsuit for breach of contract was scheduled for June 6, 1956, but never made it that far. According to Allen Yearick, Carl did not want to subject his friends to the expense and inconvenience of a trial:

> If Carl could have got his facts and figures into a court of law, I think he could have won that case. Carl withdrew from the fight because he was afraid of the hurt. When they brought in the boys [attorneys] from the big city, they were taking every little twist and turn. They were hammering from every direction—they went to strip this man of his program, and the legal battle embittered some. Carl made it known he was not going to have people like Ollie Fawcett go on trial. He didn't want to expose people he was close to.

Oliver Fawcett, one of Carl's dearest friends, recalled the trial:

The corporation was fighting Carl, and Carl went out and hired a lawyer. That was another thing—he only had so much money. He borrowed on his insurance. He finally got Dan Knittle [who] got into it, and he started to work for nothing when Carl's money ran out. I was subpoenaed, and they had me on the witness stand at one of the hearings. We had a practice session out at Dan Knittle's house the night before. Dan asked me, "You're not afraid, are you?'" I said, "Naw." But, I tell you, it wasn't pretty, pleasant days. It got pretty nasty. They wanted to know what Dan Knittle was advocating as Carl's lawyer, and what Carl was doing in regards to starting another league. That worried them more than anything. They had me on from ten o'clock in the morning, till two or three in the afternoon. Just kept peppering me. I forget what some of my answers were anymore, it was a long session. It was browbeating, is what it was. We finally ran out of money. They had two high-powered law firms—big shots came from New York. And Carl, he had but one skinny lawyer.

In the end, Carl had no chance, regardless of who his, or Little League's, lawyers were.

THE AGREEMENT

Lack of money, Carl Stotz's daughter Karen Stotz Myers recalls, was not the reason her father decided to settle his dispute with Little League Baseball, Incorporated, out of court. Instead, the reason was loyalty to his friends: "He could not bear to see his friends being hauled into court and sued by the corporation. He told people he would spend every last penny if he could, but his loyalty to his friends was more important."

Although the $300,000 lawsuit against Little League failed to win any money, Carl did gain some concessions. The document ending the dispute, signed on February 2, 1956, called for the following:

- An end to the litigation between the two parties.
- A promise by Carl to refrain from activities antagonistic to the corporation, and by the corporation to refrain from defamatory or antagonistic activities directed against Carl.
- A promise by the corporation to recognize Carl as Little League's sole founder.
- An agreement to end Carl's position as a member, director, or employee of the corporation.
- An end to the contract Carl originally signed as commissioner of Little League on June 9, 1950.
- A promise by Carl to use his "best efforts" to prevail on Original Little League to refrain from any activities competitive to the corporation, and to make its facilities available to the corporation for tournament play.
- An agreement by both parties to return any property owned by the other party.
- An agreement by the corporation to establish a method for electing field representatives to the board of directors (but allowed for Carl to run for election if he chose to).
- An agreement by the corporation to "empower the district delegates to make, amend and repeal the playing rules for local leagues of Little League Baseball."
- An agreement by the corporation to pass a resolution stating its intent to maintain its headquarters in Williamsport and to hold its annual Little League Baseball World Series there.
- An agreement by the corporation to refrain from taking any action against those "in sympathy with Carl Stotz or any activity in apparent concert with him, if such person after the date of this agreement ceases and desists from such activity and restores to the Corporation any property of the Corporation which he may have." A stipulation added, however, that the corporation could subsequently take legal action if such person "after the date of this Agreement persists in wrongful activity or fails to restore corporate property. ..."
- An agreement by the corporation not to pursue another injunction against Carl as long as he did not breach the agreement.

The document called for the agreement to expire on December 31, 1959, but for the most part, both parties adhered to it. Little League did move out of Williamsport in 1959, but only across the river to the borough of South Williamsport.◆

"GOOD FAST HANDS"

Carl Stotz did not believe in using well-known personalities to raise the profile of Little League in the eyes of the American public. He advocated a stronger "field" presence on the board—at least 50 percent representation by those closest to the grassroots of the program: managers, coaches, umpires, and league officers.

From the beginning, however, Little League's board of directors enlisted a broad cross-section of experts in fields ranging from business to the media to professional sports to medicine. One of the newest supporters of Little League in the 1950s was Walt Disney, who opined in an article for the 1955 Little League World Series program:

> To me, Little League Baseball is a valuable asset to our society because it gives boys an enjoyable experience, and yet one in which they learn to cooperate with their teammates, their families and neighbors. ... This is a competitive world where the best winning is done by observing rules of fair play and equal opportunity. Little League is valuable because the half million boys under 13 years of age who are benefiting from it may well hold the future of our country in their hands one day.

Disney could not have been more right on the latter issue. A few months before Disney's article appeared in the 1955 Little League World Series program, the father of a certain Texas Little Leaguer gives his opinion on his son's prospects: "Georgie aggravates the hell out of me at times. I am sure that I do the same to him. But then at times I am so proud of him I could die. He is out for Little League, so eager. He tries so very hard. He has good fast hands and even seems to be able to hit a little" (Former President George Bush, in an April 7, 1955, letter to his father-in-law).

Other young but promising Little League prospects during the 1950s included Bill Bradley, Dan Quayle, and William Cohen. All of them—including the boy with the "good fast hands," George W. Bush—credit Little League as having a major influence on their later successes.◆

TOP
Former U.S. Senator Bill Bradley, left, also a former Little League player, was enshrined in the Little League Hall of Excellence in 1989.

CENTER
Former U.S. Vice President Dan Quayle, pictured here as an Indiana Little Leaguer, visited the Little League Baseball World Series in 1992. He is the only sitting vice president to visit Little League in Williamsport.

BOTTOM
Former U.S. Vice President Dan Quayle's Little League glove is on display at the Peter J. McGovern Little League Museum.

And the leagues Carl expected to follow him? They took the path of least resistance. By the last week of January 1956, some 2,500 leagues already were franchised with Little League, and 50 to 100 more franchise applications arrived each day at headquarters. Although many leagues were prepared to do what Carl wanted, Karen Stotz Myers said, "It was January. It was time to franchise, time to do something. He had an injunction against him, and he wanted the boys to play ball."

Carl was ready to concede, and the attorneys met for a final round of talks. On February 3, 1956, Little League Baseball and Carl issued this statement:

> The controversy between Carl E. Stotz has been settled. Mr. Stotz is not associated with any competitive program, nor is he any longer an officer, director or employee of Little League Baseball, Inc. The settlement did not involve any financial consideration.

Before he settled, however, Carl had three stipulations: that Little League remain in Williamsport; that there be more voting representatives from field volunteers on the board of directors; and that Little League Baseball not contest his status as founder of the program.

For a while it had seemed as if Little League might be destroyed, and the story was making national news on a daily basis. The last few months of 1955 had been among the worst in Little League's history. Yet in 1956 the number of local Little League programs topped 4,000 for the first time. The exact opposite had occurred.

Brent Musburger, sports broadcaster

"I grew up on the Little League field

in Billings, Montana, and my dad was my coach.

That introduction to baseball

fueled a lifelong interest in sports."

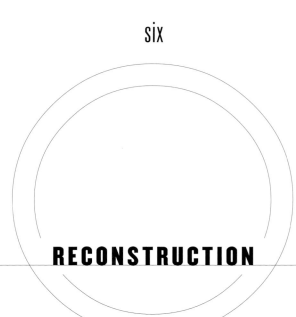

SIX

RECONSTRUCTION

Carl Stotz's exit could have been ruinous to Little League. The split between Carl and the Little League board was fodder for national wires almost daily during the court battles in December 1955, turning what was essentially a small-town feud into big news. A month earlier, Little League's founder had contacted local Little Leagues throughout the nation by mail, urging the organization to return to its original precepts. Volunteers deluged the headquarters with inquiries about the program's future.

LITTLE LEAGUE RECOVERS

But the organization emerged stronger after its civil war. Carl's break with Little League hastened momentous change for the program in 1956 and 1957: A new "congress" system allowed volunteers in the field to have more voice in rule changes; a full-time pinch hitter for U.S. Rubber was found within Little League itself; and a twelve-year-old ambidextrous Mexican boy became Little League's version of Babe Ruth, completing the organization's reconstruction.

Although the number of leagues in Pennsylvania dropped by 43 leagues to 397 in 1956, most local Little League programs around the nation flocked back to the fold in 1956, an amazing feat considering the

At a Little League World Series game in the 1950s, the seeds of friendship are sown between a player from the North, Connecticut, and a player from the South, Texas, as they sit atop a dugout and admire their trophies.

turmoil early in the year. In the June 1956 issue of the *Little Leaguer,* the lead story boasted: "More important than statistics, which indicate a new high of more than 4,000 leagues, is the evidence that Little League is wholesome, strong and has the endorsement of millions of Americans."

The question of field representation in decision-making lingered. In 1955, the board of directors was considering a way to give local volunteers some say while keeping ultimate authority in the hands of the board. Headquarters divided the world of Little League into districts, with each district's leagues electing a single representative. The representatives would help shape the future of the program.

Little League wasted no time officially putting the plan into action, which probably prevented further defections. On February 6, 1956, three days after negotiations ended the lawsuits, the board amended the corporation's bylaws, calling for the election of "field representative directors" elected from and by the leagues themselves. The original plan

"Yer Out!" A New Jersey player agonizes after being called out by the umpire in Little League World Series action in the 1950s.

called for all "district representatives" (today called district administrators) to meet annually at a convention where they were delegates to the National Congress of Little League Baseball.

In the first year under the new provision, two district representatives were elected from and by the delegates to serve on the Little League board of directors, subject to final board approval. In 1957, five district representatives were elected to serve on the board. Every year thereafter, the new bylaws called for at least one-third of the board to be elected from among delegates. That gave local volunteers some voice on the board of directors (again, subject to the board's final approval). Raymond B. Stafano of Utica, New York, and Robert S. Gordon of Birmingham, Alabama, became the first district representatives elected to the board of directors through this congress system.

That first National Congress was held on March 22–24, 1956, at the Morrison Hotel in Chicago, a significant accomplishment considering that, in some minds, the continued existence of the corporation had been very much in doubt only two months earlier. Local leagues within each district paid their share of the expenses so their delegates could make the trip. The board chose Chicago because of its central location.

According to Elmer Lehotsky, a former field representative from Ohio who later joined Little League Baseball's staff: "There was a lot of expectation. This was a whole new direction Little League was taking. Now there was democratic process in place. As for concerns, there were many. But the delegates there wanted to have some say in rules. There were rules they wanted to change, there were regulations they wanted to change, there were some policies they wanted to change. Consensus was something else."

District representatives also had some voice in changing rules, through the National Congress. The rules and franchise committees of Little League (headquarters staff employees) set the agenda based on subjects that arose most often from local league volunteer questions and comments. They debated various pros and cons of proposed changes in small roundtable discussions, then drafted a proposal for a vote by the entire delegation. If a proposal received at least two-thirds of the votes at the congress, it was submitted to the board of directors for final approval. Although the board always had the final say, no recommendation passed by the district representatives has ever been denied by the board. That system remains largely unchanged today, although meetings of the congress, now called the Little League Baseball International Congress, are currently held once every three years.

For the most part, rule changes had until 1956 been the exclusive province of Carl Stotz. At the first congress, however, some of the issues local volunteers grumbled about were addressed. Among the measures passed were:

- Local leagues were allowed to play five "special games" apiece against other leagues in the district, with the district representative's approval. "Special games" are games outside the regular season (within the league) or games in the National Tournament. Formerly, Little League teams could only play in special games against adjoining leagues.

- The local Little League division (nine-to-twelve-year-olds, often referred to as the "Major League") could include more than four teams after the first year of play, and minor-league divisions could have more than six teams. Until then, exactly four teams were required in the major league, and minor leagues were limited to six teams.

- Multiple management of local leagues was permitted, with approval of the district representative and subject to approval from National Headquarters. Until then, rules required each individual local league to have its own board of directors. But with towns growing beyond the 15,000 population limit imposed by Little League regulations for a single league, some had been forced to form a separate board of directors for a second league playing at the same site using the same facilities.

- A less restrictive rule was created for night games, placing the decision whether to play under lights in the hands of the local league and its district representative. Formerly, night games had been discouraged by the rules and could be played only "in certain climates and geographical locations," and only if Carl Stotz himself approved them.

- Delegates also recommended clarifications to playing rules, and they were passed. Until then, only the commissioner (Carl Stotz, before 1956) could change the rules.

In the second congress, delegates recommended wholesale changes that eased substitution rules, and player accident insurance became mandatory for all leagues. Board member John Lundy explained why having a voice in changing rules is the most important aspect of the congress: "You couldn't do without the congress because that's where the people vote. That's democracy in Little League."

Education became another facet of the events, with seminars and speeches by various celebrities and authorities. Among the speakers at the first congress were Illinois Governor William G. Stratton, U.S. Olympic Committee Chairman Kenneth L. Wilson, and Baseball Hall of Famer Rogers Hornsby. The 1957 congress guests included future Hall of Fame pitcher Bob Feller and Chicago Mayor Richard Daley. The list of congress guests between the first congress in 1956 and the twenty-second congress in 2001 in Ottawa, Canada, reads like a *Who's Who* of famous ballplayers, politicians, and entertainers.

Eventually, the burden of paying expenses for delegates' travel to the congress was relieved by a new plan. Starting in 1961, local leagues contributed $20 each to headquarters, which held the funds in escrow until the next congress. Later, for each team entering postseason play in Little League's National Tournament (since 1966, called the International Tournament), the local league paid an entry fee to Little League. Part of the fee was placed in escrow for district representatives' travel to the next congress.

A FOUNDATION IS BORN

Raising enough money to recover the loss of U.S. Rubber as sponsor became a priority for Little League Baseball. The sponsorship only helped to offset the deficit, as franchise fees from leagues (nearly $100,000 in 1956) now provided the bulk of Little League's income. But U.S. Rubber's support would cease at the end of 1956, so the board began searching for a financial pinch hitter almost as soon as the company announced its intention to withdraw. At the sponsor's prompting, Peter McGovern had presented a rough outline for a "Little League Foundation" at the fateful November 1955 board meeting where Carl Stotz issued his ultimatum. Part of the plan was to solicit donations from corporations and wealthy individuals, but local Little Leagues were to be its main supporters. Meanwhile, U.S. Rubber promised to continue with financial help until the Foundation was on its feet.

MAISIE CHEN GOES TO THE WORLD SERIES

Maisie Chen fled China in 1950 with her husband, Kenneth, a former Chinese diplomat. On June 9, 1956, Chen, who operated a Chinese restaurant in Manhattan with her husband, appeared on the television program "Big Surprise" and won $100,000 by answering the jackpot question in the category "Brooklyn Dodgers." The entire Chen family were Dodgers fans, so when the final question, "Who was the final out in the 1955 World Series?" was asked, Maisie easily replied, "Elston Howard."

Maisie informed Little League that she wanted to donate $2,000 to Little League Baseball's newly created Foundation, and Little League invited her and her fourteen-year-old son to attend the 1956 Little League World Series.◆

McGovern was intensely patriotic. In regular newsletters to local Little League presidents, he often exhorted volunteers to vote, to have faith in the American system and its economic system, and to support the U.S. armed forces. So it came as no surprise that the Little League board of directors settled on Flag Day, June 14, 1957, as Little League National Foundation Day. Regular-season games on that day were to include ceremonies celebrating Little League. Mid-game collections—"passing the hat" was a tradition by then—would result in the day's donations, which would be forwarded to Little League National Headquarters. The idea of setting aside a single day to collect donations and send them to Williamsport was not new. Two years earlier, Little League had spearheaded a drive to have its local leagues send one day's collection to headquarters to be donated to polio relief.

The district representatives heard of the plan for the Little League Foundation in April 1957 at the second congress, also in Chicago. Initially the goal was to make Little League independent of any need for a national sponsor by raising at least $1 million. In the June 8, 1957, issue of the *Williamsport Sun-Gazette,* sports editor Ray Keyes explained that the Foundation would ensure "the permanency, self-sufficiency and development of Little League Baseball" and that the money raised would not be used for operating expenses. Keyes, who covered every Little League World Series from 1947 until his death in 1988 at the age of seventy-two, and who frequently wrote columns that were glowingly complimentary to Little League, outlined the Foundation's objectives: (1) funding for future growth of the Little League program, (2) establishing a permanent National Headquarters building for Little League Baseball, (3) conducting expanded research, (4) creating workshops in Williamsport for local league volunteers, and (5) establishing an adult leadership training program.

The first trustees of the Little League Foundation were Peter J. McGovern, Howard J. Lamade (vice president of Grit Publishing Company), and Harry Humphries, president of U.S. Rubber. Little League secured endorsement for the Foundation from President Dwight D. Eisenhower, former President Herbert C. Hoover, and F.B.I. Director J. Edgar Hoover.

In its search for funding, the Little League Foundation sent solicitation letters to well-to-do and well-connected citizens, telling them about the Foundation and its purpose. In addition, $12,000 was collected from leagues nationwide, an amount that doubled to more than $24,000 in 1958. The average contribution per league in 1958 was $5.11, compared with about $2.50 in 1957.

Another goal of the Little League Foundation was to establish an emergency fund to keep Little League operating in the event of a financial catastrophe. As Peter McGovern left for a globe-trotting tour to promote Little League internationally in the summer of 1958, he explained the Foundation's contingency plans to a reporter from the *Montreal Star:* "What we're primarily interested in is having the money against the day when hard times come along—if they ever arrive. We wouldn't want to find ourselves in trouble and with no money to support us. We've come too far to curl up and die because we hadn't planned for an emergency."

It didn't take long to realize that the Little League Foundation's greatest support would come from large donors, which resulted in some well-known names appearing among those on the list of trustees. Luminaries such as Lawrence Welk, Bob Hope, Walter O'Malley, William A. "Bill" Shea, Walt Disney, and J. Edgar Hoover have served.

On November 2, 1959, a letter from McGovern to all the leagues reported that the Foundation had $294,000. In years following its inception, the Foundation helped fund a long list of special projects, including facility construction, research into the mental and physical effects of youth baseball, an anti-spitting-tobacco campaign, a Challenger Division for disabled children, a traffic-safety initiative, and a program to bring baseball back to inner-city areas. While the Little League Foundation was a rousing success, and thrives today, eventually Little League again accepted national sponsorship, though not from a single benefactor.

H. E. Humphries, center, an executive with U.S. Rubber, congratulates the 1959 Little League World Series champs, Kankakee, Illinois. It was the first year the series was played at the new facility, the Howard J. Lamade Memorial Field in South Williamsport.

This early-1950s action shot leaves some doubt as to the outcome of this play. Note that the ball is already in the fielder's mitt as he prepares to tag the runner diving into bag.

WHERE WILL THE SERIES BE PLAYED?

Carl Stotz's Original Little League proceeded during the 1956 season without franchising with Little League Baseball, Incorporated, and it did so with Carl at the helm as its newly elected president. That led to another controversy: Where would the Little League Baseball World Series be played?

The site for the tournament every year since 1947 had been the field at Max M. Brown Memorial Park, but the field there was leased by the city of Williamsport to Original Little League, still led by Carl. In a letter mailed in late 1955, Little League officials assured its affiliates that there would be another World Series and announced that the dates would be August 21–24, 1956. However, they did not list a location.

Through much of 1956, representatives from Original Little League, the city of Williamsport, and Little League Baseball wrangled over the use of the field, not only for the World Series but also for the Pennsylvania state tournament that was scheduled to take place before the international event. It might have been easy for the city to simply mandate that Little League could use the Original League field for the two weeks they needed, but even though the city owned the fields, such structures as the bleachers, dugouts, scoreboard, and fences belonged to Original Little League. Another sticky point was a Little League Baseball rule prohibiting tournament play on fields operated by nonsanctioned leagues.

With the city acting as intermediary, the two sides finally reached an agreement, but the accord resembled the Korean War peace negotiations of a few years earlier in its complexity. City council first passed a measure transferring control of the property during a specified period from Original Little League to the city, then passed a separate measure assigning control to Little League Baseball, Incorporated. Even the keys for various buildings went through the hands of city officials before Little League Baseball took temporary possession of the field.

Players at the 1956 World Series were blissfully unaware of the turmoil in the city of Williamsport earlier that year, particularly Fred Shapiro of Delaware Township, New Jersey. Shapiro, a slender five-foot-ten boy of 124 pounds, pitched the first perfect game in Little League World Series history as his team defeated Colton, California, in the semifinals. He was mobbed by reporters after the game, including Mike Bernardi, associate sports editor for the *Sun-Gazette,* who described a meeting between Shapiro and Vernon "Lefty" Gomez, former New York Yankee pitcher and Hall of Famer, a special guest at the Series:

> "May I shake your hand, Mr. Gomez?" Shapiro asked as he looked admiringly into the eyes of the former great, who holds the record of never losing a World Series game in six decisions.
>
> Smiling, Gomez replied, "I want to shake your hand, son. You pitched a whale of a ball game out there today."

Bernardi then explained that Fred hugged his mother, but she brought him down to earth a bit with a quiet rebuke for pounding his bat against the ground after he struck out during the game: "You can't hit every time you're up there, Freddie. I don't want to see you do that again."

WHAT *IS* ORIGINAL LEAGUE?

What's in a name? The term "Little League" was coined by Carl Stotz in 1939, but it did not refer to a wider program. In fact, for the first eight years "Little League" referred only to the original local program that Carl Stotz founded. Carl advised other local programs on how to pattern their operations after his, but the other programs were not using the Little League name. That changed in 1947 with the advent of a national championship tournament. Carl's local league was identified in the 1947 National Little League Tournament program as "Williamsport Little League." But other programs began identifying themselves as "Little League" too, so the media began calling Carl's program "Original Little League," and the name stuck.

The tournament was renamed the Keds National Little League Tournament in 1948, then it became the National Little League Baseball Tournament in 1949, then finally it was called the Little League Baseball World Series in 1950, its name ever since.

The 1947 tournament was played at Max M. Brown Memorial Park, a sprawling recreational area on the west side of Williamsport that also contains Bowman Field, a minor-league baseball facility currently occupied by the Williamsport Crosscutters, a Class A affiliate of the Pittsburgh Pirates. The baseball field within Memorial Park, where the first twelve Little League national or world championship tournaments were played, was known simply as Little League Baseball Field until 1951, when it became known as Original Little League Park. In 1954, it became Original Little League Field.

From the founding of the organization in 1939 until January 1950, the words "Little League" were still in the public domain. Anyone could have used them without having any connection to Carl Stotz or his baseball pro-

Original League players prepare for the 2000 Mac McCloskey Tournament. Although most of the rules are the same, members of Original League are not chartered Little League Baseball players, and haven't been since Carl Stotz and his local league split with the program in December 1955.

gram—and many did, to Carl's chagrin. To protect the name, U.S. Rubber convinced Carl to form a corporation and to claim ownership of the trademark in the corporation's name, which he did. The new corporation was to be known as "Little League Baseball, Incorporated."

Carl and Little League Baseball parted ways in the well-publicized court battle that began in 1955 and ended in February 1956. At the same time, Original Little League parted ways with the corporation and exists today as an independent league, although it was forced by court action on the part of Little League Baseball, Incorporated, in 1958, to drop the word "Little" from its name because it was a trademark violation. That was not uncommon, however, because even before the split from Carl's original program, Little League regularly turned to legal means to protect its trademark when nonaffiliated groups have attempted to use it.

So local volunteers formed "Original League, Incorporated" in 1958, and the name of the field was changed to Original League Field. In 1974, Original League renamed the field "Carl E. Stotz Field," although Carl's daughter

Karen said he did not approve of that.

For the first decade of its existence, Little League Baseball, Incorporated, rented office space in downtown Williamsport. Growth of the program and the need for more space made the offices barely tolerable. The field used for the Little League World Series for the past three Series (1956–58) was being "borrowed" by the corporation from Original League, Incorporated—and that was intolerable. So Little League Baseball, Incorporated, pulled up stakes and moved across the West Branch of the Susquehanna River to the borough of South Williamsport, where it remains today.

The field built for the World Series in South Williamsport was originally called Howard J. Lamade Memorial Field, named for the late vice president of the Grit Publishing Company who had been a member of the Little League board of directors from 1951 until his death in 1958. It was renamed Howard J. Lamade Stadium when the old wood and steel stands were razed and a concrete stadium was constructed in 1968.◆

Volunteers wearing white chef hats feed the masses Buckeye's Pretzels at the 1952 Little League World Series.

One celebrity at the 1956 Series was Al Schacht, known around the world then as "The Clown Prince of Baseball." Schacht got his start in baseball in 1910, earning $4 a week and board as a minor-league pitcher for several years before making it to the big leagues with the Washington Senators. He compiled a 14–10 record over three years, but his career ended with an arm injury. But then Schacht put his rubber face and nimble body to work in 1921 as a clown and performed in twenty-seven World Series. Although he had made several visits to Williamsport before 1956 to perform at Williamsport Grays games, it was his first trip in connection with Little League. He called the Little League program "the greatest thing to combat juvenile delinquency."

Thousands of fans show up for a Little League World Series game at Brown Memorial Park in the mid-1950s. Many fans spurn the benches and instead sit on the grass-covered dike or stand at the outfield fence waiting for home-run balls.

TOP
World-famous clown Emmett Kelly, on loan from the Brooklyn Dodgers, entertains the crowd between innings at the 1957 Little League Baseball World Series.

BOTTOM
A female reporter joins the ranks of cameramen and the press at an early World Series.

MEXICO'S BABE RUTH

Another famous clown visited the Little League Baseball World Series. Emmett Kelly was under contract to the Brooklyn Dodgers, and the Dodgers released him for the week to perform in Williamsport for the 1957 Little League World Series. By the time the tournament ended, however, Little League found a new star to put an exclamation point on Little League's reconstruction period.

Exactly one year after Fred Shapiro pitched the first perfect game in Little League World Series history, Mexico's Angel Macias duplicated the effort—only this time it was in the final game. Macias accomplished the feat while pitching right-handed, but he also was capable of throwing left-handed. The story captivated journalists covering the Series in Williamsport, and the team members—Macias in particular—became instant celebrities and fan favorites.

The Mexican team, Monterrey Industrial Little League, arrived in Williamsport for the Series carrying paper bags for luggage. They had good manners and voracious appe-

tites. The players were smaller than most Little League teams, yet won their way up the chain by claiming titles in their native Mexico, then in three cities in Texas (McAllen, Fort Worth, and Corpus Christi), then in Louisville, Kentucky, at the Southern Region Tournament. When asked by reporters whether the larger American kids were of concern to the Mexican team, first baseman Ricardo Trevino replied, "We have to play them, not carry them."

Upon their arrival at the World Series, all players were examined by Williamsport doctor Robert Yasui, the physician-consultant for the Little League World Series from the mid-1950s until he retired from the position in 1998. Yasui expressed amazement that Monterrey's players had nearly perfect teeth—not a single cavity. The reason, he surmised, was that they couldn't afford candy and that the water in Monterrey was heavily fluoridated.

At an average height of four-foot-eleven, most were too small to fit into any of the uniforms provided by Little League, so the team wore their home uniforms emblazoned with "Monterrey" across the front of the jersey. They had been eating well since leaving Mexico, and they gorged on food provided by Lycoming College. In fact, before the team entered the United States two weeks earlier for tournament play, the average weight per player was eighty pounds. When the World Series games actually started, many on the Mexican team had gained ten to fifteen pounds each.

By the time the final game rolled around, the boys from Monterrey were everyone's darlings. Then Angel Macias topped all the hoopla by retiring all eighteen batters he faced—the first and last perfect game in Little League World Series championship game history. He did not allow a single ball to leave the infield.

OPPOSITE PAGE
Ambidextrous pitcher Angel Macias pitched a no-hitter for Monterrey, Mexico, in the 1957 Series. Macias later played professional baseball, being drafted by the California Angels in 1962. He also played twelve years in the Mexican League.

BELOW
Angel Macias practices his pitching technique at his home in Monterrey, Mexico.

Members of the Monterrey, Mexico, 1957 Little League Baseball World Series Championship Team wave their sombreros farewell as they ride the Little League shuttle bus to the airport. The same league, Monterrey Industrial, returned to the Little League World Series in 1958.

The story made national headlines, and U.S. President Dwight Eisenhower invited the Monterrey winning team to the White House for a visit. They also met future Presidents (then U.S. Senators) Lyndon Johnson and Richard Nixon. Hollywood came calling too. A year later the team was in the film "The Little Giants," which failed to make a dent at the box office but enjoyed good public reaction when televised twice in 1960 and once in 1961 on NBC (with a new title, "How Tall Is a Giant?"). The film's distributor, Continental Distributing, Inc., wanted Little Leaguers around the country to sell tickets for the movie, but Little League Baseball—almost fervent in opposing exploitation of players by commercial interests—would not allow it. Little League continues to receive requests to use its trademarked name in movies, books, and television programs, but rarely gives permission.

The same league, Monterrey Industrial, earned a rare repeat trip to the Little League World Series in 1958 when the number of teams increased from four to seven, with three of the regions (Latin America, Canada, and Pacific) producing teams from outside the United States. Because players must be either eleven or twelve years old, most Little League Tournament teams include only a few players who are eleven, which means the bulk of the team will be too old for the Little League Division in the following season. In Mexico's case, only one player, first baseman Ricardo Trevino, participated in both tournaments. The hero the second time around was Hector Torres, who went on to a career in Major League Baseball.

Angel Macias was drafted by the California Angels in 1962 and played twelve years in the Mexican League. He earned a degree in business administration and is a public relations supervisor in Monterrey. Macias was one of nine Little League World Series participants invited back to Williamsport in 1996 to celebrate the fiftieth Series, as a member of a commemorative team made up of players from various eras. In a Little League news release in 1996, Macias said: "In the championship, I was concentrating so much on trying to win that I didn't realize I was pitching a perfect game. At the end of the game, I remember most of all [coaches] Cesar Faz and Pepe Gonzalez celebrating the triumph with us. That was the most important thing." Faz had been a batboy and clubhouse attendant for the San Antonio (Texas) Missions in the minor leagues. Gonzalez, a photographer, continues to make a pilgrimage to Williamsport every year for the Little League World Series.

Yogi Berra, former New York Yankees catcher, Baseball Hall of Famer

"I think Little League is wonderful.

It keeps the kids out of the house."

seven

LITTLE LEAGUE CROSSES THE RIVER

Little League Baseball pushed forward with more ambitious plans for 1959 and beyond. First and foremost, it acquired a new home, which was christened by one of the most dominant Little Leaguers ever, Art Deras. And in 1960, Little League expanded its program to include Little League graduates. Then the American Broadcasting Company (ABC), a distant third behind NBC and CBS in the hearts and minds of Americans in 1963, added the Little League Baseball World Series to an experiment it called *Wide World of Sports*.

NEW CHALLENGES

The idea of borrowing a baseball field for its biggest event was uncomfortable, but Little League officials also acknowledged that the original home of the Little League World Series had become too small. Seating was limited at the field at Memorial Park, sandwiched between West Fourth Street and the dike protecting Williamsport from Susquehanna River floods. More than 12,000 fans, a record for the site, were present for the 1958 Series, the last played there. (The field was named Carl E. Stotz Field in 1974.)

By the end of 1958, Little League's financial problems had been straightened out—so much so that it not only reestablished the eight-team format for the World Series but also opened the tournament to four guaranteed berths for non-U.S. teams for the first time. Until 1958, foreign teams had to play through a U.S. region, but the 1958 Series, which featured teams from Mexico, Canada, and Hawaii, convinced the Little League board of directors that diversity was a good thing, as noted in a 1958 issue of *Little Leaguer*:

The Little League World Series is more than games played on the diamond. It is boys from Monterrey singing a Mexican birthday song to a boy from Kankakee. It is lads from Valleyfield, Quebec, echoing the same sentiments with a French-Canadian lyric. And it is also Hawaiian youngsters and their mothers strumming ukuleles and singing a song of the islands for all of the team and their followers on Community Night at Lycoming College.

In three languages the boys learn about surfboarding on Waikiki, ice boating on the St. Lawrence and pitching at a piñata in Mexico. Living under one roof at Lycoming College, the lads and their leaders find Little League to be a program, which knows no barriers. … Plans for this global tournament are moving ahead … , inspired by the success and enthusiasm, which was generated by the 1958 Series just completed.

Earlier in the summer of 1958, another war of words heated up over a proposal by the Greater Williamsport Chamber of Commerce to transfer control of part of Brown Memorial Park (site of the Little League World Series from 1947 to 1958) and some of the surrounding buildings and land to Little League for development of a permanent headquarters complex. The Williamsport City Council voted four-to-one in favor of the measure, but vocal opposition by a group of Original League supporters nixed the idea, particularly in face of the opposition of one very important supporter. The *Morning Herald* of Jersey Shore (Pennsylvania) reported in its June 12, 1958, edition that Sarah Moyer, sister-in-law of the late Max M. Brown, had begun legal action to stop the move. She tried to wrest control of the property from the city—which, in her mind, had violated the terms of Brown's will—and give control of the property to Original League, which had been incorporated in 1957. Legal proceedings might have prevented Little League from using the site for its 1958 tournament, although officials of Original League, Inc., stated publicly that the Little League World Series could continue to be played there.

Other appealing possibilities existed, however. The Brooklyn Dodgers and the New York Giants pulled up stakes and moved to California after the 1957 season, leaving two empty edifices in The Big Apple. As late as July 1958, a month before the Little League World Series, questions remained about where the Series would be played. The August 1, 1958, edition of the *Williamsport Sun-Gazette* reported "serious efforts" to lure the Little League World Series away:

One of the overtures made to Little League to move to other cities came from Walter F. O'Malley, president of the [Los Angeles] Dodgers. He offered Ebbetts Field in Brooklyn, former home of the Dodgers, to Little League.

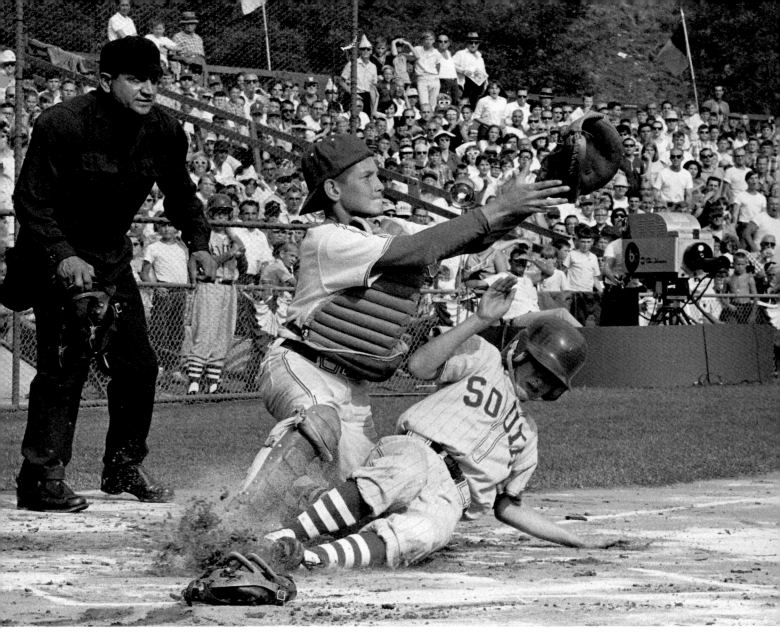

An early 1960s action shot at a Little League World Series showing umpire Frank Rizzo behind the plate. Rizzo was Little League Baseball's umpire-in-chief for many years after the organization moved to its current facility in South Williamsport.

The Polo Grounds in New York City, now also unused, has been available to the league for the asking. And Mayor Robert F. Wagner, mayor of New York City, has promised Little League "anything it wants" in New York to move its offices and series there.

Louisville, Chicago, Portland, Ore., and Staten Island, N.Y., also have offered facilities to Little League. They already have elaborate stadiums, sites of the four [regional] tournaments held prior to the World Series in Williamsport each year.

That got the ball rolling. John E. Person Jr., president of the Williamsport Chamber of Commerce and owner of the *Sun-Gazette,* convened a meeting of some of the most influential and powerful businessmen in the community to discuss ways to keep Little

HOWARD J. LAMADE

Little League's renowned stadium is named after newspaper magnate and Little League Baseball philanthropist Howard J. Lamade. Unfortunately, Lamade did not live to enjoy much of the Little League program's expansion, with which he had helped as a member of the Little League Foundation. Nor did he live to see one of the world's most beautiful fields of friendly strife settled into the green rolling hills of South Williamsport on acreage purchased for the youth program in his memory. That ballpark, now called Howard J. Lamade Stadium, annually hosts the Little League World Series.

Lamade, vice president and secretary of Grit Publishing Company, which published a popular national weekly newspaper, *Grit*, and its local edition, died suddenly on May 15, 1958, in the hospital, following a period of apparent recovery from recent surgery.

Born on January 15, 1891, Lamade was the son of Ciara Ann Rhen and Dietrick Lamade, who founded the *Grit* and served as publisher until his death in 1938. Howard earned a bachelor's degree in journalism in 1913 from the University of Missouri and then joined *Grit* as a clerk. In 1917 he was named business manager, and in 1919 he became *Grit* secretary. He joined Grit Publishing Company's board of directors in 1920 and was elected vice president and secretary in 1943.

During Lamade's tenure, the *Grit*, which leaned heavily toward positive news, homespun humor, and useful tips, grew rapidly. Its weekly national circulation at the time of his death was 1,159,000 copies, and its local, Williamsport edition provided stiff competition for the *Williamsport Sun* and the *Williamsport Gazette & Bulletin*.

As the employer of 50,000 boys as paperboys in 16,000 small towns around the United States, the *Grit* had a vested interest in youth. In the Williamsport area it made philanthropic gestures by establishing scholarships, buying land for playgrounds, and sponsoring the Pennsylvania Little League Championships every year from 1948 until 1958. In 1959, the Lamade family donated the money to the Williamsport Foundation to use for the purchase and donation of property for Little League Baseball.◆

This view of Howard J. Lamade Stadium was taken during the 1999 Little League Baseball World Series. Although the stadium itself can hold 10,000 visitors, an additional 30,000 or more may stake a spot on the hillside to watch the annual contest.

League in town. By then the Little League World Series had become far too valuable to lose, for it gave a town of about 50,000 a national identity that many larger towns envied, not to mention the economic benefits it created for local businesses, principally hotels and restaurants. The chamber estimated that visitors in town to watch the Little League World Series spent a half-million dollars in one week, figuring 10,000 or more visitors would spend $50 each, on the average, during the five-day event.

It was *Grit* publisher George R. Lamade who came up with the idea to save the Series, and that came as no surprise. The Lamade family, one of the most respected in Lycoming County, had a record of philanthropy, especially with regard to local youths. In this case, the family stepped up again and gave $35,000 to the Williamsport Foundation to purchase a twenty-nine-acre tract on U.S. Route 15 in the borough of nearby South Williamsport. The land, most of it purchased from Lycoming College, was then deeded to Little League Baseball as a memorial to Howard J. Lamade, vice president and secretary of Grit Publishing Company, who began his tenure on the Little League board of directors in 1951 and died on May 15, 1958.

The facility built on the South Williamsport site—originally named the Howard J. Lamade Memorial Field and renamed Howard J. Lamade Stadium in 1968—has been the site of the Little League Baseball World Series ever since. Thus, Little League really did leave Williamsport, but unlike the Dodgers and the Giants, who bolted across an entire continent, the move involved little more than the width of the river.

MORE MOVES

Pitching mounds around the world moved too. Based on research by Dr. Creighton Hale, Little League's vice president and director of research, the pitching distance for the 1959 season increased from 44 feet to 46 feet. In the August 24, 1958, *New York Daily News* columnist Dick Young quoted Hale's reasoning: "We have found that our pitchers, throwing the ball at about 70 mph, get the ball up to the plate in less time than a big league pitcher who throws 60 feet at 100 mph. By moving the [pitcher's plate] back two more feet, we will be giving Little League boys just about as much time to swing, proportionately, as the big leaguers have."

The Little League home plate had been slightly wider than 14 inches because Carl Stotz carved the first one out of rubber he borrowed from his father's garage, but it increased to the standard 17 inches in 1959 and thereafter. The move to a new stadium also meant the fences could be pushed back to 200 feet. The outfield fence at the Original Little League field at Memorial Park was 175 feet from home plate to the left and right field corners and 188 feet to center field. A dike protecting Williamsport from Susquehanna River floods dictated the distance to the right field fence at the old site. Fences on the new field in South Williamsport would be 200 feet from home plate at all points (they have since been pushed back to 205 feet).

Young's *Daily News* story quoted Little League Public Relations Director Robert

DR. CREIGHTON HALE

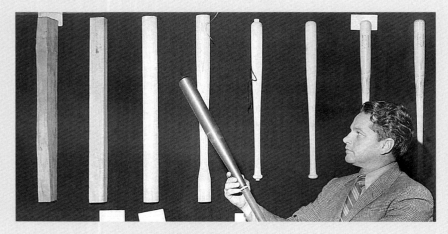

Dr. Creighton Hale examines the revolutionary aluminum bat in this 1972 photo. On display behind him is an exhibit on how wooden bats are made.

Creighton J. Hale was born February 18, 1924, and reared on a farm in Hardy, Nebraska, a town with a population of only 299. "The town was completely mesmerized about sports," Dr. Hale recalls.

His mother, Fay, was an English teacher and his father, Russell, taught science and mathematics and also was the superintendent of schools. A gifted athlete, Creighton attended the University of Nebraska on a track scholarship. Later he became a U.S. Navy officer and earned his doctorate in physiology at New York University.

Dr. Hale joined Little League Baseball as director of research in 1955, taking an extended leave from his laboratory at Springfield College. He says today, "Certain developments occur by accident and not by design," and goes on to tell how that happened:

Being keenly interested in science and sports medicine specifically, I was attracted to an issue, which was whether it was beneficial for young children to compete in high-level competition. Many of the educators, particularly the Academy of Pediatrics, took a negative view of having young children participate in a high level of competition. I was concerned that people were reacting to

the issue emotionally, without any objective data.

There was an article in the local Springfield (Massachusetts) paper which caught my attention—it announced that the president of Little League Baseball, Peter J. McGovern, ... had appointed a three-member committee to investigate the effect of competition on young children. None of the committee members had any research background. I didn't know Mr. McGovern, but my reaction ... was to write him a short note suggesting that if he wanted to give this wonderful idea any credibility ... he should consider appointing people who were known for their research, nationally.

Within a few days I had a telephone call from Mr. McGovern. He inquired if I would undertake the research studies I seemed to think were necessary. I said yes. If I had not responded to that article, I would never be here. It was purely by accident. And now I'm on the longest leave of absence from Springfield College.

Dr. Hale quickly became a friend and confidant of Peter McGovern, and in 1956 he became

assistant to the president. Two years later, Hale was vice president, and in 1971 he was named executive vice president, a position he held for two years before becoming the second president in Little League Baseball history. He was appointed president and chief executive officer in 1983. Dr. Hale retired as Little League's president in 1994 and as chief executive officer in 1996. He remains employed by Little League as senior advisor, continuing his contributions to the program in that role.

One of his first areas of research was to determine whether Little League's level of competition was deleterious or beneficial. By measuring pulse rates and blood pressures of players and coaches and managers, he found that the "emotional stimulation" of children is far less than that of adults. "The problem is, people tend to evaluate the emotional stimulation of a Little League Baseball game according to how adults felt, not children. They were overly excited."

Children, he decided, are an extension of their "overly involved" parents. "The chemistry of that is such that some parents can't control it. In college, I used to tell the students, 'It's like being out on a date—you have good intentions, but sometimes the chemistry overrides the good intentions. It's similar.'"

As Little League Baseball's research director and resident scientist, Dr. Hale was responsible for improving safety standards. While at Springfield College, he had conducted research on new helmets for baseball and for boxing.

People have said the most important thing I've done is develop the safety helmet. In order to develop the helmet, I had to develop a laboratory test method. Up to that point, in the laboratories, all they had for measurements was they would drop a weight like a shot put on a helmet—industrial or military—and then drop a plumb bob to measure the depth of penetration. Well, in baseball, you don't have shot puts or plumb bobs.

So I developed a compressed air cannon which would fire baseballs at controlled speeds and simulates exact conditions under which helmets are going to be impacted. That same test method is being used today, although the technology has been improved. It was a Rube Goldberg [invention]—original in all aspects.

In 1961, the newly patented batting helmet that covers the full head and ears, designed by Dr. Creighton Hale for Little League Baseball, became a requirement for all Little Leaguers. He also developed the catcher's helmet, using the same testing methods:

In the catcher's helmet, you have to protect the same part of the head. Secondly, you want the mask to be a part of the helmet so that when they take the helmet off to catch a foul ball, they can take the mask off and it won't be under their feet. So this was one of the big problems I had, but it was very simple after I finally recognized how to do it.

Everyone at Little League wears this helmet. It has become the prototype of the best helmet on the market that is worn by professional players.

Dr. Hale explained that Kevlar (a very tough, lightweight fiber product made by DuPont) was a result of research on military helmets. As chairman of the National Committee on Military Helmets (under the Academy of Science), he and other research scientists developed the general-issue military helmet first used in Grenada and then in Desert Storm. Kevlar is five times as strong as steel, and one of its offshoots is the bulletproof vest worn by police officers.

Another Little League safety requirement resulting from Dr. Hale's research is the standard for field-lighting. "The problem with the lighting is that very often it was for the spectators, not the players, to see," Dr. Hale said.

"There was a disagreement about whether children should play under lights. Because of the physiology of the eye, diffused lighting at dusk is difficult to pick up."

But leagues in the South and West wanted lights because of soaring temperatures during the day. "This became something of intense debate, and some of the state organizations were threatening to rebel and leave the program." At first, Dr. Hale opposed lighting baseball fields, but with his research, he was able to determine a safety standard. When artificial lighting was finally approved, he says, it proved to be "extremely helpful, because more children are getting the opportunity to play."

Dr. Hale developed an impressive, detailed data bank on all aspects of Little League injuries that has been immensely useful. "We use it to adjust the rules of the game," he says. "As an example, we found out that a large amount of money was being paid for medical expenses incurred by batters in the on-deck circle—being hit by bats and not paying attention. So Little League wiped out the on-deck circle."

Another innovation aided by Dr. Hale's research was the nonwood bat. Aluminum bats meant cost-savings for local Little Leagues because they lasted much longer than wood bats.

His latest project is representing Little League on the USA Baseball Medical and Safety Advisory Committee (the governing body for amateur baseball in the United States) and helping to determine whether the number of pitches thrown by children in games should be limited. Current rules limit only the number of innings in a week or day.

Throughout his career as a scientific researcher, Dr. Hale has been the driving force behind many improvements, not only in Little League Baseball but also in several youth sports programs. He has never received a royalty for his several patents. All were donated to Little League Baseball.◆

Dr. Creighton Hale, resident scientist for Little League Baseball, tests his compressed-air cannon while researching the impact of baseballs on safety helmets. The safety helmet became mandatory in Little League play in 1961. Dr. Hale donated his patent for the helmet to Little League Baseball.

This is the original home plate from Howard J. Lamade Memorial Field (now Howard J. Lamade Stadium), site of the annual Little League Baseball World Series. Home plate had been slightly wider than fourteen inches since Carl Stotz carved the first, but increased to the standard seventeen inches in 1959.

Students from Williamsport Technical Institute (now the Pennsylvania College of Technology) used tractors, steam shovels, and graders to clear the land for the new stadium in July 1959.

Stirrat, who explained: "When we started, few boys could reach the fences. Now, even their pops go out. The boys are much better. We are not recommending that the regular Little League parks change their fences. We feel we need it up here because we get the best hitters at the World Series." Eventually, however, Little League recommended that all fields adopt 200-foot distances to outfield fences.

THE NEW STADIUM AND HEADQUARTERS

Plans for the stadium in South Williamsport came not from an architectural firm but from a student project at The Pennsylvania State University. Tractors, steam shovels, and graders supplied by the Williamsport Technical Institute (now the Pennsylvania College of Technology) and operated by its students cleared the land, moving tons of earth and rocks. Several years before the property was purchased, earthmovers had gouged the side of Bald Eagle Mountain to use in the dikes lining the Susquehanna River, helping to spare Lycoming County residents from periodic flooding by the Susquehanna. The ground, strewn with huge boulders and crossed by streams, presented challenges for engineers and building crews.

Construction of a stadium might normally have lasted two years, because it was whittled from a rocky scar on the side of a mountain. Making matters worse, a late thaw meant that work could not begin until mid-April 1959, with the Little League World Series only four months away. But somehow it all fell together.

Williamsport Technical Institute students helping design the new Little League facility, from left, are: Robert Mondock, Jack Kavelack Jr., Dean Palmer, and Don Miller. By the time teams arrived for the 1959 Little League Baseball World Series, a stadium seating 7,000, with sunken dugouts and a large parking lot, awaited.

Local businesses and individuals donated funds as well as much of the equipment, materials, and services. Local Little League volunteers also pitched in. By the time teams arrived for the 1959 Little League World Series, a stadium seating 7,000 awaited, with sunken dugouts, a large parking lot, and a "field manicured as well as any major-league park," according to the *Williamsport Sun-Gazette*.

A year later, Little League acquired more land through donations and erected bunkhouses for eight teams and its first headquarters building, at a cost of $104,000. The January 10, 1961, headquarters newsletter to presidents of local leagues reported: "The year brought realization of a fine new Headquarters building, three stories, 120 feet long, overlooking a playing site of 35 acres on which a prototype World Series field and extended bleachers are now established. We are happy to announce that the entire site is free and clear—paid in full during the year in which it was completed. This area will be refined continuously for maximum usage until it will become one of the finest recreation areas in the land."

McGovern worked hard to persuade U.S. President Dwight Eisenhower to attend the dedication of the headquarters building during the 1960 Little League World Series. After all, Eisenhower's grandson, David, played second base at the time in the Moose Little League of Gettysburg, Pennsylvania. Twelve-year-old David even declined an opportunity to travel with his grandfather to the Soviet Union so he could continue playing Little League.

As it turned out, however, the "U-2 incident," in which American CIA pilot Francis Gary Powers's reconnaissance plane was shot down by the Soviets, nixed the visit anyway. But David's Little League participation turned out to be a factor in Ike's decision to decline the invitation from Little League. In his "regrets" letter, Eisenhower said: "His parents strongly, and wisely I believe, oppose anything that would single him out in comparison with the other members of his particular team. … I know you will understand."

David Eisenhower, twelve-year-old grandson of U.S. President Dwight Eisenhower, makes his first appearance playing second base for Moose Little League, Gettysburg, in this photo. President Eisenhower was a fan of Little League Baseball and occasionally invited Little League World Series champions to his home in Gettysburg.

The ever-expanding Little League Baseball International Headquarters complex now boasts sixty-six acres, a sixteen-team dormitory with sleeping facilities for 270, a Junior Olympic-size swimming pool, a recreation and dining facility seating more than 300, a 25,000-square-foot office/administration building, a 5,600-square-foot conference center with fourteen bedrooms, a 20,000-square-foot museum, a second stadium seating 5,000 fans, and the venerable Howard J. Lamade Stadium, at which crowds of more than 40,000 are not uncommon at the final game.

NATIONAL LITTLE LEAGUE BASEBALL WEEK

Little League made political moves as well as physical moves. The first indicator of recognition from the U.S. government came in May 1959, when the House and the Senate passed a resolution proclaiming the second week in June as National Little League Baseball Week. Five-term Pennsylvania state representative Alvin R. Bush initiated the action to mark the twentieth anniversary of Little League's founding. President Dwight Eisenhower, whose support of Little League was well known, signed the proclamation. By then, Little League boasted 25,000 teams playing in twenty-five countries. During a promotional trip through New York, on the day after the resolution passed, McGovern told the *Utica Observer Dispatch,* "Little League is no longer a fad."

Three years later, President John F. Kennedy reissued the proclamation, possibly partly because his secretary of state, Dean Rusk, had been a Little League coach in

U.S. President John F. Kennedy autographs a baseball for a Little Leaguer during the summer of 1963. The teams visited Washington, D.C., after Northern Little League of Granada Hills, California, defeated Stanford (Connecticut) Little League, 2–1.

Scarsdale, New York, before taking a position in the Kennedy cabinet. Rusk was described in the January 6, 1960, issue of *Life* magazine as "an efficient and persuasive man who took time off from the Presidency of the Rockefeller Foundation to coach Little League Baseball." Also, Kennedy's press secretary, Pierre Salinger, was a volunteer umpire in Bailey's Crossroads Little League of Falls Church, Virginia, before being added to Kennedy's team.

A FEDERAL CHARTER

The real plum came on July 16, 1964, the year of Little League's silver anniversary. On that day, President Lyndon Johnson signed Public Law 88-378, granting Little League a Congressional Charter of Federal Incorporation. New Jersey Representative William Cahill introduced House Resolution 9234 the previous year, which sailed through both houses of Congress. The certificate of charter charged Little League with responsibilities beyond simply teaching boys how to play baseball:

> Objectives … to promote, develop, supervise, and voluntarily assist in all lawful ways the interest of boys who will participate in Little League Baseball.
> To help and voluntarily assist boys in developing qualities of citizenship, sportsmanship, and manhood.

Using the disciplines of the native American game of baseball, to teach spirit and competitive will to win, physical fitness through individual sacrifice, the values of team play and wholesome well-being through healthful and social association with other youngsters under proper leadership.

Little League remains the only sports program granted a federal charter. Other similarly recognized organizations at the time were the Boy Scouts of America, the Red Cross, Boys Clubs of America, and 4-H Clubs. Congress amended the law in 1974 following Little League's longest court battle, when girls were admitted to the program.

A federal charter gave Little League even greater legal footing in protecting its trademark, because the U.S. government officially stood behind it. It also meant that the corporation created fourteen years earlier in New York could be dissolved and that Little League would report its earnings to the U.S. Congress through an independent accounting firm, and no longer to the New York State Assembly. Every year, following its annual audit, Little League has received the best possible rating.

INELIGIBILITY PROBLEMS

The first Little League World Series at the new stadium was played in 1959. It began well enough, although the European champion was a no-show, shrinking the Series field to seven teams. Bad Kissingen Army Base, a team composed of dependents of U.S. military personnel, did not make the trip because flight arrangements out of West Germany could not be completed in time.

Pitcher Art "Pinky" Deras of Hamtramck, Michigan, won nine of ten Little League tournament games via shutout. On the first day of the Series, Hamtramck's 135-pound pitcher tossed a one-hitter as his team beat San Juan, Puerto Rico, 5–0.

WHATEVER HAPPENED TO ART DERAS?

Few Little Leaguers have graduated from the Little League program with as much promise as Art Deras. News reports around the nation touted him as one of the best prospects ever to be discovered, and he was only twelve years old.

Art went on to become a star in the Pony League, leading his team to a national championship. He signed a professional contract with the St. Louis Cardinals, with a bonus of $80,000, but lasted only a few years in the minor leagues.

Deras had burned out on baseball. One day in 1968 he walked away and never looked back. "As far as I know, the Cardinals may still be expecting me to come back," Deras said in an interview with the *Detroit Free Press* in 1983. "I didn't tell them I was retiring and they didn't ask why. I guess they knew."

Deras later became a police officer in his hometown.◆

Hamtramck, Michigan, a suburb of Detroit, earned the title of early favorite, having won nine of ten tournament games with shutouts. On the first day, Hamtramck's 135-pound pitcher, Art "Pinky" Deras, tossed a one-hitter as his team beat San Juan, Puerto Rico, 5–0, extending his personal string of scoreless innings pitched to an incredible sixty-nine. He fanned seventeen, maintaining his average of 2.8 strikeouts per inning. Hamtramck defeated Oahu, Hawaii, 7–1 in the semifinal (behind a Deras grand slam) to reach the final game.

Deras took the mound for the championship game before a crowd estimated at as many as 18,000, including 150 Hamtramck residents. Surrendering only three hits, Deras pushed his scoreless streak to seventy-five innings in a 12–0 victory, unmatched for lopsided championship games until 1973, when Tainan City, Taiwan, defeated Cactus Little League of Tucson, Arizona, by the same score. Deras's single-season pitching statistics were printed in newspapers around the nation and were nothing less than staggering: 18 complete games, 18 victories, 16 shutouts, 10 no-hitters (including five straight), 298 strikeouts, and only 10 walks in 108 innings. At the plate, Deras hit 13 home runs in 13 tournament games, giving him 33 for the season, along with 112 runs batted in.

The accomplishments of Hamtramck and Deras made big news nationally, and bigger news in the Detroit area. The *Detroit Times* report of the excitement was typical of the reaction local towns had to having a Little League World Series champion:

Mayor [Albert] Zack proudly proclaimed, "It's a great day for Hamtramck—in fact it's a great day for Michigan."

Bernardine Perry, 12, rushed out to the pitcher's mound and plunked a big kiss on Deras' cheek, apologizing, "I know you don't like this but I can't help it."

Deras' cheeks showed why they called him "Pinky."

When news of the victory was brought to a bar at 9740 Dequindre, co-owner Steve Piasecki rushed to call a sign painter.

"I want a big sign, 'Welcome Home, Champs,' for my window by tomorrow noon," said Piasecki.

His partner and brother Joseph was at the title game as president of Hamtramck's Little League.

Calls asking the score clogged the police switchboard so badly that an hour after the game the department sent out sound trucks to tour the community proclaiming the final score.

But accusations saying Hamtramck used ineligible players surfaced several months after the Series, and newspapers began to speculate on the matter. A lengthy investigation by Little League Baseball's franchise committee followed, including a full hearing at the 1960 National Congress in Chicago. The franchise committee found that some Hamtramck players—regular-season players, not players on the tournament team—had been allowed to continue to participate earlier in the 1959 season, after it was discovered that they lived outside the league's boundaries (a violation of Little League regulations). A letter from McGovern to local leagues explained, "There was no proven evidence of collusion by officers of the league beyond verbal accusation," but Little League suspended Hamtramck's tournament privileges for 1960 and put the league on probation for one year for "laxity in checking residence requirements of eligibility and for failure to suspend players promptly when they were found to be ineligible."

That was not the first time the franchise committee took such action. In the summer of 1959, it suspended tournament privileges for the three leagues of Monterrey, Mexico, because they were accepting players from outside their boundaries and began practice for their all-star teams before the prescribed date. McGovern's August 1959 letter to leagues said: "This devious and disproportionate concentration upon winning tournament play could not be condoned. ... We were extremely regretful that the fine little Mexican boys were deprived of a chance to come forward because of the cynical ambitions and intentional violations of a few of their adult leaders."

BILL SHEA

The night before the big game at the 1959 Little League Baseball World Series Community Dinner at The Lycoming, New York attorney William A. "Bill" Shea explained his reasons for forming a third big league, the Continental League, to compete with Major League Baseball's monopoly. The *Williamsport Sun-Gazette* reported that Shea "emphasized that the Continental League stands behind Little League and pledged its support of the youth program."

Shea's league never materialized, but the New York Mets did, and Shea was that club's first owner. He became a hero to New Yorkers for bringing National League baseball back to the city, and a hero to Little League for the staunch support he promised, and delivered with unwavering devotion. Shea became president of the Little League Foundation in 1976, following the death of the Hon. James A. Farley. Head of the Madison Avenue–based law firm Shea, Gould, Climenko & Casey, he first was elected as a trustee of the Little League Foundation in 1960, but his relationship with the youth baseball program began years earlier.

William A. "Bill" Shea, left, plays catcher behind Baseball Hall of Fame third baseman Brooks Robinson in pre-game ceremonies at the 1978 Little League World Series. Shea, a New York attorney and frequent Series visitor, was president of the Little League Foundation and is the person for whom Shea Stadium, home of the New York Mets, is named.

Little League continues to honor Shea with the William A. "Bill" Shea Distinguished Little League Graduate Award, given annually to a Little League graduate who reaches the major leagues and exemplifies Shea's spirit. The Shea family picked up the torch too and is a strong supporter of Little League's Urban Initiative, a program to reintroduce Little League Baseball to urban areas. Now the entire Shea family are heroes to Harlem Little League in New York, founded in 1990, where more than 800 children play each year.◆

LITTLE LEAGUE ADDS BIG LEAGUE

A third division of Little League began in 1968 on an experimental basis when the Big League baseball program took shape. As with the Senior League program at the beginning of the decade, local Little Leagues that were interested in forming a Big League division (for sixteen- through eighteen-year-olds) could apply for a Big League charter.

Winston-Salem, North Carolina, hosted the first Big League Baseball World Series, which featured the host team (Southwest Forsyth Little League of North Carolina) and one team from each of the four U.S. regions: Indianapolis, Indiana; Barstow, California; New Hyde Park, New York; and Charleston, West Virginia. Charleston won it, defeating New Hyde Park 3–2.

Twenty-two leagues and 114 teams participated in the Big League program the first year. Today there are more than 1,500 Big League Baseball teams.◆

LITTLE LEAGUE EXPANDS TO SENIOR PLAY

Frankie Frisch, a Major League Baseball Hall of Fame second baseman who turned to broadcasting, brought up a subject at the 1959 Little League World Series that was on many minds, particularly with Bill Shea in town talking about a whole new major league. Frisch, in Williamsport as an announcer for television station WPIX in New York City, told the *New York Daily News:* "What happens to them after they get too old for Little League? I know, there's Babe Ruth baseball. But all too many of the kids seem to get lost. They leave the game."

Babe Ruth League, Inc., and Pony Baseball, Inc., were both founded in 1951 in Hamilton Township, New Jersey, and in Washington, Pennsylvania, respectively, following the sudden nationwide success of Little League. Both programs aimed to provide an organized baseball league to which Little Leaguers could graduate once boys entered their teens. Hundreds of similar, independent leagues already existed in towns and cities, including Williamsport, but Babe Ruth League and Pony (an acronym for "protect our nation's youth") were the first to model their programs on the Little League's template. Both gained national acceptance quickly.

Because Little League did not have a program for teenage players, the relationship between Little League and the older boys' programs remained cordial, even friendly, through most of the 1950s. In fact, advertisements for Babe Ruth League appeared on the back cover of several Little League World Series programs during the decade—and as late as 1961. Little League vigorously pursued legal action against leagues and businesses trying to trade on Little League's name, and it was successful most of the time. The U.S. Department of Commerce Trademark Trial and Appeal Board canceled the registration for Little Boys Baseball, Inc., after Little League sued, "because of the confusion created in the minds of the public with 'Little League Baseball' and the general impressions given that the programs are substantially the same," according to a letter from McGovern to all Little Leagues. The February 1962 *Little Leaguer* newsletter added, "The suit was brought without rancor or vindictiveness and on the insistence of legal counsel."

Volunteers at Little League programs in places where no Babe Ruth or Pony pro-

Moving billboards promote Little League Baseball in 1960.

grams existed asked Little League to create a program for teenage graduates. The *Little Leaguer* claimed that "less than half of those Little Leaguers reaching the age of 13 annually could be accommodated by all existing over-age programs." In 1961, Pony and Babe Ruth programs numbered about 2,500 nationally, while 5,706 Little League local programs existed. So the Little League board of directors authorized an experiment for the 1961 season in which thirty leagues were identified and permitted to operate, for the first time, another league.

All the operations of the extension program for players thirteen through fifteen years old, dubbed the Senior League, would be under the umbrella of the local Little League's board of directors. Creating a separate board of directors at the local level, the Little League board decided, would simply duplicate efforts.

At the end of the first season, nine teams from Alabama, Rhode Island, New Jersey, Ohio, Kentucky, North Carolina, and Pennsylvania traveled at their own expense to Bowman Field in Williamsport for a world series of sorts, although it was not known as such until 1962. Natrona Heights, Pennsylvania, won the tournament, which was played simultaneously with the Little League Baseball World Series across the Susquehanna in South Williamsport. That allowed the greatest number of district representatives to see the games as well, because they were in town for the Little League tournament, and then to bring news of the program back to their home leagues.

The Little League board of directors deemed the experiment a success and on October 27, 1961, voted unanimously to open the program to any Little League. However, leagues were instructed not to "raid" the other programs, and that a Senior League program could be only an extension of the base Little League organization, as explained in McGovern's October 31, 1961, letter to leagues: "The Senior Division should not aggressively promote any solicitation of leagues. Applications will be received only from already organized and franchised Little Leagues. Boundaries will be the same."

At first, policy would not allow a Senior League program in areas where another national organization offered baseball for young teens, unless the league could prove that the existing program was not serving the community well enough. Eventually, the policy was dropped to allow Senior League programs in any area where a Little League charter currently existed. Not only did Little League keep growing, it was finding new directions in which to grow.

The three largest youth baseball programs now officially competed for at least some players of the same age-group, and Pony announced plans in 1961 to start a division for players age twelve and under with this statement:

> Pony League has, ever since its start, depended upon Little League graduates to provide playing personnel for Pony League.
>
> The source now appears to be in jeopardy. Therefore, in light of the Little League action, the directors of the Pony and Colt League have directed that a national program in the age level immediately under the Pony League be organized in order to provide the necessary feeder system for Pony League.

Babe Ruth's president, Walter B. Cocks, fired back as well. In a wire-service story in early February 1962, he was quoted as saying: "We do not approve of ... the possibility of a pending monopoly. ... Control of so vital a part of our great national pastime in the field of youth activities should not be entrusted to the dictatorial powers of one league."

A few days later, Little League's Robert Stirrat responded in an Associated Press story: "The purpose of our Senior League was to accommodate our kids who could not be accommodated in other leagues. Our leagues and boards of directors felt it was desirable."

Little League, Babe Ruth League, and Pony League did agree on some things. They settled on August 1 as the common date for the "age cutoff," the same date Little League had used for a number of years. This meant that a player who had his thirteenth birthday before August 1 of the year would be considered a "league age" thirteen-year-old for the entire year in all three programs. Little League had far more players in its programs at the time, and still does, so its rules remained unchanged.

Babe Ruth added a division for younger players later. Today, all three organizations offer baseball and softball to players ages five through eighteen. The original Pony League had six teams, but now has more than 500,000 members. The original Babe Ruth program had ten teams and is now the second-largest youth baseball program in the world, with 858,000 players. Little League, with its more humble three-team genesis, remains the largest youth sports program in the world, with more than 2.9 million players in 104 countries.

LITTLE LEAGUE'S FIRST DEATHS

Reports of the first accidental death of a Little Leaguer while playing ball shocked the nation on May 19, 1961. A week later, another boy was fatally injured, then another, and then another. Parents scrambled for safety equipment to protect their sons from the fastball that seemed to have become a weapon instead of a symbol of America's pastime.

Although not injury-free, more Little Leaguers played in 1961 than ever before. The string of tragedies provided critics "with a barrel of ready-made ammunition," wrote Sid Hoos, sports editor for San Francisco's *Daily Review*. "An activity that in its first 21 years achieved the near-impossible feat of providing organized physical competition for millions of youngsters 9 to 12 years old without a recorded fatality has—in the space of 27 days—been blamed for the death of four boys."

It began with a May 22, 1961, edition of the *Houston Press*, in which columnist Bob Rule wrote:

> Nine-year-old Barry Babcock was struck directly over the heart by a pitched ball, collapsed in the umpire's arms and died before the umpire could lay him down. The pitcher, 10-year-old Michael Hanes, collapsed in uncontrolled hysterics.
>
> Little League officials, with offices in Williamsport, Pa., have taken every precaution to protect these little fellers, but national statistics still show that 15,444 youngsters have been injured seriously enough in the last five years to require treatment by a physician.

The newly patented batting helmet that covers the full head and ears, designed by Dr. Creighton Hale for Little League Baseball, became a requirement in 1961. But the new helmet, Rule wrote, came "too late to save little Barry Babcock's life." (Rule disregarded the fact that the ball hit Barry in the chest, not the head.)

Rule went on to point out that at the same time the "Batter's Protector," manufactured in Baton Rouge, Louisiana, by James J. Melton, was just coming on to the market. Three-quarter-inch foam rubber covered with canvas, which looked much like a catcher's chest protector and "in no way interferes with the batter's swing or with his running," fit under the armpit and claimed to protect the heart, collarbone, kidneys, lungs, ribs, and hips of the players. But the protector never caught on, nor did any of the myriad models that followed over the years.

Only a week after the first tragic event, a ten-year-old Little Leaguer died five days after being hit on the head by a line drive. The May 30, 1961, *Los Angeles Times* reported that George McCormick had been pinch-hitting on his first day of practice in Hinckley Park, a Chicago suburb of Park Ridge: "A line drive glanced off his head. George felt all right at first, but Sunday he began to feel dizzy. He was taken to Resurrection Hospital in Chicago, where he died. Doctors said death was caused by a brain injury."

Two weeks later, twelve-year-old catcher Brumit Estes collapsed and died on the field in Cocoa, Florida, after being struck in the throat by a pitched ball. A United Press International wire report read: "A pitched ball struck home plate and bounced up, hitting him in the throat between his chest protector and catcher's mask. 'He fell down,' said Lieutenant Ozzie Carlton, of the Cocoa Police Department, 'then got up, threw the ball back to the pitcher and collapsed again.'" It was surmised, the report continued, that "the boy's windpipe was crushed by the force of the ball."

On August 15, 1961, the *New York Mirror* reported that Patrick H. McCormack, a twelve-year-old outfielder playing in the Kalamazoo County (Michigan) Little League tournament, was wearing only a headguard when a pitched ball struck him. He was taken to a doctor's office, treated, and released. The next morning, he became ill and was rushed to University Hospital in Ann Arbor, where he died of a hemorrhage caused by the blow.

Little League has always had to strike a delicate balance between the competitive nature of baseball, and safety and cost factors. With less than three-tenths of one percent of Little Leaguers injured each year to the point of requiring medical attention, the game is relatively safe. In fact, not a single play-related death occurred in a Little League game or practice during the 1990s, even though more than 10 million games and 20 million practices were conducted in that decade.

Rules are revised when practical to reduce the number of injuries. For example, in 1995, Little League found a way to reduce the number of finger, hand, and arm injuries by prohibiting runners in divisions for twelve-year-olds and below from sliding headfirst while moving forward on the base paths. The revision did not change the competitive nature of the game (runners can still slide feet-first), but it reduced the number of injuries.

The 1961 rule requiring full helmets for batters and base runners has certainly meant fewer head injuries. There is some support for softer baseballs in all divisions of play, but Little League only makes their use optional. Little League says softer baseballs could reduce the severity of some injuries, but there is evidence they may actually make some injuries worse. More than 90 percent of local Little Leagues use the softer balls for the divisions involving players ages five through eight, but less than 10 percent use them at the nine-through-twelve level.

Little League's ASAP ("A Safety Awareness Program") initiative has also helped to reduce injuries. Started in 1995, ASAP shares the best safety ideas from local leagues and districts with all the leagues in the world. Underwritten by CNA Insurance and Musco Sports Lighting, the initiative features a monthly newsletter and a national awards program for the leagues with the best safety ideas.◆

FIRST TELECAST OF A LITTLE LEAGUE CHAMPIONSHIP GAME

The Little League Baseball World Series Championship Game was televised a few times during the 1950s, but only on a tape-delay basis and only regionally. The first live national telecast of the Series came in 1960 as Levittown, Pennsylvania, defeated Fort Worth, Texas, 5–0 on ABC. In fact, it was the first live national telecast of any kind from the Williamsport area. The signal from Lamade Field bounced along seven mountaintop relays on the way to the network headquarters in New York City, with Buddy Blattner, former New York Giants star, the lone voice behind the microphone. Peter J. McGovern's newsletter to league presidents on October 16, 1960, held promise for Little League's future on television:

> One of every three television sets in use on the afternoon of August 27th were dialed to the Little League World Series final game, according to ratings released last week. The nation-wide telecast was acclaimed by all who wrote us. It carried a great deal of respectable and straight-out entertainment values. Aside from a little unusual emphasis on commercials, everyone seemed pleased, including the sponsor. Indications are that this colorful show will again be carried coast-to-coast next year.

McGovern's prediction was not quite on the mark. New York station WPIX televised the 1961 Little League Baseball World Series, but only in New York, and on tape, with former Yankee star infielder Gil McDougald behind the mike. In fact, Little League delayed the start of the fifth inning for five minutes so the WPIX crew could change its reels. The 1962 Series also was televised only in New York on WPIX. That same year, ABC debuted its *Wide World of Sports* program, but initial reaction by critics was less than enthusiastic about the program dedicated solely to "the constant variety of sport," with nontraditional fare like skiing from Austria and sumo wrestling from Japan. A year later,

LITTLE LEAGUE AND ABC

The American Broadcasting Company and Little League Baseball team up annually to bring the Little League World Series to millions of viewers around the world.

Not many people believed ABC's *Wide World of Sports* would be successful when it started in the early 1960s. Some thought a television program dedicated solely to "the constant variety of sport" would not have enough general appeal to stay afloat. As it turned out, however, *Wide World of Sports* was at least a decade ahead of its time. In the last two decades, a host of all-sports television channels have followed. In a short time, *Wide World of Sports* became one of the most highly respected and most-watched sports programs on television.

In its second season, *Wide World of Sports* added the Little League World Series to the August lineup, and Little League has kept that position ever since. The Little League World Series is the longest continuously running sporting event in the program's history. The Little League World Series Championship Game also is the longest-running single sporting event on a single network.

Some of the biggest names in sports and sports broadcasting have graced the broadcast booth at Howard J. Lamade Stadium over the years, including Mickey Mantle, Jim McKay, Don Drysdale, Chris Schenkel, Brent Musburger, Johnny Bench, Al Michaels, Jim Palmer, Jack Edwards, Harold Reynolds, and Jackie Robinson.

The association of the Little League World Series with ABC is ensured at least through the year 2006. In 2000, ABC Sports and Little League Baseball agreed to continue their unique partnership through that year at least. ◆

TOP
Former Major League Baseball player Mickey Mantle joins Bud Palmer for ABC at the 1972 Little League World Series. Mantle nearly stole the show as ABC's color commentator during the *Wide World of Sports* broadcast.

BOTTOM
Former Major League Baseball player Carlton Fisk, on the disabled list, works for ABC's *Wide World of Sports* during the 1974 Little League World Series.

the Little League Baseball World Series was added to the late summer lineup and has been there ever since. *Wide World* not only found an audience, it blazed a trail for ESPN and its various incarnations.

Wide World didn't carry the Little League World Series live until 1989, but it did turn to color starting in 1966, the year Little League opened its first permanent regional center in St. Petersburg, Florida. Veteran broadcaster Chris Schenkel provided the live play-by-play commentary in 1963, with Les Keiter on color. A very young Jim McKay, along with Sonny Fox and Bill Veeck, handled the commentary in 1964 on tape. Some of the other better-known names in broadcasting have worked the games over the years: Brent Musburger, Keith Jackson, Bud Palmer, Jack Edwards, Bob Eueker, Al Michaels, Mel Allen, Red Barber, Curt Gowdy, Julie Moran, John Saunders, Jack Edwards, Harold Reynolds, and Terry Gannon.

The Little League World Series is now the longest-running event on *Wide World of Sports*, and each year it establishes a new record for the oldest continuous relationship between a major sporting body and a single network. In the summer of 2000, Little League, ABC, and ESPN signed an agreement that will keep the Series final on ABC through 2006.

George W. Bush, Forty-Third U.S. President

On his batting prowess at Yale University…

"Not very good.

I peaked in Little League."

eight

CHANGING TIMES

Little League had become part of the "establishment" by the 1960s, and its popularity continued to soar. By the middle of the decade, nearly 7,000 leagues were chartered. Little Leaguers, along with America, changed dramatically during the decade. And, like America in the 1960s, the Far East had a lasting effect on Little League.

HERE COMES THE WORLD

Until the mid-1960s, Little Leagues in the United States could mostly ignore the rest of the world. Little League World Series champs had always been American teams, with the exception of Mexico's back-to-back titles in 1957–58. The first team from Europe to make it to the World Series was Berlin, in 1960, when it lost in the first-round game against Monterrey, Mexico; then defeated Toronto; then lost to Pearl Harbor, Hawaii, 7–2. The Berlin team was composed of children of U.S. servicemen—a feature that would be common for most European teams both then and now. Europe's first victory in the Series did not come until 1962, when a U.S. military team from Poitiers, France, defeated Japan in the consolation bracket of the 1962 Series. That game marked Japan's first time in the Series, but it certainly would not be the last.

The 1964 Little League World Series only solidified American

In this early-1960s Little League World Series game photo, a player from Japan is safe at home after sliding.

dominance. Danny Yaccarino spun a no-hitter, issuing only one walk in the last inning, as Mid-Island Little League of Staten Island, New York, defeated Obispado Little League of Monterrey, Mexico, 4–0. The only base runner for Monterrey reached base on a high curveball with a three-and-two count on Obispado's smallest hitter in the last inning. It was the third no-hitter by a winning American pitcher in the championship game over a five-year period. (The first two were by Joe Mormello of Levittown, Pennsylvania, in 1960 and Ted Campbell of San Jose, California, in 1962.)

Staten Island's boys earned a trip to New York City for the World's Fair and, incredibly, a ticker-tape parade arranged with the help of Bill Shea. One police officer at the parade remarked for the September 3, 1964, *New York World Telegram:* "It's the first ticker parade we've ever had for kids. This time we're having one for kids we know instead of some visiting bigshot nobody knows."

The team rode in open cars through the canyons of New York as ticker tape rained down and tens of thousands of New Yorkers turned out to cheer—saving their heartiest for Yaccarino. The parade started at the Battery and ended at City Hall, where, the

September 4, 1964, *New York World Telegram* reported, Mayor Robert F. Wagner told the team: "If I read the scores correctly, I'm afraid you may be the only world championship baseball team we have this year."

Staten Island advanced to the final that year by squeaking past Tachikawa, Japan, 3–1, in the semifinals. If Japan had won, the United States would have been shut out of the championship game for the first time in Series history.

Japan's manager explained to a *Grit* reporter that his team was hampered because it had never seen a left-hander: "Japanese children are brought up to be righthanded. This is done for two reasons. It is difficult to write Japanese with the left hand, and chopsticks, which can be used for eating with either the right or left hand, are supposed to be used in the right hand by the Japanese. It is considered bad manners to use chopsticks in the left hand. If I had a son, I wouldn't allow him to be left-handed."

The next year, Canada had its first and only team in the final but lost to Windsor Locks, Connecticut. It was the last time an American team would meet and defeat a foreign team in the Little League Baseball World Series Championship Game until 1982.

Fundidora Ball Park, Monterrey, Mexico, was the site of the 1962 Latin American Little League tournament. A popular pastime in Mexico, baseball warrants a grand stadium in the impoverished country.

Former U.S. President Dwight Eisenhower greets a Japanese pitcher after the Far East's 1967 Little League Series win. Little League Baseball President Peter McGovern, right, assists in the simple ceremony in the Eisenhowers' Gettysburg home.

U.S. Vice President Dan Quayle signs autographs at the 1992 Little League Baseball World Series. Quayle visited the Series to accept his 1990 enshrinement in the Peter J. McGovern Little League Museum Hall of Excellence.

LITTLE LEAGUE AND THE EXECUTIVE BRANCH

Some notable public figures have visited Little League Headquarters over the years. State governors are regular visitors to the Little League World Series, but two men who eventually became U.S. President also have traveled to Williamsport for Little League functions.

The first, Lyndon B. Johnson, visited in the fall of 1960 to present a U.S. flag to Little League President Peter J. McGovern shortly after the dedication of the new building. At the time, only a few weeks from Election Day, Johnson was John F. Kennedy's vice presidential running mate. The flag was displayed for the first time on Monday, November 25, 1963, the first full day of Johnson's presidency, following Kennedy's assassination.

The second, George Bush, also was a candidate for U.S. vice president on the Ronald Reagan ticket when he visited International Headquarters for the World Series in 1980. Bush, who coached his sons in Little League in Texas, was Ronald Reagan's successor in the White House.

Dan Quayle, who visited the Series in 1992 to accept enshrinement in the Peter J. McGovern Little League Museum Hall of Excellence, is the only sitting U.S. vice president to visit Little League in Williamsport. No sitting U.S. president has visited, although many Little League World Series teams have been invited to the White House.◆

The Mid-Island Little League (New York) team is honored with a ticker-tape parade down Broadway after its 1964 Little League World Series win. During that year, Little League's silver anniversary, U.S. President Lyndon Johnson signed Public Law 88-378, granting Little League a Congressional Charter of Federal Incorporation.

LEFT
Little League
players swarm
television comedian
and movie star
Lucille Ball at the
1964 World's Fair in
New York. Trips for
Little Leaguers to
New York or
Washington, D.C.,
after the Series,
were common
during the 1960s
and 1970s.

RIGHT
"How's the nose?"
New York Mets
manager Casey
Stengel comforts a
1964 Little League
World Series player
during a visit to New
York. The youngster
was injured during
the tournament.

Westbury American Little League, of Houston, Texas, won in 1966, besting another American team, from New Jersey—yet another American victory. In both cases, Japanese teams reached the Series but failed to earn a berth in the championship. Nobody could have known that twenty of the next twenty-five Little League World Series titles would be won by teams from the Far East.

Although the idea of organized boys' baseball was introduced to Japan in 1950 through translated Little League films, the program in that country took root slowly. Japan franchised its first league in 1960, but Japanese teams never made it past the second round in their first four trips to Williamsport. The day before the 1967 Series began, Mike Bernardi, a sports columnist for the *Williamsport Sun-Gazette,* wrote prophetically about Japan's chances:

> The rapid growth of Japan is reflected not only in the improved calibre of play but in the number of games presently required in tournament play to decide the Pacific Region championship.
>
> In the short span of one year, the number of tournament games has doubled. Last year, the team from Osaka won the Pacific championship in only four games. This year it required eight games for West Tokyo to climb the tournament ladder from district to regional level.

After the first day, the North Roseland Little League team from Chicago appeared to be the early favorite, thanks to a no-hitter—the eighth in Little League World Series history—by Bob Stratta against Rota, Spain. Stratta's manager, Rick Dentino, commented on the twelve-year-old pitcher in the *Sun-Gazette:* "He can go through an opposing lineup once, and the second time around Bob remembers every pitch he threw to every batter." Stratta's knack for attention to detail, and his presumably "good hands," served him well later in life as a transplant surgeon at the University of Tennessee.

JAPAN TURNS THE TIDE

But the West Tokyo Little League team stole the show in the 1967 Series opener, which opened some eyes as well. Until that game, teams from the Pacific Region (later renamed the Far East Region and recently renamed the "Asia-Pacific Region") fared poorly, usually finishing in the bottom half of the eight-team field. They became known as the most well-mannered teams in the Series, bowing to umpires before each at-bat and placing the ball squarely in front of the pitcher's plate at the end of each defensive half-inning. Japanese pitchers even bowed each time a pitch came close enough to make a batter flinch.

TRAVEL ADVENTURES

In the year 2000, Little League's operations department booked more than fifty teams, or about 750 individual fares, for flights from regional tournament sites to World Series tournaments and back to the teams' homes. The airfare is paid by Little League Baseball, as are costs for room and board.

The travel misadventures for one team are legendary, though. In 1967, Pennsylvania's Newtown-Edgemont Little League team earned a berth in the Little League Baseball World Series by winning the Eastern Region title on Saturday, August 19, in Bridgeport, Connecticut. On Sunday, after a bus trip to New York, these Eastern Region champions from Pennsylvania were supposed to board a plane and fly to Williamsport. A story in the *Williamsport Sun-Gazette* explained the headaches that followed for the fourteen players, manager, coach, and small contingent of Little League officials:

The first sign of trouble was when the bus driver did not show up. He overslept. Then, to make matters worse, the taxi en route to the airport had a flat tire.

Still, with time to spare, the group got into New York City. But, near the Long Island site of the 1964–65 World's Fair, the bus driver took a wrong turn.

By the time the team got to La Guardia Airport, the Allegheny Airlines plane was beginning to warm up its engines. An attempt was made to hold the plane, but an Allegheny gate official said this could not be done.

Before LLB officials were able to find an Allegheny ticket man, who contacted the control tower in an effort to stop the plane from taking off, the aircraft was speeding down the runway and the control tower could not call it back.

Allegheny then told the team to go to Newark where another plane would be leaving in about an hour. Getting to Newark, Little League officials learned there were seats on the plane as far as Wilkes-Barre–Scranton but not to Williamsport, at least not for the entire group. Little League officials said the Delaware County team could not be split up.

It was decided to fly the team to Wilkes-Barre–Scranton and bring it by automobiles to Williamsport. However, the plane that was going to fly the boys from Newark had mechanical problems and another aircraft had to be obtained. Finally the contingent arrived in Scranton and set out by car to Williamsport. The end of the trouble was not yet in sight.

A short way from the airport, one of the cars developed mechanical trouble. Near Red Rock, on Route 118, another of the cars had a flat tire. And, a third car pulled into Hughesville almost out of gas.

Ten hours after the team left Bridgeport, it finally arrived in Williamsport.

Travel for most teams is rarely as eventful. For many Little Leaguers who make it to the World Series, either in Williamsport or any of the other seven tournaments, it is their first time in an airplane.◆

Masahiro Miyahara, a twelve-year-old pitcher with good location and an average fastball, did it all in Japan's first game of the Series, pitching a one-hitter and hitting a three-run homer as West Tokyo beat British Columbia's East Trail Little League 3–0. Even Peter McGovern expressed surprise at Japan's newfound success and was quoted in a column by Mike Bernardi in the *Sun-Gazette* titled "Times Have Changed":

First Japanese players in a Little League World Series made a big hit in 1962. Note the traditional kimono garb as the players gather at the fence to chat with their new American friends.

"That's the first home run I ever saw a Japanese team hit in Series play. I didn't think they had the power."

Although always a neutral observer at the Series, he couldn't help but feel pleased with West Tokyo's all-around performance. "This is good for our program overall and the Series."

He remembers, as do regular Series fans, back before last season when Japanese teams had only their kimono garb for color. In 1965, only going back that far, Japan

[Arakawa] suffered an 18–0 defeat at the hands of Jeffersonville, Ind., in the opening round and set a Series record it would rather forget of 13 errors.

Last year things began looking up as Osaka scored an eight-inning 6–2 opening-round victory over Rhein-Main, Germany, before bowing out in the semifinals of the Series won by Houston, Texas. Now the goal of the Japanese is to make the championship round. To do so they will have to get by Pennsylvania's Newtown-Edgemont in Thursday's semifinal game.

It's a tough order, but this year's team is well coached and poised enough to pull a major upset.

It did pull a major upset. Japan defeated the crowd favorite, Newtown-Edgemont, 4–1 in the semifinals, setting up a showdown with the team from Chicago. Bernardi's column on championship day recalled the times when American teams ruled, a dominance they never would again enjoy: "Manager [Kazuo] Hayashi has made the right choices and has his club loose and ready to play. No longer is there that underlying fear that American Little Leaguers are far superior—something that was brought up after terrible beatings during the early days of Series competition."

The 1967 Little League World Series began ominously. Rain postponed the start of the game. During the delay, baseball great Ted Williams interviewed Stratta for ABC, but refused to talk to the Japanese team. "He said he fought against them in World War II, and there was no way he was going to talk to them," Stratta recalls.

COOPERSTOWN COMES TO WILLIAMSPORT

Many National Baseball Hall of Fame members or eventual inductees have visited the Little League World Series:

Connie Mack	Jackie Robinson
Cy Young	Jim Palmer
Frankie Frisch	Carlton Fisk
Frank Baker	Bob Gibson
Lefty Gomez	Don Sutton
Ted Williams	Brooks Robinson
Joe DiMaggio	Don Drysdale
Joe Morgan	Willie Stargell
Johnny Bench	George Brett
Mickey Mantle	Robin Yount
Stan Musial	

Former Major League Baseball player Jackie Robinson visited the Little League World Series in 1962 for television commentary on WPIX, out of New York City. He signed hundreds of autographs for his fans.

But when the game finally got under way, a section of the stands at Lamade Field collapsed. Elmer Lehotsky, the public address announcer, remembers the moment of the collapse: "There was a noise like a rifle shot, and the stands just gave way in that one section." The event delayed the game for several minutes, and two spectators were slightly injured.

Stratta went on to pitch well for North Roseland, scattering only seven hits. Miyahara, however, was better, tossing a three-hitter in Japan's 4-1 win. But the incident was the impetus for building a new stadium.

It was only a sign of things to come. In the same way that America no longer completely dominated Little League, Asian industry in general, and Japanese industry in particular, were challenging to the status quo. America's economic dominance would soon be over. For a few days in August 1967, North Roseland Little League pushed news of a growing conflict in Vietnam off the front pages of the Chicago papers. The city gave their U.S. champions a parade, after the team returned from a visit to Expo '67 in Montreal. Exactly one year later, North Roseland's World Series near-miss was far from the minds of Chicagoans as anti–Vietnam War protesters clashed with police at the start of the Democratic National Convention in the city.

The showdown game in the 1968 final pitted a team from Richmond, Virginia, against Wakayama, Japan, in a new $300,000 concrete stadium that replaced the rickety stands, some of which had been secondhand in 1959, when the stadium was built. In another example of Williamsport's amazing ability to pull together to support its jewel, one-third of the funds needed for construction were raised in one week in the Williamsport area.

Hundreds of Richmond supporters made the trip to Williamsport, spicing their "Go, Go, Tuckahoe" chant by waving Confederate flags. It was probably the largest contingent of boisterous Virginians to assemble in the Keystone State since Robert E. Lee's Army of Northern Virginia fought for three summer days in Gettysburg. One Virginian planted a large flagpole bearing the Old South's standard just beyond the center-field fence, but it was quickly removed by Little League's grounds crew. It is, after all, Pennsylvania.

Japan won the title again. The Wakayama Little League team defeated Tuckahoe, 1–0, as Hideake Highashide and Roger Miller dueled through six innings, each giving up only three hits. Japan's lone run was unearned.

Still, two consecutive World Series victories hardly constituted Japanese dominance. The seeds of a dynasty were sown on a different island, many years earlier.

TAIWAN PLAYS TO WIN

Actually, Japan planted the seeds for the dynasty during its fifty-year occupation of Formosa, an island off the southeast coast of China between the East and South China seas. By the 1920s, baseball was quite popular in Japan, and American servicemen spread

Japanese players
rejoice after the Far East
team won the 1967 Little
League World Series.
The team's pitcher
tossed a three-hitter in
Japan's 4–1 win.

The Japanese catcher autographs a baseball for fans after the Far East team won the 1967 Series.

its popularity to its possessions, including the island later known as the Republic of China, or Taiwan. Servicemen also introduced baseball to the Chinese in the larger cities of Shanghai and Peking while stationed there in World War II. When the Nationalist Chinese, called the Kuomintang, fled mainland China and the Communist army in December 1949, they took baseball with them, although it took nearly two decades for the game to become popular.

One of those who fled was Wu Ming-Tien, who learned baseball as a boy from the Japanese army, the same way Japanese boys learned it from the U.S. Army and Navy. He became a teacher in an isolated east coast village, adding baseball—or something like it— to the school curriculum in 1963. Syndicated columnist Bob Considine wrote: "They are, by all odds, the strangest ball club ever assembled. They are mountain boys, aborigines whose forebears practiced head-hunting until the 1930s. Incredibly, their primitive school has only 16 students."

Ming-Tien did not have baseball equipment at his disposal when he began teaching the sport in the village, so he improvised with bamboo sticks for bats, and stones for balls. A strict disciplinarian, he conducted hours-long drills without gloves. The village team eventually gathered enough real equipment for proper baseball games and requested a charter from Little League in 1968.

1969: A MEMORABLE SERIES

The year 1969 was a memorable year in many ways. Neil Armstrong and Edwin Aldrin walked on the moon a month before the Little League World Series that year. The Woodstock music festival near Bethel, New York, a two-hour drive from Williamsport, ended on Sunday, August 17, the day the last teams arrived for the Series.

Those who attended the 1969 Little League World Series recall it as one of the most memorable too. Taiwan wowed the crowds with the first of its seventeen titles, and Mickey Mantle nearly stole the show as ABC's color commentator during the *Wide World of Sports* broadcast.

For Williamsport residents, the 1969 Series remains memorable because it was the last time a team from that city advanced to the Series. Having won the Eastern Region title in Belleville, New Jersey, Newberry Little League, managed by Fred Heaps, was the first Williamsport team to win a state title since state tournaments began in 1949. Ace pitcher Don Cohick, who went on to fly jet fighters for the U.S. Air Force, was one of nine players from different eras invited back to Williamsport as part of the 50th Little League Baseball World Series Commemorative Team in 1996. The commemorative team also included two others from the 1969 Series. One was Tsai Ching-Fong, a player with the Taiwan 1969 champions who went on to coach professional baseball in Taiwan. The other was Carney Lansford, a star for the Santa Clara, California, team. He broke his arm in the semifinal game and did not play against Taiwan in the championship, but later he played fifteen seasons in the major leagues for the Oakland Athletics, the Boston Red Sox, and the California Angels.◆

TOP
Don Cohick pitches for Williamsport's Newberry Little League team in the 1969 Little League World Series.

BOTTOM
The Chinese Taipei pitcher celebrates with his catcher in its first Little League Baseball World Series victory in 1969. The team, the Golden Dragons, traveled 9,000 miles to Williamsport.

Chef Yen Yu-Cho serving Taiwan's players, most of whom had never eaten Western-style food. Yen was brought in by Taiwan's embassy in Washington, and he enjoyed the experience so much that he and his family decided to open a restaurant in South Williamsport.

Some inkling of their baseball prowess came late that year when they played against a traveling team of Japanese players, some of whom were on the 1968 Little League World Series Championship team, and beat them. Having played its one requisite season on probation, Taiwan entered the International Tournament in 1969 with a team practiced to near perfection. They won the Taiwan national title, then took to the air for a 3,900-mile trip to defeat Guam, 16–0. A week later, they flew another 1,400 miles to defeat Japan's national champion 3–0. That earned a 9,000-mile trip to Williamsport for the team nicknamed the "Golden Dragons." A Chinese report after the victory against Japan illustrated the peculiar way "baseballese" is translated into other languages:

With two men on the piles [bases], our guerilla [shortstop] in whom we had great hope to hit a good ball was killed [struck out]. At this time we all felt a cold shiver.

But luckily Yu Hung-Kai mounted the field [came to bat]. He is our famous attacker. And so it happened that he made a two pile safe hit to center. The crowd was stunned.

In fact, Taiwan's reaching the Series on its first try stunned everyone, except maybe the Taiwanese. The Japanese were so confident of earning a berth in the Series that one Japanese businessman promised to underwrite the cost of the team's travel to the United States, even though the Far East regional tournament had not begun. As a result, nine Little League teams attended the 1969 Series, with the Japanese team taking part in all the events except the games themselves. Little League had to change plans too, as uniforms with "Japan" on the chest were relettered with "Republic of China."

The Taiwanese boys never had eaten Western-style food before coming to the United States, so a Taiwan government official sent a letter to Little League requesting that the team be allowed to eat at a Chinese restaurant. Williamsport did not have a Chinese restaurant at the time, but the team didn't have to abide hamburgers, hotdogs, French fries, and sodas the first year. The Miao family of Williamsport, natives of Korea, volunteered to prepare the team's food. After that, however, a chef from the Republic of China Embassy in Washington was brought in to supply a special diet each time a team from Taiwan earned a berth in the Series.

The chef, Yen Yu-Cho, enjoyed Williamsport so much, in fact, that he and his family eventually settled there and opened the area's first Chinese restaurant: Yen King. The restaurant is still popular, and Yen Yu-Cho still talks to visitors about the early years of Taiwan's World Series success.

The Golden Dragons entered the Series as an unknown quantity, but soon they established themselves in a way that characterized Taiwanese teams in the Series for almost three decades. Playing flawless defense, Taiwan erupted for five runs in the twelfth inning to defeat Valleyfield, Quebec, in the opener. Chen Chi-Yuan pitched the first nine innings, striking out twenty-one batters. He explained to an Associated Press reporter through an interpreter how he came to be so successful on the mound after only playing baseball for one year: "At school, I practiced every day. I have a coach at school and I also have a volunteer coach who is an [alumnus] of my school." Playing baseball in school, and Little Leagues composed of players from one school instead of geographical boundaries, became a hallmark for Taiwan, but it also proved to be the reason Taiwan would drop out of Little League in the 1990s.

Taiwan made it to the World Series in 1970 but failed to reach the final. Starting in 1971, however, Taiwan began an incredible streak of thirty-one straight victories in Little League World Series games, stretching over eleven years.

Kevin Costner, actor, director

"Little League Baseball was such a huge part

of my life. As a kid and as a father, the memories are,

in fact, so thick that I have to brush them

away from my face. Thank God for Little League

Baseball and how it's managed itself."

nine

GIRLS, GIRLS, GIRLS

For its first thirty-three years, Little League was a male-dominated institution—in almost every respect. Men comprised the vast majority of Little League volunteers. A female coach or umpire was a rarity—even an object of curiosity. Women traditionally occupied administrative or domestic positions in Little League, such as auxiliary members or concession-stand workers.

On the field, too, Little League was for boys alone. The earliest Little League rules referred only to boys because, well, because girls just didn't play baseball. So there was no need to have a rule specifically barring girls. According to Carl Stotz, quoted in a May 1973 issue of the *Detroit News*: "When we started the Little League, the idea of a girl playing baseball, even with other girls, was simply unthinkable."

Carl Stotz was not alone in his views. It is fair to say that American society has never been entirely comfortable with the idea of girls playing baseball. In 1885 a writer told the *St. Louis Globe-Democrat*: "The female has no place in base ball, except to the degradation of the game."

Many Americans shared that view. Even as late as 1971, a Connecticut judge was quoted as saying: "Athletic competition builds character in our boys. We do not need that kind of character in our girls."

Nevertheless, one can find instances of girls playing baseball as far back as the late 1800s. Usually they played informally with other girls in

MARGARET GISOLO

American Legion ball, which predated Little League as a baseball program for boys, was for teenagers age fourteen and above. The first season of American Legion ball came in 1926, and it took only two years for a girl to try to break the gender barrier. Fourteen-year-old Margaret Gisolo was drawn to athletics, so her debut for Blanford, Indiana, in the boys' world of baseball made sense to her: "It was just as easy for me to stop doing the dishes and go out and play some. I'd play catch. My brother taught me how to slide into base. He played with the local team, and when they put together an American Legion team, they needed a second baseman."

Margaret's skill helped her make it onto the roster, and in one game against Clinton, a cross-county rival, she drove in the winning run. Clinton lodged a protest that made its way to the national level. After consulting with Kenesaw "Mountain" Landis, the commissioner of Major League Baseball, American Legion officials decided Margaret could stay on the team. Newspapers picked up on the novelty, and a few other girls followed suit in other areas. Margaret proved she could perform too, flawlessly playing at second base and compiling a .429 batting average through the playoffs. Blanford won the state championship and reached the national semifinals before bowing out.

But American Legion ended the experiment the next year by reversing itself and officially barring girls, citing economic reasons for the decision. It would have been too costly, officials said, to provide separate facilities for males and females while traveling.

Margaret played for barnstorming teams for several years, which helped her earn money for college. She received her bachelor's degree in 1935, a master's degree in 1942, became an officer in the U.S. Navy, and retired as a full professor in 1980 from Arizona State University after elevating the "Modern Dance" section of the physical education curriculum to a "School of Dance." Margaret received an honorary doctorate in fine arts from Arizona State in 1995 and lives in Tempe, Arizona.◆

Margaret Gisolo of Blanford, Indiana, at the age of fourteen. Gisolo was the first girl to play in American Legion Baseball, paving the way for many other barrier breakers.

boarding schools and, rarely, on organized teams with boys. The first celebrated example of a girl playing competitive baseball with boys is Margaret Gisolo, who played American Legion ball for Blanford, Indiana, in 1928. Margaret was an accomplished player who helped her team capture the state championship. But the following year American Legion ended the experiment by officially barring girls, citing economic reasons. It would have been too costly, officials said, to provide separate facilities for males and females while traveling.

For Little League, the issue of girls playing baseball did not surface until the program began to expand beyond Pennsylvania's borders and the possibility of girls invading the all-male bastion increased. In 1951, a single line made its first appearance in the Little League regulations: "Girls are not eligible under any conditions."

Baseball did not stand alone as the all-male sport of choice for girls to invade. Basketball, football, and wrestling programs were not immune to lawsuits alleging discrimination. But Little League leadership knew, long before the 1970s, that the high-profile nature of the organization made it a target for lawsuits. It's fair to say that the 1972, 1973, and 1974 seasons were the longest in Little League history.

IT HAPPENED IN HOBOKEN

Back in 1846, Alexander Cartwright probably did not envision women or girls playing the game when he came up with some rules of play. That's when the New York City resident assembled a team, the New York Knickerbocker Baseball Club, and met the New York Baseball Club at a spot called Elysian Fields in Hoboken, New Jersey. Historians generally regard the June 19 contest as the first true baseball game, and Hoboken as baseball's birthplace.

Nobody is sure who might have been the first girl to play in Little League. Maria Pepe was not the first girl ever to play in an official Little League game, but she might be the girl who had the most impact on Little League. When Maria fought to play with the boys, she fought to play at Hoboken Little League, only a few blocks from the place the first baseball game had been played.

Maria's saga began in the spring of 1972 when she tried out for and was selected to play on a team in Hoboken Little League. She wanted the competition Little League offered: "They don't [have anything] for girls in Hoboken, only for boys," she told the *Bergen Record* of New Jersey in 1972. Maria played in the first three games of the season for the Hoboken Young Democrats team, but more attention was paid to her than to her team's success, or lack of it, because she was a girl. The attention didn't stop there, however.

Word of her presence on the team reached Little League Baseball's headquarters in Williamsport, where similar issues had been handled before. Pulling the local Little League's charter is the heaviest penalty headquarters can levy on one of its local programs. Charter revocation—seldom used unless the league willfully or persistently violates rules,

OPPOSITE PAGE

OPPOSITE PAGE
Maria Pepe fought to play with the boys at Hoboken Little League (New Jersey). In 1972 the National Organization for Women sued Little League Baseball on her behalf, and in 1974 Little League finally admitted defeat, agreeing to permit girls to play.

RIGHT
Catcher Kelly Craig of British Columbia Trail Little League (Canada) played in the 1990 Little League Baseball World Series.

BELOW
Victoria Roche, a player for the 1984 European team, is the first girl to play in a Little League Baseball World Series.

regulations, or policies—is at times the only effective means of convincing a recalcitrant local Little League to toe the line. It means, among other things, that the league can no longer call itself a "Little League," that the players can't wear the Little League patch, and that the league cannot enter teams in tournament play. Also, a league that is prevented from applying for a charter cannot purchase group accident insurance through Little League. In Hoboken's case, Little League told the local league's leadership that its charter would be revoked if Maria were allowed to continue on the Young Democrats team.

The Hoboken Little League reluctantly dismissed Maria from her team, and Little League reinstated its charter. If similar to previous cases, that would have been the end of it, as indicated by Robert H. Stirrat, Little League's vice president and public relations director, in the May 28, 1972, edition of the *New York Sunday News:* "Under the conditions that the girl was removed from the team, the charter and insurance have been returned. As far as we're concerned, the incident is closed."

Little League had reason to believe that it would win a court battle anyway, given a victory in Massachusetts earlier in the year. The judge there said the courts had no jurisdiction over Little League in such cases. But Maria Pepe and her family were not willing to surrender. The incident, already fodder for New York media, grabbed heavier headlines. The New York Yankees honored Maria and her family with a special day at Yankee Stadium, where General Manager Lee MacPhail personally presented her with a New York Yankees shirt.

COURT BATTLES

Throughout the ensuing court battles, Little League presented two main reasons for the ban on girls. The first was physical differences between boys and girls. Dr. Creighton J. Hale, promoted from Little League executive vice president to president in October 1973, presented Little League's case as reported in an Associated Press story:

> Dr. Hale, who holds a Ph.D. in physiology, says: "There are differences between the male and female, in spite of the trend now to try and say there aren't any differences."
>
> He contends that boys are born with more muscle fibers, and by age 10 the muscle fiber ratio is 3–2 in favor of the boys.
>
> "These are the power units that drive the human body, how fast they can go, how hard they can hit," says Hale. "So consequently you can expect boys as a class to run faster and hit harder and the consequence in any contact sport may be an injury."
>
> The American Medical Association's Committee on Medical Aspects of Sports classifies baseball as a contact sport. But it points out that the potential for injury is far less than in such contact sports as football or ice hockey.
>
> He also cites test results that show girls have a slower reaction time than boys, and discounts the argument that girls outdistance boys in developing coordination.
>
> "Girls may develop body tissue quicker," he said. "They may be taller or heavier at 10 or 11, but it doesn't mean they have more muscle fibers and this is where we're thrown off in my opinion. We look at somebody and evaluate them based on height and weight and you can't do that. It's like giving a doctor two drops of blood and saying, 'Now are there any differences?' Well, you can't without a microscope know this."

It is important to note that Dr. Hale no longer holds such views. In fact, he says today, "I think it's one of the best things that happened. Very few girls have played Little League Baseball, but the opportunity's there for them to do it. On a personal note, I have a granddaughter—I have five granddaughters—but a granddaughter that is very athletic and plays Little League in Westerville, Ohio. This year she became the first girl ever selected to play on the Little League Baseball tournament team there. What goes around, comes around." Still, at the time of the court battles, his opinion was influential.

The second and most compelling aspect of Little League's argument was the wording of its federal charter, granted by the U.S. Congress in 1964, specifically charging the organization with administering a program for the betterment of boys. Allowing girls into the program would, in effect, abrogate the terms of the charter. In an interview with the Associated Press at the time, Hale said: "If we permit girls to play we are in violation of the law. Only Congress can change this law. It's as simple as that."

Little League's position did not go unchallenged on either argument. Newspapers carried statements from doctors refuting Hale's statements. Others pointed out that Little League could simply petition Congress to change the charter. NOW took up Maria's struggle and sued Little League in the New Jersey Division of Civil Rights. The suit charged that Little League was using public land to discriminate against females because it "promulgated, published and enforces a regulation which states 'Girls are not eligible' to compete in Little League Baseball. This rule denies girls the advantages, facilities and privileges of a public accommodation by specifically excluding them from competition … solely because of their sex."

The case dragged through the summer and into the next year. By then, Maria had turned thirteen and was too old to play, because Hoboken Little League did not offer a Senior League program. But the suit continued, and others cropped up around the nation. In 1974, legal action was under way or pending against Little League in twenty states—all to force the program into admitting girls.

Little League actually won more cases than it lost. One high-profile case in the U.S. Federal District Court in Ypsilanti, Michigan, ended in a clear Little League victory, and the hope that it established a precedent. Judge Ralph M. Freeman denied an appeal for injunction from Ypsilanti Little League against Little League. Peter McGovern's July 17, 1973, newsletter to all of Little League's presidents explained the outcome and provided leagues with news that Little League would institute a new program specifically for girls:

> Allegation was made that a 12-year-old child, Carolyn King, had been discriminated against "solely on the basis of sex" by the enforcement of Little League Regulation IV(i) which declared her ineligible to play on the same team as the boys. The hearing was carried on for four days and every aspect of the plaintiff's appeal was examined scrupulously by the court to determine, first, whether jurisdiction was involved (the court ruled this case would have to be dismissed for lack of jurisdiction) and, second, whether … there was, as alleged, any evidence of discrimination on the basis of sex. (The court ruled that the goal of safety is a legitimate concern of Little League Baseball, Incorporated and that the court could not say that the rule in question is not rationally related to the effectuation of this reasonable goal.)
>
> Since this is about the fourth federal case to be decided in favor of Little League Baseball along the same general lines, it should stand as firm precedent for all local league presidents when future cases crop up as they have been doing in many parts of the country during the past several months. It is not just a coincidence. At the 1973

Giselle Hardy of the 1991 European team (Saudi Arabia) also was a Little League Baseball World Series player.

DID THE LAWSUITS KILL THE ERA?

In 1972, American politicians were mulling over two important pieces of legislation dealing with women's rights. One, Title IX, became law when President Richard M. Nixon signed it on June 23. Title IX is generally credited with providing unprecedented opportunities for girls and women in school-related athletics.

The other was the Equal Rights Amendment to the U.S. Constitution. The ERA passed the U.S. Senate by a vote of 84 to 8, but constitutional amendments are, by design, more difficult to enact. After passage by two-thirds of the House and the Senate in the spring, the amendment went to each of the fifty state legislatures, where eventually it failed to win ratification by the required three-fourths of the states within ten years.

Also in the spring of 1972, Maria Pepe and other girls around the United States tried out— and some *tried* to try out—for Little League teams previously populated only by boys. When denied a spot on the roster, some sued, and some of the suits were supported by the National Organization for Women. The suits were based on the assumption that Little League was and is a public accommodation and, as such, should be open to girls too.

While the idea won support in some quarters, it's safe to say that most Little Leagues opposed it. In New Jersey, for instance, hundreds of leagues suspended registrations in 1974 while they awaited final word on the outcome of NOW's lawsuit on Pepe's behalf. Only after a judge forced the leagues to begin registrations and accept girls did the local programs back down.

It's also safe to say that men in leadership positions dominated Little Leagues in the early 1970s. Almost all the managers and coaches were men, and the majority of the local boards of directors were men. Men in such positions were also more likely to be registered voters, and actively interested in political matters. Even those men not involved with Little Leagues might have cringed at the idea of the heretofore all-male enclave of Little League being invaded by girls.

Is it possible, then, that Little League Baseball helped kill the ERA in the first few critical years of the ERA's one-decade life? Alvin Bush recalls the legal troubles Little League went through, and thinks that could be the case. Bush spent parts of three decades in Pennsylvania politics, in the state house and the state senate. He personally supported the Equal Rights Amendment but was not a voting member of either body at the time Pennsylvania ratified it. "There would have been resistance in some quarters, certainly, because of the backlash," he said. "It might have been a miscalculation on [NOW's] part."

The real victory for girls came when Title IX was passed. In 1972 there were fewer than 32,000 women competing in intercollegiate athletics. Women athletes were receiving just 2 percent of all monies, and nothing was in the form of scholarships. Today, more than 110,000 women participate in college sports. The number of female athletes in high school has increased from about 300,000 to more than 2,000,000.

As for Little League, relatively few girls play on baseball teams. But the Little League Softball program, starting with fewer than 30,000 players in 1974, now boasts more than 390,000 participants.◆

International Congress in Tampa, a motion for consideration of a program for girls of comparable Little League age was adopted by the delegates in assembly. Many leagues have already activated such programs usually in the area of softball teams using the same premises. It is recommended that this might be looked into.

But the real precedent was set by the New Jersey case. In November 1973, New Jersey became the first state in the nation to order Little League to permit girls to play. An Associated Press story reported the decision:

"The institution of Little League is as American as the hotdog and apple pie," Hearing Examiner Sylvia Pressler of the state's Civil Rights Division declared Wednesday. "There is no reason why that part of Americana should be withheld from girls.

"We must start somewhere in reversing the trends in this society. Girls should be treated no differently than boys."

The ruling, which covers only New Jersey teams, followed a complaint by a Hoboken girl against Little League Baseball, Inc. of Williamsport, Pa., after the girl was ejected from a [league] whose charter had been threatened by the national organization.

The complaint by Maria Pepe, 12, was prepared by the National Organization for Women.

Attorneys for Little League Baseball said they would appeal Mrs. Pressler's ruling to the Appellate Division of Superior Court, the state's second highest tribunal, and to the State Supreme Court if necessary.

Mrs. Pressler's ruling was made after psychologists and physicians gave conflicting testimony in a series of hearings in the past few months.

"I have no doubt they're reputable psychologists who would agree with 'the birds of a feather' theory," Mrs. Pressler said. "However, the extension of that theory is that whites like to be with whites, blacks like to be with blacks, and Jews like to be with Jews. That whole theory is in contradiction with the laws of this state.

Krissy Wendall of Brooklyn Center, Minnesota, hits at the 1994 Little League World Series.

Sayaka Tsushima, the sixth girl to play in the Little League Baseball World Series, was starting center fielder for Japan in 1998.

"The sooner that little boys realize that little girls are equals and that there will be many opportunities for a boy to be bested by a girl, the closer they will be to mental health.

"I am satisfied that children between 8 and 12 perform differently on an individual basis not on a sexual class basis," Mrs. Pressler concluded.

The key was the designation of Little League as a public accommodation. Although Little League is a private organization, NOW successfully argued, Little League accepts public funds, uses public property, and solicits membership from the general public. Little League appealed, telling leagues in New Jersey to suspend registrations for the 1974 season until the matter could be resolved. But the court intervened, forcing Little League to inform its chartered programs in the state that local Little Leagues refusing to admit girls would have their charters revoked.

The first appeal failed in the Appellate Division of the Superior Court of New Jersey on March 29, 1974, and McGovern sent a four-page letter to leagues and districts that very day. Among his comments were these:

The newspaper, radio and television stations have been covering these stories with a great deal of misinformation ever since the decision was rendered by a Civil Rights Hearing Examiner in Newark on November 7, 1973. The complaint was filed by the Chairman of the National Organization for Women through its Essex County Chapter President, Judith Weiss, and heard by woman examiner, Sylvia B. Pressler, under the most prejudiced of conditions in which the examiner acted as judge, jury and prosecuting attorney.

Alicia Hunolt (center), in 1999, was the seventh girl to play in the Little League Baseball World Series.

It is obvious that this is an outrageous and punitive order conceived in vindictive and prejudicial fashion of the worst kind. … Little League Baseball has been vilified in a manner which is unbelievable as a lawbreaking agency and during the past two years, 12 cases of litigation have been brought to bear by various segments of the National Organization for Women, in each of which case Little League was the defendant.

Needless to say, Little League Baseball faces a very serious decision. Currently the Civil Rights Order is leveled against the leagues of New Jersey, but the precedent is established through NOW's ubiquitous grapevine to affect every state in the nation. … It is time now that everyone in Little League Baseball become articulate. We ask you to contact the local leagues in groups and by person to urge them to demand equal time on television, radio and in newspapers, to state candidly that Little League is in danger of being destroyed by a power-mad current combine of ambitionists who have overreached themselves. These women, under a strange breed of leadership, have no design whatever on putting girls on the same teams as boys. The children are being used as pawns to accommodate their own ulterior motives.

McGovern's words were heeded by some. A pamphlet created by the "Pennsylvania Little League Action Committee," a group of three volunteer district administrators, was circulated among the districts in an effort to rally support for fending off more attacks: "After much discussion on how we can further act, we feel we made a major breakthrough—we feel we have the perfect answer to the individuals of NOW—the members of our Ladies Auxiliaries! Who could better stand up to those NOW invaders than the Women Volunteers of our program?"

Little League lost its next appeal too, and a superior court judge ordered headquarters to notify its 330 New Jersey leagues "in no uncertain terms" that they must comply with the ruling. In the end, the Little League Baseball International board of directors threw in the towel because of "the changing social climate." The U.S. Congress agreed to change the federal charter, but a news release on June 12, 1974, gave one parting shot to NOW:

> In reaching a decision on an issue of landmark significance, the Board has taken the position that it would be imprudent for an organization as large and universally respected as 35-year-old Little League Baseball to allow itself to become embroiled in a public controversy. Implication that the program is unwilling to change or incompetent to solve its own problems is simply not true. The Board believes that its concern and reaction to the recent intrusion into the administrative affairs of Little League by various self-interest groups was justified since they have opted to ignore the purview of Constitutional Law and have breached, as well as demanded abrogation of, the rights of others.

SO, WHO *WAS* THE FIRST GIRL TO PLAY LITTLE LEAGUE?

Since Little League's battles over gender in 1972–74, stories commemorating various regional court battles have appeared in which the claim to the title "first girl to play Little League" belonged to various girls in various locales. Twice in the past twenty-seven years since the controversy ended with Little League's admittance of girls, Kathryn Massar, a U.S. Air Force veteran and trauma nurse at Rideout Hospital in Marysville, California, felt compelled to contact Little League Baseball International Headquarters.

When Kathryn was a little girl, she lived in Corning, New York (about ninety minutes north of Williamsport, Pennsylvania, and three hours southwest of Cooperstown, New York), and her last name was Johnston. The first time she wrote to Little League was in June 1974. Addressed to Robert H. Stirrat, Little League's vice president and director of public relations, her letter reads:

> Dear Mr. Stirrat,
>
> Throughout the past year, I have found articles regarding girls in Little League somewhat amusing. As far as girls having equal competency in baseball skills as boys, I can assure you they do.
>
> In 1950, I played Little League Baseball in Corning, N.Y. At that time it was called Midget League, and I feel that this was the first time a girl ever played Little League Baseball.
>
> I am enclosing a picture of myself and a couple of articles to verify that I actually played on the King's Dairy team in Corning under the name of Tubby Johnston.
>
> With warm regards,
> Kathryn Johnston Massar

Among the clippings from the *Corning Leader* was a column by Sports Editor Frank E. Watts Jr. that appeared in spring 1950.

Don't look now but it may be only a few years before the fair sex take over the Midget Baseball League. … In the starting line-up for the King's Dairy team was "Tubby" Johnston, daughter of Mr. and Mrs. Malcolm Johnston of 108 Gorton Street. She is a student at the North Street Junior High School and can hold her own with the other male members of the team. In her initial appearance against the WCBA team, she drew three walks. The youngster also fielded her position well.

Stirrat investigated the claim and replied on July 9, 1974:

Dear Mrs. Massar:

Thank you for sending along the clippings about Tubby Johnston and the Corning Midget League, which did indeed become a Little League in 1950.

If there are no other aliases which come to light we can safely assume that you were the first girl to participate.

Cordially,
Robert H. Stirrat
Vice President

LEFT
Kathryn "Tubby" Massar may be the first girl to have played Little League. Tucking her hair under her hat, she tried out as a boy and played Little League Baseball for the King's Dairy team in 1950 in Corning, New York. Today she is a U.S. Air Force veteran and trauma nurse at Rideout Hospital in Marysville, California.

RIGHT
Betty Speziale earned the honor of being the first female umpire at the Little League Baseball World Series. Here she works the bases in 1989.

At the time, Little League was not inclined to give the "girls in Little League" controversy any more publicity than it already had, so the letters and clippings were filed away. Other than mentions of Kathryn's on-field exploits in the *Corning Leader* in 1950, her story never appeared again—until now. After her second contact with Little League Baseball International Headquarters, this time by telephone in the spring of 2000, public relations officials located her 1974 correspondence in a little-used filing cabinet.

Kathryn first tried out for Little League along with her brother, Tommy, on the King's Dairy team. Tucking her hair under her baseball cap, she hid her gender until she was selected. She used the nickname "Tubby," a character in her favorite comic strip, "Little Lulu." Even when Kathryn revealed her secret, the rest of the team didn't mind, she said. After all, she was a good player, having been trained by her father, Malcolm "Johnny" Johnston. She recalled:

> He [her father] always took me out, and we'd play. He'd throw the ball and I would bat. I was pretty good, so when the little boys came to the door, they'd always ask, "Can Kay come out?"
>
> I was very little for my age, so they didn't question anything. I had short hair anyway, so I threw it up under a cap and went out for the team.
>
> [Tommy] didn't think I'd make the team, but I was better than him. Once I was on the team, I talked to the coach in the dugout and told him I was a girl. He said, "Well, you're good enough to make the team," so they let me stay.
>
> In fact, I was a drawing card in Corning, because once they found out I was a girl, more people came out to see the games. But I was a tomboy and it made no difference to me. … I had a lot of fun doing it.

Kathryn said she would have played the 1951 season too, but that's when Little League rules began specifically prohibiting girls, so she was dismissed from the team. Her father teased her about the rule. She recalled: "He told me I couldn't play because of the new rule and said, 'Look what you've started!'" It is possible that Massar is responsible for the 1951 "no girls" ruling and that she precipitated Pepe's struggle against Little League in 1974.

Kathryn played softball after that for a few years and later became an Air Force nurse. She met her future husband, Cyril Massar, a 1957 graduate of the U.S. Military Academy at West Point, who was an officer in the Air Force in Biloxi, Mississippi, while they were in the service. Their family eventually settled in California, and Kathryn's place in Little League history largely was forgotten until the early 1970s, when reports on "pioneer" girls challenging Little League's all-boys participation regulation began peppering the news.

Perhaps, like Kathryn Massar, there were other little girls masquerading as boys to play Little League Baseball. Maria Pepe, however, did not use an alias. She tried out and made the Hoboken Little League Young Democrats team as a girl. And whereas Kathryn,

BOYS IN SOFTBALL

Although plans for a girls-only softball program had been made previously, the softball program began in 1974 amid lawsuits in twenty states in which girls sued to be allowed to participate in Little League Baseball programs. At the same time that the baseball regulations were made non-gender-specific, a softball program for girls was created. More than 29,000 participated in the first year, with the regulations specifically allowing only females to participate.

Over the years, the program grew to an all-time high of more than 400,000 in 1998. Currently, about 392,000 participate in the various divisions of Little League Softball.

In 1985, through an out-of-court settlement in California, boys were allowed to play, in that state only. In 1995, a similar out-of-court settlement in Vermont allowed boys to play in that state too. The following year, because challenges in other states based on gender, reminiscent of those in the 1970s over girls in baseball in other states, seemed imminent, the Little League Baseball International board of directors voted to open the softball program to both genders in all states and countries.

In 1998 and 1999, several teams that had boys on the rosters reached the regional level of tournament play, bringing comparatively little interest from the media and only a few complaints. In August 2000, however, a Senior League Softball team from Arizona for players ages fourteen through sixteen—with five boys on the roster—advanced to the Senior League Softball World Series in Kalamazoo, Michigan, causing an uproar at the tournament and elsewhere. The Canadian team also showed up with one boy on the roster. Forty-three news organizations requested interviews from the Little League media relations department on the subject over a two-week period. In Kalamazoo, things got ugly as jeering by spectators prompted officials to halt the games temporarily and appeal for calm.

A male runner for the Santa Cruz Valley Little League of Eloy, Arizona, slides into home plate and a female catcher in the 2000 Senior League Softball World Series.

An all-girls team from the Philippines played the Arizona team twice, defeating the coed players 3–2 early in the tournament but losing to them 4–3 later. In the championship game, the two teams were to meet again, but Philippines manager Damaso Sancon forfeited rather than allow his team to take the field, claiming he was concerned for his players' safety. That was the first time a team had purposely forfeited a world championship game in any level of Little League World Series competition. Ironically, the only other time there was a forfeit in a final game was in the 1992 Little League Baseball World Series, when another team from the Philippines, Zamboanga City, defeated Long Beach, California, 15–4, but was subsequently disqualified for using ineligible players.

The vast majority of players in the Little League Softball divisions are girls. After the 1999 season, Little League conducted a survey of its leagues, and 65 percent of the leagues responded. The results indicated that 99.75 percent of the regular season players in Little League Softball programs, ages 5–18, were girls. In tournament play, the total was 99.85 percent.

Still, the uproar caused Little League's board to direct the headquarters staff to resolve the situation one way or another, so that the softball program can legally be limited to girls only in the 2001 season and beyond. As a result, Little League added all new divisions for boys ages five to eighteen who want to play softball, while limiting the girls softball program to females.◆

as her father teased, may have been the catalyst for the "no girls" rule in the book, Maria's landmark lawsuit definitely removed it.

PAVING THE WAY FOR MILLIONS

It has been more than a quarter-century since Little League's three-year battle to prevent girls from playing on Little League's baseball teams. Maria Pepe continues to receive acclaim and was featured in a two-hour cable television special on "Barrier Breakers in Women's Sports." Although she was allowed to play in only three Little League games before her manager was forced to pull her from the roster, Pepe's hometown of Hoboken still takes pride in her "breaking the barrier" and invited her as a guest of honor on Baseball Day in 1996. Now controller at the Hackensack University Medical Center in Hackensack, New Jersey, she commented on her contribution to women's rights in a profile of Fairleigh Dickinson University alumni: "Although it was emotional for me as a kid, I've grown a lot from that experience. I was a key figure in the 1970s evolution of girls' sports, and I've had an influence on many girls' lives."

After her civil rights struggle, Pepe continued to compete athletically, playing on community softball and basketball teams and earning a spot on the varsity softball team at Saint Peter's College, Jersey City, New Jersey. "I believe that being involved in organized sports all of my life has helped me in the professional world," she says. "The interaction within a sports team is similar to the team spirit on the job."

Have it your way! Girls joined Little League and played a softball tournament during the 1975 National Championship held at Howard J. Lamade Stadium. Note "poofy" hat as part of uniform.

TOP
Members of the Toms River East American Little League of Toms River, New Jersey, celebrate their 12–9 victory against Kashima, Japan, in the 1998 Little League Baseball World Series.

BOTTOM
Dugout, Little League Baseball's mascot, is a favorite of fans and players at the Little League Series. Here Dugout dances with members of both 1999 Little League World Series Championship teams.

TOP

TOP

Pin-trading is one of the more popular events at the Little League Baseball World Series, as hundreds of children and adults from around the world compare and trade collectors' pins.

BOTTOM

Fans at the 2000 Little League Baseball World Series show their colors proudly.

Fans of the U.S. South team from Bellaire, Texas, cheer on their team in the 2000 Little League Baseball World Series.

Dugout leads the Parade of Nations at the 1999 Little League Baseball World Series.

Academy Award winner, actor, and director Kevin Costner speaks to Little League players in the dugout during the 2000 World Series Jamboree. Costner played baseball at Saticoy Little League in Ventura, California, during the 1960s.

Howard J. Lamade Stadium in the borough of South Williamsport can accommodate up to 45,000 fans. No admission is ever charged for a Little League Baseball World Series game.

TOP LEFT
Mike Mussina's Little League baseball glove and homemade trading card. Mussina played at Montoursville (Pa.) during the 1970s and 1980s.

TOP RIGHT
Cody Webster pitched a four-hitter for Kirkland, Washington, National Little League in the 1982 Little League Baseball World Series to defeat Taiwan 6–0, ending a streak of 31 consecutive World Series victories for the Taiwanese, dating back to 1970.

BOTTOM LEFT
Little Leaguers play ball on the White House lawn during a visit to Washington, D.C., to see President Reagan.

BOTTOM RIGHT
Sean Burroughs, of Long Beach, California, pitches in the championship game of the 1993 Little League Baseball World Series. Burroughs, a first-round draft choice of the San Diego Padres in 1998, played for Team USA, which won the gold medal in the 2000 Olympic Games in Sydney, Australia.

Chris Drury pitches his way to victory in the 1989 Little League Baseball World Series Championship. Drury pitched for Trumbull, Connecticut, and later went on to play hockey in the National Hockey League, winning Rookie of the Year honors in 1999 as a member of the Colorado Avalanche.

In 1974, Mark McGwire was an 11-year-old Little Leaguer in Claremont, California. In 1998, McGwire hit 70 home runs for the St. Louis Cardinals, setting the record for most home runs in a single season.

Gary Sheffield, far right, is shown here with teammates from the Belmont Heights, Tampa, Florida, Little League team that played in the 1980 World Series. Sheffield is now an outfielder for the Los Angeles Dodgers.

Derek Bell, who played for the New York Mets during the 2000 season, is only a blur as he fires a pitch in the 1981 Little League Baseball World Series for his Belmont Heights Little League team.

The jerseys Gary Sheffield and Derek Bell wore during the 1980 Little League Baseball World Series. Sheffield and Bell are the only two players from a Little League World Series team to end up playing on the same Major League team (San Diego Padres, 1993).

TOP LEFT
Far East pitcher from Hirakata, Osaka, Japan, winds up at the 1999 Little League Baseball World Series Championship.

TOP RIGHT
Pitcher for Mission Viejo, California, plays in the 1997 Little League Baseball World Series.

BOTTOM
Sierra Maestra Little League of Maracaibo, Venezuela, celebrates its victory after the 2000 Little League Baseball World Series championship.

The short uniforms worn by girls during the 1975 Little League Softball World Series make the players look more like Rockettes.

"ONE OF THE BEST THINGS THAT HAPPENED"

Little League Baseball has never asked its local leagues for figures on the number of girls who have played in the baseball programs over the years, so there is no way to determine the exact figure. Certainly, establishing an all-female softball program in 1974 resulted in many girls signing up for softball when they might have played baseball—if it was the only sport offered by Little League. A girl did not show up in the Little League Baseball World Series until 1984, when Victoria Roche, an American, played on the European entry from Brussels, Belgium. Only six others girls have made it into the Series since then. The softball program, made up entirely of girls until 1985 and still almost exclusively populated by females, now has about 392,000 players.

The first season of Little League Softball and Senior League Softball came in 1974, amid the turmoil of the lawsuits. Lost to the public, for the most part, was the fact that nearly 30,000 girls around the nation signed up in the first year. Little League did not maintain statistics on the number of girls playing in the baseball programs.

At the outset, the rules for Little League Softball for girls age eight to twelve called for a slow-pitch style of play in which stealing and sliding were outlawed. Since then, the softball rules have evolved to become more competitive. In 1978, a division for sixteen-to eighteen-year-olds, the Big League Softball Division, was added.

Fifteen years ago, one of every ten Little Leaguers was a softball player. In the year 2000, one in seven plays softball. More important, however, is that in 1974 one in twenty-seven girls played a high school sport, while today one in three play. That's reason enough for the program's existence, says Dr. Creighton J. Hale, whose earlier research and testimony initially helped to keep girls out of Little League.

Billy Hunter, executive director of the National Basketball Players Association, former National Football League player

"Playing baseball instilled in me

a hunger I just couldn't quench. Little League Baseball

was the catalyst to get me into other sports.

It created within me a desire to excel not only on the

athletic field, but also academically."

ten

DYNASTY FROM THE EAST

It took only a few years of domination at the Series for observers to won-der out loud why the Taiwanese were constantly defeating the Americans at their own game. When Taiwan won its first Little League World Se-ries in 1969, fans at Lamade Stadium cheered. They cheered when Tai-wan won in 1971. But by 1972, Little League fans in the United States began to ask questions. After victories in 1973 and 1974, they were tired of this winning streak. For the rest of the decade—and in the 1980s and part of the 1990s—fans and journalists wondered whether Taiwan was cheating. But it was another nation—a former U.S. territory, the Philip-pines—that had a desire to win the Series that reached new levels, even at the cost of being caught blatantly cheating.

TAIWAN GAINS INTERNATIONAL FAME

To say Taiwan was proud of its 1969 Little League World Series victory is an understatement. It was the first time that country had ever won any international athletic event. The *New York Times* reported on June 15, 1970:

> When the Chinese team beat Japan, the usual regional champion, for the Pacific title, the local population was quite pleasantly sur-prised. When the Golden Dragons went on to sweep the Little

League World Series in Williamsport, Pa., the citizens of Taiwan were rapturous.

Because of the difference in time zones, the games in Pennsylvania were played while it was night in Taiwan. But thousands of families stayed up to listen to the play-by-play [radio] broadcast by a Chinese announcer who traveled with the team. After the last out clinched the Chinese victory, telephone circuits were nearly overloaded as people spread the good news, firecrackers were set off in the streets, and storekeepers began to prepare red and gold banners to hang over their shop entrances.

The newspapers also found a moral in the victory. The championship, observed the *Evening News,* "fully proved that the rising generation of Chinese youth is not inferior to any other people in physique and intelligence."

President Chiang Kai-shek and his wife invited the team to the capital in Taipei, where they were honored in a ceremony. Madame Chiang placed all fourteen boys in a better school in southern Taiwan, in preparation for a college education provided by a provincial education fund and personal help from the president's wife. The government even issued a postage stamp commemorating the team's victory.

In May 1970, more than 30,000 people jammed tiny Taiwan Municipal Little League Stadium for the opening game of the Taiwan national tournament, which sent its winner to Williamsport. That team suffered a rare loss, bowing out of the Series in the first game.

Twenty years earlier, most American boys who played a team sport in a typical town played only baseball. By the start of the 1970s, however, more diversions arose as soccer, basketball, and individual sports surged in popularity. Meanwhile, Little League fever gripped Taiwan. Nothing illustrated that better than the events surrounding the illness and death of a certain national hero nine months after Taiwan won the 1972 Little League World Series. Twelve-year-old Lin Hsiang-jui, winning pitcher from the 1972 Series, succumbed to blood cancer. Associated Press told the story:

[Lin] was credited with winning the world Little League championship last year for Taipei City where Little League Baseball is football, cricket, bicycle-racing, boxing and the Kentucky Derby combined.

Since Taiwan first won the world championship in 1969, Little League Baseball has become one of the few points around which a major sense of nationalism and pride has grown up in the island.

The Nationalist government, set back by repeated diplomatic losses to mainland China, regards the game as a symbol of prestige.

So Lin's death after a two-month struggle with his illness hit Taiwan not as the death of just a Little League Baseball player, but also as the death of a real national hero.

He was treated at Taiwan's best hospitals at government expense. His death May 12 filled fully half of all television news programming during the next day. Newspa-

pers during the past week have been full of details of his life. One Taipei paper is publishing daily excerpts from Lin's diary.

The funeral Sunday resembled something close to a state occasion.

The boy's father was a laborer. Lin was quoted a week before he died as having told his parents he would one day buy them a house to replace the cramped apartment in the poor section of town in which they lived. Cash donations poured in—enough to buy his family a home of their own.

SPORTSMANSHIP AND SCUFFLES

The euphoria over winning a second Little League Baseball World Series title in 1971 did not last long in Taiwan. Nationalist China suffered a crushing defeat when it was booted out of the United Nations in favor of the People's Republic of China. Questions about Taiwan's future in Little League arose, but Little League President Peter J. McGovern told the *Williamsport Sun-Gazette:* "As far as we know, Taiwan is expected to continue its membership in Little League."

McGovern added that he found that the Taiwanese boys adhered "to the highest tenets of sportsmanship, displaying Little League class on and off the field." The same could hardly be said for some of those who attended the Series. At the 1969 Series, a minor scuffle broke out between supporters of two factions, one being natives of Taiwan and the other being those who fled the China mainland in 1949 after the Communist takeover. In 1971, a larger fight broke out, delaying the championship game and causing the state police to bring in more officers by helicopter. By the time the reinforcements arrived, however, the fight had ended.

A team from the national capital of Taipei made it to the championship game in 1972, beating Hammond, Indiana, 6–0, for the title. Fervor for Taiwan mounted, as *Grit* estimated that one in every six spectators was of Chinese descent, and more than 8 million Chinese watched the game live via satellite in the wee hours back home. Once again, however, tempers between factions flared, as detailed in an August 27, 1972, *Grit* story:

The festivities, glamour, and excitement of the Series were marred for the second year in a row by an outbreak of fighting among factions of Chinese fans.

Two Chinese fans were admitted to Williamsport Hospital for observation as a result of injuries suffered in the clash.

[South Williamsport Police Chief Charles E.] Smith indicated that he had talked with the two factions of Chinese during the game, and apparently the fight was planned.

About 10 minutes after the game the two groups squared off behind the left field fence. They swung at each other with 4-foot sticks that are one-and-three-quarters inches in diameter and very heavy, according to Smith. They also threw stones at one another.

TOP
The Taiwan team
visits President
Chiang Kai-shek
and his wife after
the 1970 Series.
Starting in 1971,
Taiwan began an
incredible streak of
thirty-one straight
victories in Little
League World
Series games,
stretching over
eleven years.

BOTTOM
Chiayi Little League
represented Taiwan
in the 1970 Series
and suffered a rare
first-round loss. This
photo shows the
team upon its return
home.

Anderson Little
League of Gary,
Indiana, played in
the 1971 Little
League Baseball
World Series—
the first all-black
team to do so.

"THESE BOYS ARE LITTLE LEAGUERS": AFRICAN AMERICANS REACH THE PLAYOFFS

The *Williamsport Sun-Gazette* brought two facts about the Little League Baseball World Series to the public's attention in the August 26, 1971, edition. Madrid, Spain, had become the first European team to win a first-round game, and Anderson Little League of Gary, Indiana, nick-named the Yankees, was "the first all-Negro team to gain the championship bracket."

Fortunately, times had changed in the sixteen years since an all-black team from Charleston, South Carolina, made it to the Series as invited guests but did not even get to play. Every other league in the state, then, was composed of white boys, and all the teams refused to play the Charleston team. Without a tournament, the Charleston players could not advance, but they received an invitation from Little League anyway.

A story in *Tuesday at Home* magazine in May 1972 explained how the Anderson Little League players were treated when they were guests in the homes of whites during their travels:

The parents confessed to previously unexpressed apprehensions that welled up when the boys first went on the road in the play-offs. However, [Anderson Little League President Phillip G.] Hudson indicated that the boys experienced almost no racial incidents. He cited as typical a conversation with one counterpart, a white official in another town where the Yankees would be visiting: "I called and told him, 'My boys are black, will there be any problems?' He told me, 'Mr. Hudson, these boys are Little Leaguers. We will accept them, no matter what color they are, as Little Leaguers. And more important, we will accept them as human beings.' I said, 'That's all I wanted to hear.' And everywhere our boys went they were accepted by the [host] family as one of the family." ◆

Political unrest between Taiwan and the Republic of China is evident even at the Little League World Series. Fans display homemade protest signs. Unrest also grew between the Americans and Taiwan. It took only a few years of domination at the Series for observers to ponder aloud why the Taiwanese constantly defeated the Americans at their own game.

The fighting did not last long, however. Fans and journalists watched as a state police helicopter parked behind the stadium took off shortly after the incident began and hovered about 150 feet over the belligerents, scattering them. Six were injured in the melee, and two people required a trip to the hospital. The next year, just before the Series, Williamsport residents received a four-page letter from the Reverend Song Chaonseng and the "Formosan Christians for Self-Determination," an anti-Nationalist group supporting independence for Taiwan. Song explained his group's position, criticizing the Nationalist "regime" in Taiwan, as well as U.S. President Richard M. Nixon, for making overtures to the People's Republic of China. The letter also appealed to Williamsporters to "do whatever is in your power to ensure that the Little League World Series this year will be a truly exciting and joyous sports event not marred by any politically motivated action of violence and disorder" and refuted claims that the "Taiwanese watchers of the game were communist instigated."

Taiwan's second straight World Series title and its third in four years brought a few complaints from American fans. Taiwanese boys also kept to themselves, mostly, and ate their own food, so Americans got the impression they were being shunned in their own country. A mother of a New City, New York, player in the Series described some of her feelings to *Grit:* "When we saw the Chinese boys going to practice carrying their bats in leather cases, like pool players carry their cues, we knew our sons didn't have a chance." In fact, the Taiwanese players got along very well with the Americans and everyone else as they struggled with language barriers to play Ping-Pong, trade mementos, and swim together.

THE MOPTOPS GET A HAIRCUT

The Wayne, New Jersey, team in the 1970 World Series and the Chiayi Little League team from Taiwan presented stark contrasts. Wayne's team earned the nickname "moptops" during their dash to the Series, but ran headlong into Little League's conservative bent. In previous World Series tournaments, Little League had no reason to dictate the grooming habits of players—as well as managers and coaches—on World Series teams. But when Wayne players Mark Epstein and Craig Kornfield, as well as Manager Gene Cancellieri and Coach Tom DeAngelis, showed up with long locks, they were ordered into the barber's chair before the first game.◆

LEFT
Wayne, New Jersey, won the 1970 Little League World Series over Campbell, California, but not without haircuts provided courtesy of Little League Baseball.

RIGHT
Wayne's fans were proud of their team's long locks.

THE BEST ON THE PLANET

When it came to baseball, though, Taiwan was all business. The headline for *Sun-Gazette* Sports Editor Mike Bernardi's column after Taiwan defeated New City 9–0 in the 1972 World Series opener queried "Is There a Dynasty in Making?"

To nobody's surprise, Taiwan won the Little League Baseball World Series again in 1973. It's the *way* it won that raised hackles in the United States, and even brought boos from some fans at the Series. Taiwan crushed a team from Bitburg Air Base in Germany 18–0 in the first game, then beat Tampa, Florida, 27–0. On championship day, Taiwanese rooters handed out miniature versions of the island nation's flags at the Lamade Stadium entrances to Chinese and Americans alike, but the team hardly needed the support as it blasted Tucson, Arizona, 12–0, in the final game.

During the three Series games, Taiwan's pitchers did not allow a single hit, and its batters belted a dozen home runs, racking up a team batting average of .417. Of the fifty-four outs for Taiwan's defense, forty-six were via strikeout. The August 31 issue of Arizona's *Phoenix Gazette* said: "The Republic of China's team beat the American teams at their own game because of serious, intensive preparation and unsurpassed motivation. Until the United States is willing to pay the same price, foreigners will continue to surpass Americans in sports."

Could it have been as simple as a general attitude of dedication to a cause? Some Americans, like the *Arizona Gazette* writer, hypothesized that Taiwan's crushing defeats

LLOYD McCLENDON

On Taiwan's second trip to the Little League World Series, in 1970, no fewer than forty Taiwanese journalists trailed along. Chiayi Little League reached the final eight, but fell to Nicaragua, 3–2, in the first round. Taiwanese television transmitted the game back to Taiwan live via satellite, another first for Little League. Despite the game's airtime of 2:00 A.M. in Taiwan, more than half of that nation's population of 14 million was estimated to have been watching.

The Wayne, New Jersey, Little League won the title in 1970, defeating Campbell, California, 2–0, in the final game. This ended a string of three straight titles by non-U.S. teams and put America's pastime back on the right path—or so it seemed. But it was the last time a U.S. team won the title (with foreign competition in the Series) until 1982.

Starting in 1971, however, Taiwan just didn't lose, and even managed to defeat one of the most dominant players in Little League history, Lloyd McClendon. The five-foot-eight pitcher/catcher from Gary, Indiana, hit a pair of home runs in each of his team's first two games and was intentionally walked in the remainder of his at-bats. That set up a showdown in the final between Gary and Tainan, Taiwan, for the championship.

The game began with McClendon turning the power on again with a three-run home run in the bottom of the first inning. Taiwan pitcher Hsu Chin-Mu intentionally walked McClendon each time after that, bringing raucous boos from the crowd, which until that Series had favored the Taiwanese. With McClendon on the mound for Gary, the teams remained deadlocked 3–3 after eight innings before Taiwan erupted for nine runs in the top of the ninth. McClendon took himself out after he gave up the seventh run and Taiwan won 12–3.

In the spring of the following year, *Tuesday at Home* magazine profiled the Gary team and talked about how it was reacting to the defeat. McClendon was recovering.

After the decisive game against the Taiwan team, a perceptive newsman noted the tears that streamed down Lloyd's strongly handsome face and observed that he had witnessed one of nature's most touching metamorphoses: the man on the field became a boy of twelve. There are few more telling indicators of an individual's basic humanness. (Later, this year, at the invitation of his Chinese competitors, Lloyd will visit Taiwan.) When he talked with us, Lloyd was beginning to gain a better perspective on losing, and we suspect that the haunted look which fleetingly veils his eyes is really a vision of the future when, on other fields, he'll rewrite the story with a different ending.

McClendon finished the Little League World Series with a record five home runs in five official at-bats, a feat they still talk about in Williamsport. His reputation grew after the Series, and he became a professional ballplayer, with nine seasons in the major leagues for the Giants, Cubs, and Pirates. In 2000 he was named the first African American manager of the Pittsburgh Pirates.

Twenty-five years after that memorable Series, McClendon said his fondest memory of the Little League World Series was trading pins with the Taiwanese players. ◆

Lloyd McClendon pitches at the 1971 Little League Baseball World Series. The team from Gary, Indiana, lost to Taiwan 12–3, but McClendon finished the Series with a record five home runs in five official at-bats.

This shot of the Howard J. Lamade Stadium shows the crowds of the Little League World Series final. The stadium got a facelift in 1971 when "wings" were added down each of the foul lines, increasing seating capacity from 4,600 to 10,000. The next major improvements came just recently, in 2001, when areas beneath the stadium were converted into meeting and office space.

of American boys could be traced to a higher sense of values and work ethic in Taiwan's players. Even those who believed the "higher work ethic" theory, however, were critical of the Taiwanese for producing emotionless robots whose sole purpose was domination of the youth baseball world.

Others assumed Taiwan's players were too old—the most common complaint yet the easiest to refute. After the 12–0 drubbing, Tucson Manager Ralph Lanik said his team was still "the best Little League–age club here." He continued: "There is no way that kid [Taiwan pitcher Huang Ching-hui] can be eleven years old." Actually, Huang had just turned twelve, well within the limits for Little Leaguers.

Birth records in Taiwan were meticulously maintained, and military conscription for a male not enrolled in a university was compulsory at age eighteen, so falsifying birth records was a serious offense. Consequently, following extensive investigations, there was never a shred of evidence that Taiwan's players were too old. Taiwan's supporters pointed out that in Taiwan the competition between leagues was extreme, so any cheaters would have been caught within their own country.

Ray Keyes, the veteran sports editor of the *Sun-Gazette,* who had covered every Little League championship since the first Little League National Tournament in 1947, told the *Philadelphia Inquirer* he thought the flap was "largely a lot of sour grapes on our part" and added, "I don't think those kids were older than ours. Maybe they excel at the game because that's all they do."

Keyes was right. The truth was that Taiwan's baseball program—the Chinese Taipei Baseball Association—was and is a quasi-government organization. As such, Little League became an instrument of a single ruling party in a country where martial law was only lifted in 1987, after thirty-eight years, where emergency rule ended in 1991 and where its first direct presidential election did not occur until 1996.

Winning the Series made headlines and heroes for a few days in American cities lucky enough to welcome a champion home from Williamsport. But Taiwan saw winning the Little League World Series not only as a source of pride but also as a way to solidify its place among the nations of the world. The United Nations might have booted Taiwan out, and many in the world diplomatic community might recognize the one billion people living across the Taiwan Strait as the "real" China, but nobody could dispute Taiwan's identity as having the best youth baseball teams on the planet.

Responding to charges that Taiwan must have been cheating, McGovern appointed a committee to investigate Taiwan's Little League operations. "The tension was at a high point at times here during the Series," he said in a *Sun-Gazette* interview. The committee, composed of Little League volunteers from Japan, Hong Kong, and the Philippines, visited Taiwan for a week. McGovern reported the findings back to the leagues in a newsletter following the Little League board of directors' fall meeting:

> [The committee was] given a pledge that discrepancies in the operation of the program chiefly through misunderstanding, i.e., use of school teachers as coaches and managers, baseball training during school hours and early selection of tournament teams, would be curbed to bring the program in better conformity with all Rules and Regulations of Little League Baseball. … In recognizing the many and unusual problems that are native to developing areas of the world, and particularly in the Far East, it was the Board's judgment that the broad interests of Little League may best be served by accepting the recommendations of the committee.

ED VOSBERG: ONE OF A KIND

Ed Vosberg was first baseman for the Cactus Little League from Tucson, Arizona, in the 1973 Series final, after pitching a one-hitter against Birmingham, Alabama, in the semifinals. He earned a baseball scholarship to the University of Arizona, where he played on a national championship team in 1980.

After a circuitous journey through several years in the minor leagues, Ed made it to the major leagues, and eventually to the Florida Marlins. That's where he made history in 1997 as the only person to play in all three of the biggest world series tournaments baseball has to offer: the Little League Baseball World Series, the NCAA College World Series, and the Major League Baseball World Series.◆

Ed Vosberg pitches for the Cactus Little League of Tucson, Arizona, in the 1973 Little League Baseball World Series. Vosberg is the only person to play in the Little League World Series, the College World Series, and the Major League World Series.

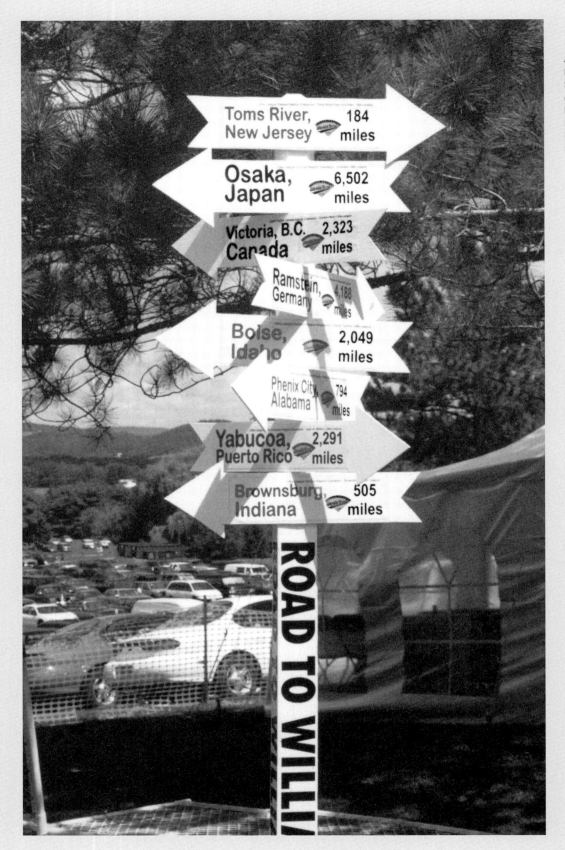

A signpost outside Howard J. Lamade Stadium gives distances to the homes of the teams in the 1999 Little League World Series.

Double-elimination is played at most levels of the Little League International Tournament, which includes a full tournament structure in eight divisions of baseball and softball. More than 7,000 teams begin the tournament in the Little League Baseball division. More than 6,500 are eliminated in the first three weeks of tournament play.

The most basic level of play takes place at the district level. Most district tournaments begin around the first week of July and last one to three weeks. Some large districts, or districts whose teams are widely dispersed, play in area tournaments before advancing to a district final or semifinal. Some district tournaments are played in a modified Olympic Pool Play Format, similar to that used in the Little League World Series.

The next major level of play is the state, province, or country level, but in some states, provinces, and countries that have a large number of leagues, a sub-tournament is played. State, provincial, or national tournaments are generally played about the last week of July or the first week of August, and most are played in a standard double-elimination format.

The third level is the regional tournament. In some areas, there may be one or two pre-regional tournaments (section or division tournaments) before advancing to the regional level. Regional tournaments are usually played in the first or second week of August. Most are double-elimination, but some use the pool play format.

The final level of tournament play is the World Series. There are eleven World Series tournaments played in the Little League program: Little League Baseball, Junior League Baseball, Senior League Baseball, Big League Baseball, Girls Little League Softball, Girls Junior League Softball, Girls Senior League Softball, Girls Big League Softball, Boys Little League Softball, Boys Senior League Softball, and Boys Big League Softball. The various World Series tournaments are played in the third or fourth week of August. At the start of the Series, eight teams remain from the more than 7,000 that started tournament play less than two months earlier.

With four exceptions, the Little League Baseball World Series has been an eight-team tournament. The first, in 1947, called the National Little League Tournament, featured eleven teams. After that, the tournament was structured for eight teams. Starting in 1958, international teams no longer had to play through a U.S.-dominated regional qualifier to reach the World Series, because separate regions were created for Canada, Latin America, the Pacific region, and Europe. However, the European entry did not show up in 1958 or 1959, so only seven played in those years. In 1975, the Little League Baseball International board of directors barred international teams from the Series, and only four teams played. Little League found that many of the other countries were placing too much emphasis on reaching the World Series and not enough on developing local league programs for the average players. The following year, international leagues were allowed to return.

But one concession was made to the U.S. interests. From that point forward, the World Series became a two-bracket affair in which the international teams and the U.S. teams were separated. The policy guarantees a U.S. finalist each year in the World Series, as well as a non-U.S. finalist, drawing fire from those who believe the entire tournament should be a "blind draw" without regard to country, and from those who believe the United States should have more of an advantage because the vast majority (about 94 percent) of Little Leaguers are in the United States.

Until 1992, a single loss at the Series eliminated a team from having any chance at the championship. It was a single-elimination tournament, with losing teams in the first and second rounds dropping into a consolation bracket. Without lights, a double-elimination tournament would have meant a longer stay for the eight teams. A one-game championship also suited ABC when it began annually televising the final, starting in 1963.

In 1992, the pool play format was devised to give each team at least two and possibly three meaningful games. The total number of games increased from twelve to fifteen, and lights were added to Lamade Stadium to allow night games. The first night game of the Series was played on Monday, August 24, 1992, when Hamilton Square, New Jersey, defeated Lake Charles, Louisiana, 5–0.

The pool play format has three distinct segments and, once a segment is completed, games played previously have no bearing on the next segment, with the exception of rules and regulations regarding rest periods for pitchers.

In the first segment, the pool play round, the eight teams are divided into international and U.S. pools. Each team in the International Pool plays the other three teams once. Each team in the U.S. Pool plays the other three teams once. The two teams with the best records in each pool advance to the next round. If the two teams cannot be determined using records in pool play, a tie-breaker system rewards defensive play by advancing the team that gives up the fewest runs per inning played on defense in the three pool play games.

The second segment is the semifinal round (International and U.S. Championships). Regardless of the results of pool play, the winners of the International and U.S. Championships advance to the third and final segment of the World Series—the World Championship Game.

Starting in 2001, the Little League Baseball World Series will expand for the first time, to sixteen teams. Dormitories for sixteen teams were actually built in 1991 with an eye toward expansion. Construction began in spring 2000 on a second stadium (unnamed as of this writing) at the Little League Baseball International Headquarters. The new stadium will seat about 5,000 and will be used for pool play games in the first few days of the tournament, along with Lamade Stadium, which can accommodate up to 45,000.◆

Dr. Creighton Hale, Little League's newly elected president, meets with representatives from both baseball and softball teams competing in the 1975 Little League Championship Series. From left, players include Gary Edwards, Jay Teitelbaum, Wendy Wills, and Robin Heidt.

Thus, Taiwan was placed on probation for the 1974 season. In addition, there was to be an annual review by the board to ensure that all overseas programs were moving toward achieving total conformity to Little League regulations.

Of the three charges leveled against Taiwan by McGovern, only one—technically—could be called a violation of Little League rules and regulations. Little League's tournament rules clearly prohibited a league's all-star teams from being named, much less practicing, until two weeks before the tournament began. But because of the school-related nature of the youth baseball program in Taiwan, the rule could be circumvented. Basically, talented twelve-year-old male athletes in Taiwan played baseball in school. Their Little League coach was also their coach at school. Under those conditions, Taiwan did not have to cheat.

But Taiwan's system went against one of Little League's tenets as a program primarily focused on local Little League operations: The World Series provides a stage for a few players to be showcased, but Little League's priority is the individual player's relationship to his team. For instance, after the first few years of its existence, Little League outlawed individual awards to players for athletic accomplishments, in order to promote the team concept. Little League still tries to strike a balance in the public's eye between the pageantry and glamour of reaching the World Series and its goal of providing a wholesome, fun program for as many children as possible.

THE YEAR WITHOUT THE WORLD SERIES

With Taiwan officially on probation for the 1974 season, the Little League World Series might be more competitive, but Taiwan swept all three divisions of Little League Baseball play: the Little League Baseball World Series; the Senior League Baseball World Series in Gary, Indiana; and the Big League Baseball World Series in Fort Lauderdale, Florida. At the title game in Williamsport, pitcher Lin Wen-hsuing struck out fifteen and was four-for-four at the plate as Taiwan blasted Red Bluff, California, 12–1.

Complaints poured in. Headlines began appearing, such as "Break Up the Taiwan Monopoly" (*San Bernardino [California] Sun-Telegram*, August 27, 1974); "Taiwan Plays Ball Like It's Tong War" (*Philadelphia Inquirer*, August 25, 1974); and "'Basic American Laziness' Cited in Taiwanese Success" (*Washington Post*, August 23, 1974). Nothing had really changed in Taiwan, but reports received from other countries were saying that their systems, though far less successful than Taiwan's, were also focusing too much on winning the World Series.

Little League's board of directors took action. It decreed that each of the four international regions (Far East, Canada, Latin America, and Europe) would conclude tournament play in the Little League Division at the regional level, thus shutting them out of the World Series. Instead, only the four U.S. regions (West, South, East, and Central) were eligible to meet in Williamsport for the "1975 Championship Series." At the same time, the Little League Softball World Series—also a four-team affair—could be played simultaneously at Lamade Stadium. The decision did not affect the Senior League and Big League baseball tournaments, both of which were won by Taiwan that year.

The media and some in the public reacted as if Little League had barred Taiwan altogether. In a November 1974 letter to district administrators, Dr. Creighton J. Hale, Little League's newly elected president, explained that Little League's position was not simply a one-year deal:

> Over-emphasis of tournament play became increasingly apparent to the Board during the past two years. Countries began practicing players throughout most of the year under the tutelage of skilled baseball coaches. The success of these countries in tournament play led to the inevitable spread of this extended and concentrated training period to other countries where it would have continued to spread unless checked.
>
> Extended training programs have proven highly successful in developing superb athletes for international competition. For example, the training program for young swimmers in preparation for the Olympic games and other international competition includes workouts of 7 to 8 hours a day, 7 days a week, 11 months of the year. The obvious reason for the rigorous and extended program is to win in international competition.
>
> The Little League approach to the international competition has not and should not be the Olympic concept. Regrettably, there has been an erosion of the Little

League concept and a trend toward the Olympic concept. The Board moved to de-emphasize the Little League World Series in order to restore the original perspective of Little League Baseball.

The rationale that the national tournament played in Williamsport can no longer be referred to as a World Series is fuzzy. Prior to foreign teams participating, the tournament was called a World Series, and the professional baseball major-league tournament, in which no foreign team has played, is referred to as a World Series.

The designation of the tournament is inconsequential. What is important is the realization that children 8–12 years of age should have an opportunity to engage in a wide variety of sports and not be forced to concentrate on one sport because of the tournament aspirations of adults.

Little League got a black eye anyway. An August 8, 1975, story in the *New York News* prefaced that year's tournament with a stinging commentary:

Red, white and blue banners no longer proclaim this hamlet as the Little League Baseball capital of the world. Instead, the talk of the town is not so much that the championship series has suddenly replaced the World Series but that the Chinese have gone and the girls have arrived.

Yes, score a blow for détente and a victory for women's lib. The girls will have equal time with their 12-year-old counterparts on a baseball diamond this afternoon when Mary Lucina Engle, Ms. Pennsylvania Teenager, will throw out the first ball in the doubleheader that begins the four-day championship. Henry Kissinger reportedly was not offered an RSVP.

The team from Tampa, Florida, lost a close final to Taiwan in the 1980 Little League World Series. Tampa's team featured Derek Bell (standing, sixth from left) and Gary Sheffield (kneeling, far right), now Major League Baseball players.

THE BELMONT HEIGHTS MACHINE

Belmont Heights Little League of Tampa, Florida, came the closest of any league in the United States to a World Series dynasty. In a nine-year period beginning in 1973, Belmont Heights made it to the Little League World Series four times, more than any other single American league. The league finished as the runner-up three times, but never won the world championship. In fact, Belmont's championship game losses were by scores of 4–3, 4–3, and 4–2. Two players on the 1980 team went on to become stars in the Major Leagues: Derek Bell of the New York Mets, and Gary Sheffield of the Los Angeles Dodgers, who were key players in Belmont Heights' run to the final game.

Belmont Heights Little League is located in a mostly African American neighborhood of Tampa, a city that has become known for producing great baseball talent. Dwight Gooden (another Belmont Heights product who played in the Senior League Baseball World Series), Tino Martinez, Dave Magadan, Wade Boggs, Fred McGriff, Tony LaRussa, Lou Pinella, and Steve Garvey are just a few of the major-leaguers whose first taste of baseball came on the Little League fields of Tampa.◆

"I guess we all have regrets that there is no international flavor at Williamsport," said LL President Dr. Creighton Hale before changing a sad grimace into a smile. "But, then again, we never had girls before."

And the boys couldn't be any happier about the new look at Williamsport this season. No, they really don't care one stick of bubblegum about pigtails sprouting from under a baseball cap. No sir. Baseball is first and, with Taiwan's big yellow machine [victors the last four years] out of the way, there's a one in four chance they'll be leaving with the championship trophy.

For the record, the 1975 final was a nail-biter—the first close championship game in five years—as Lakewood, New Jersey, squeaked past Belmont Heights Little League of Tampa, Florida, 4–3. But the foreign leagues clamored to be allowed back in—most arguing that their programs were not breaking the rules.

The Little League board of directors took a step back and called for a survey of district administrators on the issue, but Peter McGovern's November 1975 letter to them left little doubt that the 1976 tournament would revert to a true world series. The letter even contained an admission, of sorts, that a mistake had been made:

> Prior to the Board meeting on October 31, we contacted each of the foreign regions to ascertain their interest and their points of view. It was the unanimous and urgent vote of all the regions outside the United States that they be granted the privilege of returning to the Series. They included expressions of concern that if they were denied entry, it would be almost impossible to hold their chartered leagues, many of them American dependents. …
>
> The pivotal crux at issue, of course, was Taiwan. Many believed the violations occurred in use of overage players. This was not true. Taiwan did overemphasize the training of their Little Leaguers stating frankly that they did not violate anything in the Rule Book and that "if you enter a game, you play to win." The Orientals look at things somewhat differently, but this was an adult point of view and as such, it is correctable.

In the meantime, three other regions were similarly barred from the World Series which manifestly was not fair. Canada, Europe and Latin America also ask urgently to be allowed to re-enter their championship teams to play in the 1976 World Series at Williamsport. Senator K. C. Hsieh, President of Taiwan Little League, as well as the Taiwanese Embassy in Washington have asked for consideration and stated frankly that they will agree to any stipulations of tournament conduct set forth by Williamsport in agreement with other members of the Far East Little League countries if they are allowed to return. …

It must be considered that denial of the foreign participants in the Series would be, from a practical point of view, a loss of popular international prestige and stature which only Little League has earned, as well as a considerable loss of strength and revenue.

LEVELING THE PLAYING FIELD

Taiwan failed to take the Far East title in 1976 as Chofu, Japan, went on to win the Little League World Series title, 10–3, against Campbell, California. But Taiwan got right back on track the next year and every year after that until 1982, when Cody Webster pitched

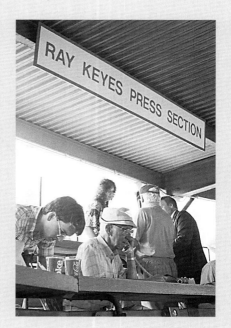

Ray Keyes covered Little League Baseball for the *Williamsport Sun-Gazette* from the very beginning in 1939 until his death in 1988. Here he sits in the press box at Lamade Stadium named in his honor.

RAYMOND J. KEYES

Known as the "dean" of Williamsport-area sportswriters, Raymond J. Keyes was a veteran journalist and beloved sports director of Williamsport's daily newspaper, the *Sun-Gazette*. A 1935 graduate of Williamsport High School, Keyes joined the newspaper staff in 1937. In 1969, he married Elsie Guinn. Among his many community service awards were accolades from the Shrine Club, the Knights of Columbus, and Kiwanis. His military record includes serving in the Army Air Corps with the U.S. Army 14th Air Force in China, Burma, and India, and he was a member of the American Legion and the Elks.

Keyes is the only newspaperman to continuously cover all Little League World Series, which he did with a paternal eye, until his demise. During his lifetime, he promoted the organization throughout the world, penning articles for noted magazines, including *Reader's Digest* and *Woman's Day*. He also served as official scorer for many World Series games.

He died on December 11, 1988, at the age of seventy-two after an extended bout with cancer. Despite numerous hospitalizations during his fight, Keyes manned his desk at the *Sun-Gazette* until a few days before his death. He wrote his final "Sun Rays" column on November 25, 1988, the same column that had introduced the residents of North Central Pennsylvania to Little League Baseball in 1939.

Before his death, Little League bestowed on him two significant honors: the inaugural W. Howard Hartman Little League Friendship Award (which he called the greatest award he had ever received) and the naming of the press box at Howard J. Lamade Stadium after him. In 1986, as part of the observance of the fortieth Little League World Series, Keyes participated in the first-pitch ceremony. ◆

and hit the Kirkland, Washington, team to a stunning 6–0 upset against Pu-tzu Town, Taiwan, in the championship game. Kirkland's victory ended an incredible thirty-one game winning streak in World Series games, dating all the way back to 1970. After a three-year absence from the World Series, Taiwan rolled to three more titles in 1986, 1987, and 1988 before Chris Drury, a future National Hockey League star, pitched Trumbull, Connecticut, to a 5–2 victory against Kang-Tu.

Taiwan won the first two Series tournaments of the 1990s, but the Philippines surprised everyone, except those who assembled the team, by winning the 1992 Far East Region tournament and advancing to Williamsport for the first—and so far only—time.

That year, 1992, the Little League World Series tournament format changed for the first time, from single-elimination to Olympic-style pool play, where each of the four teams in the two groups (the International Pool and the U.S. Pool) play each other once in the first round. The top two teams in each pool play off again for the international and U.S. titles, with the two finalists playing in the championship. The system gives a team a chance at the title, even after one or even two losses in the first round. It also allows all eight teams a chance to play at least three games.

The extra games meant either that the tournament would have to be extended or that games would have to be played at night. Because many schools are already in session by

Chen Chin-Feng played for Taiwan in the 1990 Little League World Series. The Los Angeles Dodgers later drafted him.

the time the Little League World Series final is played (always the weekend before the Labor Day weekend), making the tournament longer was unacceptable. As a result, lights were installed at Howard J. Lamade Stadium.

The first Little League World Series night game was played on August 24, 1992. Singer Lou Rawls entertained the crowd at the opening ceremonies, and several celebrities showed up to receive honors. Tom Selleck, Kareem Abdul-Jabbar, George Will, and Vice President Dan Quayle were on hand to accept enshrinement into the Peter J. McGovern Little League Museum Hall of Excellence.

ELIGIBILITY PROBLEMS

The Philippines' Zamboanga City Little League lost its pool play game against Epy Guerrero Little League from Santo Domingo, Dominican Republic. In previous years, such a loss meant no chance to reach the championship, but Zamboanga came back to beat the Dominicans in the International Championship game, then defeated Long Beach, California, 15–4 for the world title. Behind the scenes, however, there were allegations that the Philippines team and the Dominican Republic team were using ineligible players. Without time to effectively investigate, however, the games went on as scheduled.

After the tournament, the allegations continued—and turned out to be true. The Filipino adult organizers admitted to assembling a national all-star team that only loosely resembled the original team. Eight players, it turned out, were living far outside the established boundaries of Zamboanga City Little League. Several players, it seemed, had been dropped from the roster—and others added—as the tournament progressed.

According to the rules for the Little League International Tournament, a team found to be breaking eligibility rules would only forfeit the last game won by that team, though further punishment in the form of suspension or revocation of the league's charter was possible. Little League's International Tournament Committee convened and decided that the Philippines should be stripped of its championship—an intensely embarrassing turn of events for Filipinos, who had taken pride in their team's achievement. By the rules, therefore, Long Beach was declared the winner, 6–0.

As a result of more allegations the following year, the national championship teams of several countries were declared ineligible. Long Beach made a rare return in 1993 and won the title on the field in one of the most thrilling finals in Little League World Series history, defeating a team from Panama 3–2.

After back-to-back titles in 1995 and 1996 for Taiwan, Little League took a proactive approach to ineligibility, particularly with Taiwan. Little League informed Taiwan that the rules regarding eligibility would have to be strictly enforced, with no exceptions, including residency requirements.

Residency rules in effect since 1992 call for one of two methods to be employed: (1) A league, from which one all-star team is chosen for tournament play, could include play-

TOP
Let there be light! The first night game in the history of the Little League Baseball World Series was played on August 24, 1992.

CENTER LEFT
Actor Tom Selleck in his Little League days. Selleck was enshrined in the Peter J. McGovern Little League Museum Hall of Excellence in 1992.

CENTER RIGHT
Writer George Will in his Little League days. Will was enshrined in the Little League Museum Hall of Excellence in 1991 and accepted it in Williamsport in 1992.

BOTTOM
Tom Selleck, George Will, and Kareem Abdul-Jabbar attend the 1992 Little League Baseball World Series and are enshrined in the Peter J. McGovern Little League Museum Hall of Excellence.

Members of the Zamboanga City (Philippines) Little League celebrate after the 1992 Little League Baseball World Series championship. The team defeated Long Beach (California) Little League, 15–4, but was subsequently stripped of its title because it used ineligible players.

ers from boundaries with a total population of 20,000 or less, or (2) if schools ally with the Little League system, one league could be formed for every 1,000 students in grades Kindergarten through Seventh. The latter method was the one used by Taiwan, but many Taiwanese schools had far more than 1,000 students. Officials from the Chinese Taipei Baseball Association asked for a waiver to allow one all-star team in schools with more than 1,000 students, but Little League refused, saying that such a waiver would give each league a distinct competitive advantage over those in the rest of the world.

TAIWAN DROPS OUT

On April 16, 1997, the Associated Press reported that Taiwan had dropped out:

> The crowds in Williamsport, Pa., used to boo when the team from Taiwan took the field for another Little League World Series championship run.
> Now, after 12 championships in 23 years and numerous blowout victories during that span, Taiwan is quitting Little League Baseball over a rule dispute.
> "I think that Taiwan looks to it as a symbol of pride," said David Tsai of the Center for Taiwan International Relations in Washington. "Whichever team made it to the World Series—it has a lot of prestige for that school or county. This is a loss."
> On Wednesday, CTBA faxed notice of its withdrawal to Williamsport.
> "We cannot deny that LLB has played a very important role in popularizing and prospering Taiwan's development of baseball in the past years," the fax read. "How-

ever, due to the diversity of society status and culture, we have difficulty in implementing completely in compliance with LLB's regulations."

A flurry of media discussion followed. Some accused Little League of booting Taiwan out of the program without cause. Others predicted that Taiwan's absence would cause the number of countries involved in Little League to decrease from its level of 83 nations because the most successful country in the tournament in the past three decades was no longer competing. Today, Little League is played in 104 countries.

Little League's president and chief executive officer Stephen D. Keener clarified the reasons Taiwan left Little League:

They explained that it was very difficult for them to comply with that regulation. In their culture, in their system, they wanted to have one school, one team, and play against other schools. They understood that this is not the way it was done in many other places. We felt very strongly, in an effort to ensure a level playing field for everybody, that they had to conform with that rule.

When it was clear to them that they couldn't do it, they came to us and said, "We don't want to have any dishonor brought to our country. We don't want to cause Little League Baseball any embarrassment or difficulty. Therefore we've made the decision to withdraw from the Little League program."

We told them we certainly were sorry they felt compelled to make that decision, however we understood. We essentially parted ways on very friendly terms and told them at any point in the future, if they could comply with the regulation on how the league would be formulated, we would welcome them back into the program. The door remains open.

We'd be willing to meet with them and welcome them back.

They were an important part of the World Series for many years; wonderful people. The players were always so highly regarded by people here. The kids fit in and they made friends. A lot of people didn't see the behind the scenes, see the kids swimming, playing Ping-Pong and enjoying the international spirit of friendship that exists here. It's sad that the kids won't have that opportunity.

But, on the other hand, we have an obligation to all the other Little League teams in the country that are complying with those regulations. In order for everyone to benefit the most, the playing field has to be level.

George Brett, former Kansas City Royals third baseman, Baseball Hall of Famer

"When I played Little League,

it wasn't something you did because

your parents wanted you to do it

or because it was your job.

It was fun."

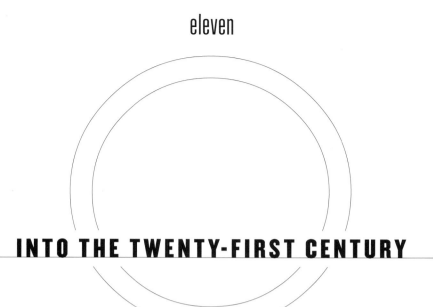

eleven

INTO THE TWENTY-FIRST CENTURY

As Little League Baseball turns the corner into the twenty-first century, it carries with it some old problems—and a few new ones. The basic tenets of the program have changed very little in sixty-two years: Its goal is to use baseball and softball in ways to create good citizens and to help solve some of the world's social ills.

PROTÉGÉ

The modern era of Little League Baseball began at Jersey Shore Little League, not far from Williamsport, nearly thirty years ago, when a twelve-year-old boy named Steve Keener came to bat in a game that would help to define him. He was a good baseball player, perhaps one of the best in his league. Like most Little Leaguers, he vividly remembers his first Little League home run, and in his case it came after an unsuccessful time at bat. He tells the story:

> I struck out on three pitches and I never swung. I was embarrassed and I was frustrated. I made up my mind: When I came up the next time, I didn't care where the ball was, I was going to swing, because I wasn't going to strike out looking at three pitches. And somehow, on the first or second pitch—I don't remember which one it was—

LITTLE LEAGUE FOUNDER DIES

When Carl Stotz died on June 4, 1992, thousands in the Williamsport area reeled with the implications of that event. It meant that the founder of Little League Baseball would never be reunited with the program he had created in 1939.

Although millions of people had never heard of "Uncle Tuck," residents of North Central Pennsylvania had been regaled with stories and details every August at the beginning of the Little League World Series. Newspapers, television, and radio personalities made a point of telling their customers that the *original* home of Little League is located on West Fourth Street, across the street from historic Bowman Field. Carl Stotz, they reminded all, still volunteered at Original League, pushing up his shirtsleeves and sometimes raking the field.

His daughter Karen Stotz Myers said he was a humble yet stubborn man who wanted to give credit where it was due. In 1989, he built a monument that lists what he called his "Founder's Group," the early organizers and managers of his original Little League, even though he injured his back making it himself. "He would not accept any help, because that was his tribute to the volunteers."

From the 1950s on, Stotz lived in the Williamsport suburb of Old Lycoming Township, where he was municipal tax collector and a frequent VIP at community events. *Sun-Gazette* reporter James P. Barr grew up a few blocks from Stotz and, as a teenager, became his newspaper delivery boy. When Stotz died, Barr wrote a commentary piece for the *Sun-Gazette* about coming of age in Williamsport's Little League–saturated culture and how he and his contemporaries were affected by the rift between Little League Baseball and its founder:

My first memory of Carl Stotz is a vision of him standing on the brightly lit stage of the Roosevelt Junior High School auditorium. I, a short, skinny 9-year-old, had just finished my first year playing organized baseball in the Old Lycoming Township league. As impressed and impressionable as I was, I remember being thoroughly awestruck when the master of ceremonies announced that "the founder of Little League Baseball" would speak to us and hand out the trophies.

Sitting in the gloom of the darkened auditorium—a huge place by the standards of an untraveled 9-year-old—I marveled at the thought that such a great personage would deign to come to our awards ceremony. After all, our league was not even part of the "real" Little League. One of the first things you learned when you joined our league was that no matter how good you or your team might be, you would never, ever get a chance to play in the Little League World Series, which at the time was held in Memorial Park, an easy bike ride from my Fox Street home.

Sometime later, I acquired the knowledge that Stotz lived on Wheatland Avenue, less than half a mile from my home. From then on, whenever I walked or rode by his modest white house, a chill of reverence passed through me, as if I were passing a religious shrine.

I also learned, somehow, that the reason our township league was not part of Little League was because of some ill-defined feud he had with the famous organization. The feud was beyond my understanding or caring, though. Just another puzzle of the adult world.

As an adult, I could appreciate Stotz' objections to the organization he fathered becoming a glitzy, high-powered international organization. I especially admired him for sticking to his principles

that Little League should be for the enjoyment of the kids, not for garnering big-money product endorsements and television contracts.

I value what Little League has done for my hometown, though. I take pride in being able to say, "I'm from Williamsport. You know, home of Little League Baseball." So I also can appreciate that such efforts are needed to maintain a massive, worldwide organization.

I understand, having done a couple of stories on Stotz, that the estrangement was as much his doing as anyone else's. Still, writing his obituary the other day left me with an inexpressible sadness and sense of injustice: sadness that the man who started the largest athletic organization in the world was largely ignored and neglected through its glory days, and a sense of injustice that the community he has raised to world fame could not see its way to honor him better while he was alive.

As a reporter, I have encountered presidential candidates, Nobel Prize winners and important people all up and down the social ladder. None of them made me as nervous as interviewing my former paper route customer, probably because you never quite get over the first great man you ever met.

PROPOSED STAMP

On the eve of what would have been the ninetieth birthday of Little League Baseball founder Carl Stotz, an effort was launched to have Stotz honored with a postage stamp issued by the U.S. Postal Service. In 2002, Carl will become eligible to have his likeness considered for a stamp. Supporters can continue to forward petitions to the Stamp Committee at: U.S. Postal Service, 475 L'Enfant Plaza S.W., Room 4474 East, Washington, DC 20260.◆

This montage of Little League's founder, Carl Stotz, and Original League players, by photographer Jonathan Smith, is used to promote issuance of a stamp by the U.S. Postal Service.

TOP
**Howard J. Lamade
Stadium during the
Little League World
Series from center
field in 1998.**

BOTTOM
**The Peter J. McGovern
Little League Baseball
Museum is located in
South Williamsport
adjacent to the
International
Headquarters. The
20,000-square-foot
museum houses
artifacts from former
Little League and
Major League
baseball players.**

Steve Keener, President and Chief Executive Officer of Little League Baseball, right, with former Pennsylvania State Representative Tom Dempsey at the Little League World Series. Keener is the first graduate of Little League to hold either of those positions.

I swung. The bat met the ball—it must have been just the right way, because the ball went. I just stood there in amazement, because I had never hit a home run before, and watched it go over the left field fence.

I don't remember if we won or lost the game, quite honestly. What I remember is my mom was quite excited for me. She gave me two dollars and said, "That's for hitting a home run." Of course, that was terrific.

My dad was standing off to the side, and as I was heading to the concession stand he stopped me and said, "I know your mom gave you that two dollars, but this is a team game and I've coached for a lot of years. I just want you to understand you don't play for your own personal achievements, and your own accomplishments. What's most important in a team game is what the team does, and you've contributed to that and that's great. You played well, and I'm happy you hit the home run. But I just don't want you to think you should try to hit home runs because you're going to get rewarded every time you do that."

I didn't quite understand it at the time. He said, "You can keep the money, or you can do what you want with that, but I just want you to understand."

I don't know why, but I gave my mom the two dollars back. I said, "I don't need it."

The point is, I was very fortunate to have a father who was a coach and a teacher and understood those things about playing games and being part of a team, and wanted me to understand what it was about. I don't think he intended for me to give the two dollars back, but I did. As time has gone by, I've remembered that as one of the lasting impressions from my own Little League experience. And I think it was a good one.

Penny and Jim Vanderlin, volunteers at Original League, are driving forces behind reconstruction of the birthplace of Little League Baseball and the maintenance of the historic field and small museum.

RESTORING ORIGINAL LEAGUE FACILITIES

Jim and Penny Vanderlin, volunteers at Original League, Inc., have become the driving force behind restoring the historic birthplace of Little League and improving what has become a living-history museum. Each day, except Sundays, volunteers use the facilities on West Fourth Street in Williamsport to practice teams and play baseball games. Since it was last used for Series games in 1958, the ballpark had become well worn, the grass had died during a previous drought, and the chain-link fence was sagging.

In 1995, the Pennsylvania Historical and Museum Commission recognized the significance of the ballpark with a historical site marker. Substantial grants from the Williamsport-Lycoming Foundation, from John W. Lundy, and from interested banks and business owners made it possible for the Vanderlins and other Original League volunteers to forge ahead with more than $200,000

in improvements. A kick-off event featuring major-league pitcher Mike Mussina announced: "We're going to restore the birthplace of Little League Baseball, and we need your help."

The restoration revitalized not only the field but also the community's interest in the ballpark. Even Jim and Karen Stotz Myers, who lived in Muncy when the effort began, committed themselves to restoring Original League. The amount of time and energy needed for the project persuaded them to move back to Williamsport. Karen said, "I never thought I'd move up here, but that's Little League. We were involved with Original and getting the restoration going. We were spending every night at the field. My husband was vice president of the league and I was in the concession stand."

For Penny Vanderlin, Original League is a home-away-from-home. At the small museum, she can take visitors from one display case to

another, telling stories and anecdotes about the boys who played and are immortalized in the Stotz memorabilia on display during baseball season. Her husband, Jim, the quiet driving force behind the improvements, continues to beautify the facility, with the help of volunteers and community members. Anyone can use a rake or pick up trash, he reasons. His gardening skills are evident throughout the grounds, which are resplendent with lush flowers and foliage in season.

Karen marvels at the popularity of the facility. "We have found that people like to have a part in helping Original. If they can, they donate things at cost. People give a lot of in-kind things."

And Original League sponsors are on a waiting list, she added. "A lot of people look at Original as unique, and we are. They think we're special, and we are. They think we're perfect, and we're not."◆

Don Keener, Steve's dad, became an instructor at Lock Haven University after teaching and coaching basketball at Loyalsock Township High School near Williamsport. During the summers, however, Don worked part-time as a counselor at Little League's summer camps. Dr. Creighton J. Hale, Little League's president at the time, recalls his impression of a young Steve Keener:

> I first knew him when he was a gym rat, probably five or six years old. His father was my older son's basketball coach. Steve went to Westminster College [in New Wilmington, Pennsylvania], and his dad called to ask if I had any recommendations about what Steve could do during the summer since he had no plans. So I created an internship for the summer to keep him busy. By the end of the summer I was certain that he had great leadership potential. I created a new full-time position for him, assistant director of public relations for Little League Baseball, and he's never worked for anybody else.

Steve became director of public relations for Little League Baseball in 1984 and was elected first vice president in 1991. Three years later he was president of Little League Baseball, and in 1996 also became chief executive officer—the first Little League graduate in either of those positions. For Dr. Hale, who is credited with inventing the modern batting helmet and assisting in creating the protective helmet worn by U.S. military forces, as well as numerous other innovations, bringing Steve Keener to Little League Baseball is one of his proudest accomplishments.

"I can't think of anything else I'd want to do," says Keener. For him, leading Little League Baseball is a dream job:

> When you can walk into your office every day and look out the window and see a baseball field and realize it's the centerpiece of a program that provides benefits to millions of kids every year, you have to feel good about that. This organization, Little League Baseball, is one of the few enduring institutions in this country, and around the world, that hasn't strayed from its initial purpose. It's different, but it's the same—if that makes sense. Sounds like something Yogi Berra would say.

RECENT INITIATIVES

During Steve Keener's tenure, Little League has created new initiatives to improve the condition of boys and girls around the world—initiatives that *do* seem to stray from simply teaching teamwork, sportsmanship, and fair play through baseball and softball. But the Little League Baseball International board of directors believes children's membership in Little League can be used to reach them in other areas of their lives.

The Little League Child Protection Program, for instance, created in 1996, seeks to educate local Little League volunteers and children in ways to protect themselves against

TOP
Little League Baseball has enlisted the help of Olympic gold medalist and softball pitcher Michele Smith to promote the sport. Trading cards are sent to players as part of Little League's initiatives.

BOTTOM
Just like Major Leaguers, today's Little Leaguers often have their own trading cards.

pedophiles through pamphlets, videos, trading cards, and printed guidelines in the Little League Operating Manual. Now that there are hundreds of boys and girls in most local programs, Little Leaguers can become targets for sexual predators, and have in some cases. As a result, Little League now strongly recommends that its local Little Leagues conduct background checks on volunteers. Implementation of background checks, however, presents other issues, such as privacy and the cost of conducting such checks. Mandatory screenings are not possible at this point, because each state has its own laws regarding background checks and the extent to which a person's history can be investigated by a nongovernmental agency.

Some states are considering legislation to force programs like Little League, Boy Scouts, Girl Scouts, 4-H Clubs, and others to screen their volunteers. Some municipalities have already enacted such laws. More access to information has helped, as computer databases listing sexual predators have weeded out some potentially disastrous problems.

The Little League Child Protection Program also teaches children and adults how to spot the most common indicators that a pedophile might be involved in the league. Trading cards bearing the photographs of U.S. Olympic gold-medal winning softball pitcher Michele Smith and former Little Leaguer and current St. Louis Cardinals slugger Mark McGwire are printed by the millions and mailed to local Little Leagues, with the back of each card listing ways children can stay safe. Such a program would never have existed fifteen years ago.

Other campaigns during the past ten years include the Little League Anti Spit-Tobacco Education Program, which warns Little Leaguers about the dangers of smokeless tobacco through trading cards, pamphlets, and videos; the Little League Drug and Alcohol Awareness Campaign; the Little League Traffic Safety Initiative, a campaign in conjunction with the National Highway Traffic Safety Administration to persuade children to wear seatbelts in cars and helmets while riding a bike; and ASAP (A Safety Awareness Program), an education program designed to share the best safety ideas from local Little League volunteers around the world. ASAP has been very successful, as injuries continue to decline overall, helping to keep insurance costs down.

Dwight Raiford and his wife, Iris, founded Harlem Little League in 1989. Dwight is chairman-elect of the Little League Baseball International board of directors.

Some of the programs have drawn big names to help support them. The tobacco program, for instance, has former major-league catcher Joe Garagiola as its pitch man. Garagiola, who has seen friends suffer and die from the use of smokeless tobacco, is a willing participant. He spoke to delegates at the twenty-first Little League Baseball International Congress in San Antonio, Texas, in 1998 about his crusade: "We've got an epidemic on our hands, and it's up to guys like us—good, God-fearing fathers and grandfathers who have the guts to take this on. Kids think they're invincible. They say, 'Hey, you got to die of *something.*' That's what I used to say when I was eighteen. After you get to be fifty years old, you don't say it but maybe once a year. When you get to be sixty or seventy, you don't say it ever. What you do is go to the Bible and look for a loophole."

Another program is the Little League Baseball Urban Initiative, designed to bring baseball back to areas of cities in which the sport has been neglected or abandoned altogether. Two "test case" areas in which the program flourishes are Harlem, New York, and South Central Los Angeles. Little League now is expanding the scope of the Urban Initiative to other cities, using funding from its first capital campaign.

In Los Angeles, near the site of the 1993 riots following the verdict acquitting the police officers in the Rodney King beating, hundreds of children play in four Little League programs. The programs, in operation only a few years, received major support from the Hilton Foundation, the Los Angeles Amateur Athletic Foundation, the Los Angeles Dodgers, the Los Angeles City Council, and the Los Angeles Recreation and Parks Department.

The Harlem Little League was founded in 1989 by Harlem residents Dwight and Iris Raiford. Iris is a trustee of the Little League Foundation, and Dwight is chairman-elect of the Little League Baseball International board of directors—the first African American elected as an officer of Little League.

Until recently, Harlem Little League shared public facilities with municipal softball programs in the city, but through the Urban Initiative it now has its own place to play. Groundbreaking on the Bill Shea Harlem Little League Friendship Field took place in

This artist's rendering of the new Little League World Series stadium (foreground) was prepared by the stadium architects, Larson Design Group, of Williamsport. Howard J. Lamade Stadium is in the center, and the Little League Baseball International Headquarters building is in the background.

the spring of 1998, and dedication took place in 1999. Harlem Little League now boasts more than fifty teams. "I think, for many parents in Little League, it's almost a babysitting service—a place for the kids to get out of the parents' hair," said one Harlem Little League volunteer, mother of two players in the league. "But in this organization you see lots of parents involved on a daily basis. That's because, for us, it's not babysitting—it's surviving."

New York attorney William A. "Bill" Shea was chairman of the board of trustees for the Little League Foundation and was responsible for bringing the New York Mets into existence in 1962. He was a Little League supporter for decades, and his family continues to support programs like the Urban Initiative. "I wish my father could have been here to see this," said one of Shea's daughters, Kathy, at the dedication, "because you kids sum up his heart."

THE CAMPAIGN FOR THE FUTURE

The Urban Initiative, fostering growth of baseball and softball leagues in urban areas, is only one beneficiary of "A World of Opportunity: The Little League Baseball Campaign for the Future," the first national capital campaign in Little League's sixty-two-year history. The campaign was officially launched on August 26, 1999, during the week of the Little League Baseball World Series. On September 13 the same year, Pennsylvania Governor Tom Ridge announced that he would approve the appropriation of $3 million in funding toward improvement of the facilities at the Little League Baseball International Headquarters.

LITTLE LEAGUE COMES TO BOSNIA

By Jeff Elijah, Editor and Publisher,
"International Baseball Rundown"

It was the winter of 1998–99 in Mostar, Bosnia-Herzegovina. Inside an apartment building with one wall blown away—one of many reminders of the bitter conflict surrounding the breakup of former Yugoslavia—a curious thing was happening. About a dozen young people had gathered in the apartment of Terry Hardesty. Spread out on the floor was a posterboard mock-up of a baseball field, drawn and pieced together. A marble skittered across the board, sometimes colliding with chess pieces representing defensive players. Terry was teaching the young people the rules of baseball.

"Baseball," said one of the boys, "is a strategy game without fighting. It is strategy without war."

Bosnia-Herzegovina and the city of Mostar were devastated by the civil war between rival ethnic groups in the early 1990s. By 1995, more than 2 million people in the country were homeless, and another million had fled the country. In Mostar, more than 5,000 inner-city buildings were damaged. Industry and infrastructure were ruined. About 2,000 people were killed and at least 26,000 were driven out as refugees. Before the war, Mostar's economy was based on high technology, agro-industry, and tourism. Its university and high schools were among the best in the former Yugoslavia. After the war, despite an ongoing rebuilding effort, its institutions and lifestyle are nothing like they once were.

Into that scenario last August stepped sixty-two-year-old Terry Hardesty, recently recovered from two heart bypass surgeries, and his wife, Sandie. They sold their house and other belongings in Arkansas and moved to Mostar. Terry, forced to retire from the construction business because of the surgeries, wanted to help children in Bosnia-Herzegovina. But how?

Children of the Mostar City (Bosnia-Herzegovina) Little League practice baseball in a park amid war-damaged buildings. The league was sanctioned in 1998, making Bosnia-Herzegovina the ninety-ninth country to hold a Little League charter.

"We came to Mostar not knowing what we were going to do when we got here," Terry recalls.

Unsure about how to start a conversation with children who had been through a war in a culture far removed from Arkansas, Terry eventually thought of baseball. He got his hands on a ball and bat sent to him by a friend in the United States and walked outside with those in hand. He recalls:

A little girl came up to me and asked, "Is that a baseball?" I told her it was a softball. "Would you throw it to me?" she said. I pitched it to her underhand from about thirty feet away, and she tried to catch it with her foot. Soccer is a popular sport in Mostar. I threw it to her again and she tried to catch it stiff-handed, screaming about how much it hurt. I showed her how to catch the ball and noticed a fifteen-year-old boy watching us from a distance. The next time she caught it, and the time after that she caught it easily. The boy began hollering to throw the ball to him. I did and he tried to catch it stiff-handed. That began the sequence of events that led to Bosnia-Herzegovina eventually joining Little League as its ninety-ninth affiliated country.

The Mostar City Little League received its charter in February 1999 and, later that spring, received a "starter kit" of brand-new equipment from Rawlings Sporting Goods, a Little League corporate sponsor at the time. (Wilson Sporting Goods provides the kits now.) But before all that happened, Terry found himself last October [1998] with enough kids to get started, winter coming on, and no indoor facilities available.

"We started playing baseball inside the apartment we live in," he said. "I made a big field out of posterboard, and used a marble, chess pieces and a pencil for a bat. I started showing them what baseball is all about. We had as many as twenty-five kids in here playing the baseball game, and by the spring they had the rules down pretty well. They practically live here now, and they call us grandma and grandpa."

The players in the Mostar City Little League, which completed its second season in Spring 2000, are a mixture that might have seemed impossible only a few years ago. Croats, Muslims, and Serbs play together on teams, even though many of the children had lost one or both parents in the war. Says Hardesty, "If these kids can come to know there is more to life than war and that they can be friends with anyone, not just their kind, it will all be worthwhile." ◆

Little League's European Headquarters is located in Kutno, Poland. Here, Poland's President, Aleksander Kwasniewski, visits Kutno in 1996 with bat in hand.

The goal of the campaign is to raise $20 million to fund a variety of projects, including enhancement of educational programs for players and volunteers (such as tobacco, drug, and alcohol education, and prevention of child abuse); improvement of communications at all levels of Little League through technology; expansion of Little League's facilities in South Williamsport; completion of the Little League European Leadership Training Center in Kutno, Poland; and construction of the Southwest Leadership Training Center in Waco, Texas.

Some of the contributions made in the first year of the campaign, in addition to the contribution from the Commonwealth of Pennsylvania, are $1 million from myteam.com (the official Internet service provider of Little League Baseball), $1 million from the Conrad N. Hilton Foundation, $300,000 from Major League Baseball, $500,000 from CNA Insurance, $500,000 from the Masons of Pennsylvania, and $360,000 from The RoberT Plan Corporation. At the 2000 Little League Baseball World Series, Steve Keener, Little League president and chief executive officer, announced that the total pledged to that point was $15 million.

Improvements at the Little League Baseball International Headquarters in South Williamsport include a second stadium with seating for 5,000. The second stadium—just north of Lamade Stadium—allows the number of teams that play in the World Series each year to double to sixteen, the first expansion of the Series since its inception. The cost for stadium construction, along with a new concession facility to serve both stadiums and other improvements, is $6.5 million.

Little League's European Headquarters in Poland is the focal point for more than fifty nations in Europe, the Middle East, and Africa where Little League is played. A little more than a decade ago, Little League had no programs in Eastern Europe, but the fall of the Iron Curtain and demise of the Soviet Union have allowed those nations to embrace Little League. "It's only a matter of time before the Eastern European countries are able to compete with the American kids," said Frank Lupacchino, Little League's director of international regions.

THE CHALLENGER DIVISION

Created in 1989, the Challenger Division of Little League is another important recent initiative of Little League, and one that Dr. Creighton Hale is also particularly proud of. The Challenger Division has modified rules that allow mentally and physically disabled youth to play baseball with the help of "buddies," able-bodied children who assist the Challenger player around the baseball diamond. For example, a buddy can help push a Challenger's wheelchair down the base path, if needed. The buddy's assistance varies depending on the need. Most Little Leagues use players from other divisions as buddies during a Challenger game. The benefit for the able-bodied person is friendship and a greater understanding of the disabled.

The philosophy behind the Little League Challenger Division is to provide the framework for fair play; the value is found in the strengthening of self-esteem and the discipline of teamwork. At first, Little League officials worried about injuries, Dr. Hale said, "but it's almost injury-free because everybody is so careful."

Little League had accommodated—even nurtured—millions of boys and girls, and yet, "There was this group of disabled children who loved baseball, so I just decided to see if it were possible to organize a program," Dr. Hale said. "I went to see my friend Senator [Bob] Dole, because he is disabled, and we put together a feasibility committee."

Dr. Hale also spoke with officials of the Special Olympics, including Sargent Shriver, about adding baseball to the competition. He was told that Special Olympics works specifically with mentally disabled people and was not prepared to assimilate physically disabled athletes into its sports activities. But Dr. Hale persevered. "Even though the experts said you couldn't put the mentally and the physically disabled children together, Little League did it," he said. "And it's very successful. It's one of our pride and joys, because there's nothing more pure than a Challenger game. Parents on both sides are applauding all of the kids."

Challenger Baseball helps build confidence, said Ed Beardsley, who served on the national task force headed by former Senator Dole to promote baseball for the disabled. His son, Dave Beardsley, is a graduate of the Challenger Division at Edgewood Little

Dave Beardsley, a "buddy" and a graduate of the Challenger program in Connecticut, assists a disabled youth.

LEFT
Little League created its Challenger Division in 1989 to give disabled children the opportunity to play baseball with the help of "buddies." Here Theodore Wilson Jr., a member of the Williamsport Challenger League, waits to score a run.

League of Bristol, Connecticut. In 1998, Ed was honored by Little League Baseball with the inaugural Challenger Award for his decade of volunteerism.

Ed remained with the Challenger program. "First of all," he said, "when you see something this big happening, you know it's going to be difficult to drop. One of the biggest reasons we started this was, when [Dave] was eight years old, he was having a very difficult time. That was in May. In September, for the first time, he really started to improve in school. He began to pick up on the reading and the math. It was kind of like a mental block had broken."

Playing baseball with his peers gave Dave confidence. "He learned how to catch," Ed marveled. Ed helped other parents of disabled children "learn to let them fail wherever they fail and go on from there and develop their own independence." Says Ed, "I really feel my son will make it, and any parent in this position would love to see that. When the kids get out in the field they get motivated, and when the parents see that they get motivated."

Dave Beardsley remained with the program for eleven years as a Challenger before joining the league himself as a volunteer. He has become a "buddy" for other children, so he knows firsthand how important a buddy can be.

About 1,500 Challenger Division teams exist, most in the United States, making up less than one percent of Little League's total number of teams. It remains, however, one of Little League's "crown jewels."

A YEAR-ROUND ENDEAVOR

Running Little League Baseball has been a year-round venture ever since 1948, when U.S. Rubber hired Carl Stotz to manage it. Still, some are surprised that a baseball and softball league has full-time employees—more than 100, in fact. Considering all the facets of operating the world's largest organized youth sports program, however, Little League hardly has enough time in a year to accomplish everything.

With its own printing department, Little League prints and mails more than 3 million pieces each year, and some larger jobs are printed commercially. Most of them are mailed throughout the year to local Little League volunteers and district administrators. About 750,000 rule books are printed each year, with every league receiving two free copies per team. Local Little Leagues and district administrators also receive free manuals and brochures every year that help guide them through the season.

Supplies are mailed when the charter committee accepts a local Little League's application. Leagues are required to establish their own boundaries, without encroaching on another chartered league's boundaries.

Little League also maintains several branch offices in the United States. These miniature versions of International Headquarters have small staffs but full facilities, such as stadiums, practice fields, dormitories, dining halls, and so on and are located in St. Petersburg, Florida; San Bernardino, California; Indianapolis, Indiana; and Bristol, Connecticut. A new state center is under construction in Waco, Texas. The Little League Baseball European Leadership Training Center in Kutno, Poland, is the first full-service center established outside the United States. Offices also are maintained in Tokyo, Japan; Caparra Heights, Puerto Rico; and Ottawa, Ontario, Canada.

Headquarters also processes all insurance claims for leagues that purchase group coverage through CNA Insurance. With a staff at Williamsport specifically dedicated to handling claims, insurance costs for leagues are kept low. Depending on the division of play and the state, Little League accident insurance costs the local Little Leagues between $1 and $3 per player per year.

Marketing is an important aspect of Headquarters operations, as about one-third of Little League's annual revenue is generated through licensing and sponsorship. Long gone are the days when Carl Stotz believed a sponsor should donate money philanthropically. Manufacturers who want to use Little League's name in promotions, advertisements, or on the product itself sign a licensing agreement with Little League after the product or service is evaluated. If the product is a piece of equipment, it is usually tested at an independent laboratory at the manufacturer's expense, then tested at a Little League summer camp, before the licensing agreement is signed. Little League then receives royalties on each unit sold.

Corporate sponsorship, first sought by Carl Stotz in 1948 when he convinced U.S. Rubber to help, is an area where Little League tries to strike a delicate balance between overcommercialism and fiscal survival. Little League does not reveal the cost, but sponsorship revenue is more than $2 million annually. Steve Keener, who has often said he "won't allow Little League to become a race car," explained:

Our corporate sponsors, who are so valuable to us, allow us to offer affiliation for about $13 a team as the charter fee. The most direct benefit to the leagues is that they keep affiliation affordable: about $1 a player. If we took that sponsorship away, the fee could be $30, $40, or $50 per team.

The reality is, you can't ask a corporation to make that obligation and not provide them with some opportunity to benefit themselves. They should be entitled to some benefit for the support they're providing. When we say, "We won't let Little League become a race car," what we mean is we will certainly seek corporate support and will provide a minimal amount of visibility and exposure for those corporations for the help they provide us. But we draw the line at putting corporate names on uniforms, or signs on the outfield fence, or throughout the stadium. The exception is the scoreboard.

We'll also limit it. We won't have fifty sponsors, and we won't have three. We try to keep less than twelve.

In terms of the commercial aspect, when I played for Little League I played for Milo's Sub Shop. The point being, sponsors have been a part of Little League since it began with the first three teams in 1939. I understand the economics of what many professional teams and universities do—they have to have revenue and that's one way to get it. But I think Little League needs to maintain as much of a pure and commercial-free atmosphere as possible.

EYE ON THE FUTURE

When Little League first became popular in Williamsport, it was the only game in town. As Art Kline explains, "There was no television, no organized type of summer activity. The only thing you did in those days was play ball."

For decades, participation numbers soared, but not recently. During the most recent years the number of Little Leaguers in America has fallen—about one percent each year since 1998. How does that bode for Little League's future? Steve Keener explains:

We look at reports that we receive from, for example, the Sporting Goods Manufacturers Association. They did some recent surveying of teenagers, and they found participation in team sports was on the decline.

The overall number of different activities that are out there compared to twenty, thirty, forty years ago is greater. Now, Little League Baseball is maybe only one of ten or fifteen things that may be available. You've seen a growing interest in everything from roller blading to computer camp.

We have to be attentive to social and economic changes and times and be willing to adapt to that. We've already made some changes that ten years ago wouldn't even be considered. In the softball program, we've liberalized playing rules and allow them to travel and play in more tournaments. It wasn't the wrong decision at that time to prevent it several years ago, but times are changing.

We've had to be more conscious of single-parent homes. There was a time when a child's legal residence was with the parent that had legal custody. Well, today we allow the child and parent to make a choice. If the child lives with mom nine months and then lives with dad for the summer, then they decide which of the two leagues to play in.

We have to constantly be looking at our rules and regulations and see how they reflect society today. You'll always have to have rules and regulations. That's the foundation of this program. But that's not to say those can't be tweaked when it's appropriate.

The issue of boys trying out for softball programs, originally intended for girls, also is facing Little League. In several cases boys have been placed on regular-season softball teams, and although no court has forced Little League to admit boys to its softball program, several challenges to the all-girl rules ended in out-of-court settlements. In 1995, the rules were rewritten to eliminate specific references to eligibility by gender. A recent Little League survey found that there are five male softball players for every 2,000 females in the Little League Softball divisions.

The difficulty arises during tournament play, Keener said, when an all-girls team runs up against a team with male players. "I find it odd that a male, particularly when he gets to be fifteen or older, would get any real satisfaction out of being on a team or appearing to excel against a team of female participants. Conversely, we all seem to marvel at a female who can compete and excel in a program that is predominantly a male program." Little League's solution was to create separate softball programs for boys and girls.

Little League's leader, Steve Keener, and his wife, Cheryl, are experiencing the Little League Baseball program from an entirely different perspective: as Little League parents and volunteers at the Newberry Little League in Williamsport. In making everyday decisions affecting nearly 3 million children and a million adults in 104 countries, Steve uses his experiences with his sons, Joshua and Nicholas, and his own experiences from when his father coached him. "It's really about teaching them how to win, and be humble. To lose gracefully, and not get too upset about it, as long as they've played their best. Go back to 'the home run story.' It's far more important to just be part of a team, part of a group working toward a common goal. Those are all lessons children learn in this program."

Appendixes

APPENDIX 1. CAPSULE HISTORY OF LITTLE LEAGUE

1939	Little League Baseball is founded in Williamsport, Pa., by Carl Stotz, with help from others in the community. Stotz, George Bebble, and Bert Bebble are the first three managers. … A $30 donation is sufficient to purchase uniforms for each of the first three teams.
1940	Little League expands to include a second league.
1941–46	Little League Baseball expands to 12 leagues, all in Pennsylvania.
1947	The Hammonton, N.J., Little League becomes the first league established outside Pennsylvania. … The first Little League World Series is won by the Maynard Midgets of Williamsport.
1948	Little League grows to 94 leagues. … Lock Haven, Pa., wins the second Little League World Series, defeating a team from St. Petersburg, Fla.
1949	Little League expands to 307 leagues in the United States.
1950	The shortest Little League World Series game ever, lasting exactly one hour, is played between Hagerstown, Md., and Kankakee, Ill. … The first leagues outside the U.S. are formed at each end of the Panama Canal.
1951	The first permanent Little League outside the United States is formed in British Columbia, Canada. … Little League grows to 776 programs.
1952	Peter J. McGovern becomes the first full-time president of Little League Baseball. … Baseball immortal Connie Mack is a visitor at the World Series. … Little League expands to more than 1,500 programs.
1953	The Little League World Series is televised for the first time by CBS, with rookie announcer Jim McKay behind the mike. Howard Cosell handles the play-by-play for ABC radio. … Birmingham, Ala., defeats Schenectady, N.Y., 1–0, in one of only two 1–0 finals in World Series history.
1954	Boog Powell, who later played for the Baltimore Orioles, participates for Lakeland, Fla., in the World Series. … Ken Hubbs, who would win the 1962 National League Rookie of the Year Award with the Chicago Cubs, plays in the Little League World Series for Colton, Calif. … Little League Baseball expands to more than 3,300 leagues.

1955	Cy Young makes his last visit to the Little League World Series before his death in September. ... Morrisville, Pa., defeats Delaware, N.J., 4–3, in seven innings (the first extra-inning Little League World Series championship game). ... Little League is now played in all forty-eight states. ... Near the end of the year, founder Carl Stotz initiates court action to gain control of Little League from the board of directors.
1956	An out-of-court settlement ends with Carl Stotz leaving Little League. ... The Little League Foundation is created. ... The first Little League World Series perfect game is pitched by Fred Shapiro of Delaware Township, N.J. ... Little League grows to more than 4,000 leagues. ... The first Little League Congress takes place in Chicago.
1957	Monterrey, Mexico, becomes the first non-U.S. team to win the Little League World Series as Angel Macias pitches the first perfect game in a championship final.
1958	Monterrey, Mexico, becomes the first Little League to win consecutive World Series championships. ... Hector Torres, who would later play in the major leagues, plays for Monterrey. ... Rick Wise, who would also play in the major leagues, plays for Portland, Ore., in the World Series.
1959	The modern protective helmet is developed by Dr. Creighton J. Hale, then director of research for Little League Baseball. ... The World Series is played for the first time at its present site in the borough of South Williamsport. ... Little League Baseball now has more than 5,000 leagues. ... The second week of June is proclaimed National Little League Week by President Dwight D. Eisenhower.
1960	The first European entry in the Little League World Series is Berlin, Germany. ... The World Series final is broadcast live, by ABC, for the first time. ... More than 27,400 teams participate in more than 5,500 Little Leagues.
1961	Senior League Baseball is created for players thirteen to fifteen years old. ... Brian Sipe, who would later play quarterback for the Cleveland Browns, plays for the World Series champions from El Cajon, Calif. ... More than 5,500 teams participate in Little Leagues.
1962	Little League Summer Camp opens in Williamsport. ... Jackie Robinson is inducted into the Baseball Hall of Fame and is a guest at the Little League World Series. ... National Little League Week is proclaimed by President John F. Kennedy.
1963	ABC-TV and its *Wide World of Sports* show televises the Little League World Series championship game for the first time, with Chris Schenkel calling the play-by-play.
1964	Little League Baseball is granted a Charter of Federal Incorporation by the U.S. Congress. ... Danny Yacarino pitches a no-hitter and hits a home run to lead Mid-Island Little League of Staten Island, N.Y., against Monterrey, Mexico, 4–0, for the Series title.
1965	Venezuela and Spain are represented in the Little League World Series for the first time.
1966	Little League Baseball's first regional headquarters, the Southern Region Headquarters, opens in St. Petersburg, Fla. ... A rain delay during a World Series game holds up the contest for an hour and thirty-three minutes. ... The game is broadcast in color for the first time, on *Wide World of Sports*.
1967	West Tokyo, Japan, becomes the first Far East team to win the Little League World Series title.

1968   Big League Baseball for players sixteen to eighteen years old is started. ... Darrell Garretson, now head of the NBA Officials Association, is manager of the Garden Grove, Calif., team in the World Series. ... Turk Schonert, future NFL quarterback, is a member of Garretson's team. ... Little League grows to more than 6,000 programs.

1969   The Western Regional Headquarters of Little League Baseball in San Bernardino, Calif., is opened. ... Newberry Little League participates in the World Series, becoming the first Williamsport-area team to play in the World Series since 1948. ... Taiwan wins the first of its seventeen Little League World Series.

1970   The Canadian Headquarters of Little League Baseball opens in Ottawa.

1971   Lloyd McClendon, now manager of the Pittsburgh Pirates, hits five home runs in five at-bats during the World Series for Gary, Ind. ... One of the longest games in World Series history is played over two hours and fifty-one minutes as Gary and Tainan, Taiwan, battle for nine innings. ... A Little League State Center opens in Waco, Texas. ... Howard J. Lamade Stadium is expanded to increase seating capacity to 10,000. ... The aluminum bat, developed in cooperation with Little League, is first used.

1972   Taiwan wins a second consecutive World Series championship for the Far East Region. ... Title IX, giving women and girls greater opportunities at higher levels of athletics, is signed into law by President Richard M. Nixon.

1973   Dr. Creighton J. Hale is elected president of Little League Baseball, only the second full-time president in thirty-five years. ... Future major-leaguer Ed Vosberg (now pitching for the Phillies) plays in the Little League World Series for the runner-up team from Tucson, Ariz., and goes on to become the only person to participate in the Little League World Series, the College World Series (University of Arizona, champions, 1980), and the Major League World Series (Florida Marlins, champions, 1997).

1974   Little League rules are revised to allow participation by girls. ... Little League Softball and Senior League Softball programs are created.

1975   Non-U.S. teams are barred from advancing beyond regional play. ... Lakewood, N.J., defeats Belmont Heights, of Tampa, Fla., 4–3, in the World Series final.

1976   Baseball Hall of Famers Joe DiMaggio, Ernie Banks, and Bob Gibson are Series guests as Chofu, Japan, wins that country's third championship.

1977–78 Future major-leaguer Charlie Hayes (now playing for the Brewers) plays in the 1977 Series for Hattiesburg, Miss. ... Little League grows to include more than 6,500 Little Leagues for nine-to-twelve-year-olds; 2,850 Senior Leagues for thirteen-to-fifteen-year-olds; and 1,300 Big League programs for sixteen-to-eighteen-year-olds. ... Little League and Senior League softball teams total more than 7,400.

1979   Junior League Baseball is created for thirteen-year-olds.

1980   George Bush, a former Little League coach who is elected Vice President of the United States three months later, throws out the first pitch for the World Series championship game. ... Big League Softball is started for players sixteen to eighteen years old. ... Belmont Heights reaches the finals again, falling 4–3 to Taiwan. Gary Sheffield and Derek Bell, now playing for the Dodgers and Mets, respectively, are teammates for Belmont Heights.

1981	Dan Wilson, now catching for the Seattle Mariners, plays for Barrington, Ill., Little League in the Little League World Series.
1982	The Peter J. McGovern Little League Museum opens at the Little League International Headquarters complex. ... Future major-leaguer Wilson Alvarez (now pitching for the Tampa Bay Devil Rays) plays for the Maracaibo, Venezuela, team in the Series. ... Kirkland, Wash., defeats Taiwan, 6–0, before a then-record World Series crowd of 40,000 as Cody Webster tosses a two-hitter in the final game.
1983	Major League Baseball Commissioner Bowie Kuhn throws the ceremonial first pitch for the Little League World Series championship game, and musical star Chuck Mangione plays the Dominican Republic National Anthem. ... East Marietta (Ga.) National Little League wins the World Series with future major-leaguer Marc Pisciotta (now pitching in the Indians organization) on the mound.
1984	Seoul, Korea, wins that country's first Little League World Series championship, defeating Altamonte Springs, Fla., 6–2. One Altamonte Springs player is Jason Varitek (now catching for the Red Sox). ... Peter J. McGovern, Little League board of directors chairman for more than thirty years, dies on June 30.
1985	For the first time, ABC-TV carries the Little League World Series championship game live on *Wide World of Sports*. ... For the first time in baseball history, ABC mounts a micro-miniature camera on the mask of the home-plate umpire.
1986	Baseball Commissioner Peter Ueberroth makes his first visit to the Little League World Series for the championship. ... Bill Shea, president of the Little League Foundation and the namesake of New York's Shea Stadium, throws the ceremonial first pitch.
1987	The 1947 Little League World Series champions, the Maynard Midgets of Williamsport, are reunited on the field before the championship game.
1988	The press section of Howard J. Lamade Stadium is named in honor of Ray Keyes, the only sportswriter to cover every Little League World Series from 1947 to 1988. ... Tom Seaver, a graduate of the Spartan Little League in Fresno, Calif., becomes the first player to be enshrined in the Peter J. McGovern Little League Museum Hall of Excellence.
1989	Little League Baseball celebrates its fiftieth anniversary. ... Poland receives four Certificates of Charter for the first Little League programs in a former Eastern Bloc country. ... Trumbull, Conn., National Little League becomes the first U.S. team to win the World Series since 1983, before a crowd of 45,000, with future NHL star Chris Drury on the mound.
1990	Little League Baseball launches the first full season of the Challenger Division for mentally and physically disabled children. ... Little League Baseball is now enjoyed by children in 39 countries. ... Taiwan regains the championship of the Little League World Series with a 9–0 victory over Shippensburg, Pa.
1991	Taiwan defeats Danville, Calif., 11–0 in the final game of the Little League World Series.
1992	Carl E. Stotz, founder of Little League, dies. ... The Little League World Series undergoes a series of changes. A "pool" format, in which each team is assured a minimum of three meaningful games in World Series play, is adopted; a state-of-the-art Musco

Sports Lighting System is installed at Howard J. Lamade Stadium; and the first Little League World Series night game is played. ... Long Beach, Calif., Little League is named World Series Champion following the disqualification of Zamboanga (Philippines) City Little League. ... Guests at the Series include Kareem Abdul-Jabbar, George Will, Tom Selleck, and U.S. Vice President Dan Quayle.

1993	Long Beach becomes the first U.S. team in history to win consecutive Little League Baseball World Series championships with a thrilling 3–2 victory against a team from Panama.
1994	After a record three-hour, six-minute rain delay, Coquivacoa Little League of Maracaibo, Venezuela, becomes the first Latin American team to win the Little League World Series since 1958. ... Stephen D. Keener becomes the first Little League graduate to be named president of Little League Baseball, succeeding Dr. Creighton J. Hale.
1995	Hall of Famer Stan Musial throws out the ceremonial first pitch for the Little League World Series. ... After a three-year drought, Taiwan regains the world championship, defeating Spring, Tex., 17–3.
1996	Little League celebrates its fiftieth World Series. ... Little League's first full-service regional headquarters outside the United States is opened in Kutno, Poland. ... The Little League Education Program for Managers and Coaches is launched. ... The John W. Lundy Little League Conference Center is dedicated. ... Taiwan wins its seventeenth Series title.
1997	Little League and Major League Baseball enter an agreement for the first time, co-producing a magazine that is mailed free of charge directly to 1.9 million Little Leaguers. ... An all-time record 2,993,760 Little Leaguers participate. ... Sharon Robinson, daughter of the late Jackie Robinson, is a guest at the Little League World Series. ... For the first time, U.S. regional championship games in Little League Baseball are televised nationally on ESPN2. ... A Jamboree Hitting Contest and All Star Game are added to the Little League World Series, and both are televised nationally on ESPN2. ... The Little League Softball Advisory Committee is formed. ... Linda Vista Little League of Guadalupe, Mexico, wins the Little League World Series with a four-run rally in the last inning.
1998	Little League expands to include 95 countries. ... Toms River, N.J., East American Little League wins the Little League Baseball World Series, defeating Kashima, Japan, Little League 12–9 in a championship game featuring eleven home runs and 41,200 fans at Lamade Stadium. ... Late in the year, it is announced that the Little League World Series will expand from eight teams to sixteen in 2001, and a second stadium will be built.
1999	The number of countries with Little League programs hits 100 as Burkina-Faso joins. ... Hirakata Little League of Osaka, Japan, wins that nation's first World Series title since 1976, defeating Phenix City, Ala., 5–0. ... Little League begins the first capital campaign in the program's history, to raise $20 million for a variety of projects.
2000	Construction begins on a yet-unnamed stadium just north of Lamade Stadium in preparation for expansion of the Little League World Series from eight to sixteen teams in 2001.

APPENDIX 2. THE COUNTRIES OF LITTLE LEAGUE (THROUGH JANUARY 5, 2001)

EUROPEAN REGION
(includes Africa and the Middle East)

Albania
Armenia
Austria
Bahrain
Belgium
Bosnia and
Herzegovina
Bulgaria
Burkina Faso
Cameroon
Croatia
Czech Republic
Egypt
England
Georgia
Germany
Ghana
Holland
Ireland
Israel
Italy
Jordan
Kazakhstan
Kenya
Kuwait
Kyrgyzstan
Latvia
Lesotho
Lithuania
Luxembourg
Macedonia
Mali
Malta
Moldova

Nigeria
Norway
Pakistan
Poland
Qatar
Romania
Russia
Saudi Arabia
Scotland
Slovakia
South Africa
Spain
Sweden
Togo
Turkey
Ukraine
United Arab
Emirates
Uzbekistan
Zambia
Zimbabwe

LATIN AMERICAN REGION

Antigua
Argentina
Aruba
Bahamas
Barbados
Belize
Bermuda
Bolivia
Brazil
British Virgin
Islands
Chile
Colombia
Costa Rica
Cuba
Dominican Republic
Ecuador
El Salvador
Guatemala
Guyana
Honduras
Jamaica
Mexico
Netherlands Antilles
Nicaragua
Panama
Puerto Rico
St. Vincent & the
Grenadines
Trinidad & Tobago
U.S. Virgin Islands
Uruguay
Venezuela

FAR EAST REGION

American Samoa
Australia
Guam
Hong Kong
India
Indonesia
Japan
Korea
Northern Mariana
Islands
Malaysia
Micronesia
New Zealand
Palau
Republic of Papua
New Guinea
People's Republic of
China
Philippines
Sri Lanka
Thailand

CANADA

UNITED STATES OF AMERICA

1947	Maynard, Williamsport, Pa.	16
	Lock Haven, Pa.	7
1948	Lock Haven, Pa.	6
	St. Petersburg, Fla.	5
1949	Hammonton, N.J.	5
	Pensacola, Fla.	0
1950	National, Houston, Tex.	2
	Bridgeport, Conn.	1
1951	Stamford, Conn.	3
	North Austin Lions, Austin, Tex.	0
1952	National, Norwalk, Conn.	4
	Optimist, Monongahela, Pa.	3
1953	Southside, Birmingham, Ala.	1
	Schenectady, N.Y.	0
1954	National, Schenectady, N.Y.	7
	Colton Lions, Colton, Calif.	5
1955	Morrisville, Pa.	4
	Delaware, Merchantville, N.J.	3
1956	Roswell Lions Hondo, Roswell, N.M.	3
	National, Delaware Township, N.J.	1
1957	Monterrey, Mexico	4
	La Mesa Northern, La Mesa, Calif.	0
1958	Monterrey, Mexico	10
	Jaycee, Kankakee, Ill.	1
1959	National, Hamtramck, Mich.	12
	West Auburn, Auburn, Calif.	0
1960	American, Levittown, Pa.	5
	North East Optomist, Ft. Worth, Tex.	0
1961	Northern, El Cajon, Calif.	4
	El Campo, Tex.	2
1962	Moreland, San Jose, Calif.	3
	Jaycee, Kankakee, Ill.	0
1963	Northern, Granada Hills, Calif.	2
	Original, Stratford, Conn.	1

1964	Mid-Island, Staten Island, N.Y.	4
	Liga Pequena, Monterrey, Mexico	0
1965	Windsor Locks, Conn.	3
	Stoney Creek, Ontario, Canada	1
1966	Westbury American, Houston, Tex.	8
	American, West New York, N.J.	2
1967	West, Tokyo, Japan	4
	North Roseland, Chicago, Ill.	1
1968	Wakayama, Osaka, Japan	1
	Tuckahoe, Richmond, Va.	0
1969	Chinese Taipei	5
	Briarwood, Santa Clara, Calif.	0
1970	American, Wayne, N.J.	2
	Campbell, Calif.	0
1971	Tainan, Chinese Taipei	12
	Anderson, Gary, Ind.	3
1972	Chinese Taipei	6
	Edison, Hammond, Ind.	0
1973	Tainan City, Chinese Taipei	12
	Cactus, Tucson, Ariz.	0
1974	Kao Hsiung, Chinese Taipei	12
	Red Bluff, Calif.	1
1975	Lakewood, N.J.	4
	Belmont Heights, Tampa, Fla.	3
1976	Chofu, Tokyo, Japan	10
	Campbell, Calif.	3
1977	Li-Teh, Chinese Taipei	7
	Western, El Cajon, Calif.	2
1978	Pin-Kuang, Chinese Taipei	11
	San Ramon Valley, Danville, Calif.	1
1979	Pu-Tzu Town, Chinese Taipei	2
	Campbell, Calif.	1
1980	Long Kuong, Chinese Taipei	4
	Belmont Heights, Tampa, Fla.	3
1981	Tai-Ping, Chinese Taipei	4
	Belmont Heights, Tampa, Fla.	2

| 1982 | National, Kirkland, Wash. | 6 |
| | Pu-Tzu Town, Chinese Taipei | 0 |

1983	National, East Marietta, Ga.	3
	Liquito Hernandez, Dominican	
	Republic	1

| 1984 | National, Seoul, South Korea | 6 |
| | National, Altamonte Springs, Fla. | 2 |

| 1985 | National, Seoul, South Korea | 7 |
| | Mexicali, Baja Cal, Mexico | 1 |

| 1986 | Tainan Park, Chinese Taipei | 12 |
| | International, Tucson, Ariz. | 0 |

| 1987 | Hua Lian, Chinese Taipei | 21 |
| | Northwood, Irvine, Calif. | 1 |

| 1988 | Tai Ping, Chinese Taipei | 10 |
| | Pearl City, Hawaii | 0 |

| 1989 | National, Trumbull, Conn. | 5 |
| | Kang-Tu, Chinese Taipei | 2 |

| 1990 | San-Hua, Chinese Taipei | 9 |
| | Shippensburg, Pa. | 0 |

1991	Hsi Nan, Tai Chung,	
	Chinese Taipei	11
	San Ramon Valley, Danville, Calif.	0

| 1992 | Long Beach, Calif. | 6 |
| | Zamboanga City, Philippines | 0 * |

| 1993 | Long Beach, Calif. | 3 |
| | Chiriqui, Panama | 2 |

| 1994 | Coquivacoa, Maracaibo, Venezuela | 4 |
| | Northridge, Calif. | 3 |

| 1995 | Shan-Hua, Tainan, Chinese Taipei | 17 |
| | Spring, Tex. | 3 |

1996	Fu-Hsing, Kao-Hsuing,	
	Chinese Taipei	13
	Western, Cranston, R.I.	3

| 1997 | Linda Vista, Guadalupe, Mexico | 5 |
| | South, Mission Viejo, Calif. | 4 |

1998	Toms River East American,	
	Toms River, N.J.	12
	Kashima, Japan	9

| 1999 | Hirakata, Osaka, Japan | 5 |
| | National, Phenix City, Ala. | 0 |

2000	Sierra Maestra, Maracaibo,	
	Venezuela	3
	Bellaire, Tex.	2

* Disqualified (forfeit)

APPENDIX 4. JUNIOR LEAGUE BASEBALL WORLD SERIES CHAMPIONS

1981	Boardman—Boardman, Ohio		1991	Northwest 45—Spring, Tex.
1982	Belmont Heights—Tampa, Fla.		1992	Sunnyside—Tucson, Ariz.
1983	Manati—Puerto Rico		1993	Cayey—Puerto Rico
1984	Pearl City—Pearl City, Hawaii		1994	Thousand Oaks—Thousand Oaks, Calif.
1985	Tampa Bay—Tampa, Fla.		1995	South Lake Charles—South Lake Charles, La.
1986	Waldorf—Waldorf, Md.			
1987	Rowland Heights—Rowland Heights, Calif.		1996	Northwest 45—Spring, Tex.
			1997	Salem Youth—Salem, N.H.
1988	Lugo Buzo Montez—Mexicali, Mexico		1998	South Mission Viejo—Mission Viejo, Calif.
1989	Manati—Puerto Rico		1999	Arroyo, Puerto Rico
1990	Juan Antonio Bibiloni—Yabucoa, Puerto Rico		2000	Aeia, Hawaii

1961	Natrona Heights—Natrona Heights, Pa.
1962	West Hempstead—West Hempstead, N.Y.
1963	Del Norte—Monterrey, Mexico
1964	International—Massapequa, N.Y.
1965	Del Norte—Monterrey, Mexico
1966	East Rochester—East Rochester, N.Y.
1967	Westbury—Westbury, N.Y.
1968	New Hyde Park—New Hyde Park, N.Y.
1969	Airport—Sacramento, Calif.
1970	West Tampa—Tampa, Fla.
1971	East La Habra—La Habra, Calif.
1972	Meiho Pingtung—Chinese Taipei
1973	Taipei—Chinese Taipei
1974	Ping Tung—Chinese Taipei
1975	Meiho Pingtung—Chinese Taipei
1976	Meiho Pingtung—Chinese Taipei
1977	Hau Hsing—Chinese Taipei
1978	Jong Kung—Chinese Taipei
1979	Tung Feng—Chinese Taipei
1980	Ping Tung—Chinese Taipei
1981	Georgetown—Georgetown, Del.
1982	Golita Valley—Santa Barbara, Calif.
1983	Mei—Ho Ping Tung—Chinese Taipei
1984	Altamonte Springs—Altamonte Springs, Fla.
1985	Ping Tung—Chinese Taipei
1986	Taipei—Chinese Taipei
1987	Athens—Athens, Ohio
1988	Taipei—Chinese Taipei
1989	Ping Tung—Chinese Taipei
1990	Ping Tung—Chinese Taipei
1991	Ping Tung—Chinese Taipei
1992	Ping Tung—Chinese Taipei
1993	La Vega—Dominican Republic
1994	North Brandon—Brandon, Fla.
1995	Dunedin National—Dunedin, Fla.
1996	Coquivacoa—Maracaibo, Venezuela
1997	San Francisco—San Francisco, Venezuela
1998	Diamond Bar—Diamond Bar, Calif.
1999	Kissimmee, Fla.
2000	Curundu—Panama City, Panama

APPENDIX 6. BIG LEAGUE BASEBALL WORLD SERIES CHAMPIONS

1968	Charleston—Charleston, W.V.
1969	Mojave Desert—Barstown, Calif.
1970	Lincolnwood North—Lincolnwood, Ill.
1971	Cupertino—San Jose, Calif.
1972	Orlando South—Orlando, Fla.
1973	Lincolnwood North—Lincolnwood, Ill.
1974	Ping Tung—Chinese Taipei
1975	Taipei—Chinese Taipei
1976	Ping Tung—Chinese Taipei
1977	Ping Dong—Chinese Taipei
1978	Taichong City—Chinese Taipei
1979	West Hempstead—West Hempstead, N.Y.
1980	Buena Park—Buena Park, Calif.
1981	Ping Tung—Chinese Taipei
1982	San Juan—Puerto Rico
1983	Taipei—Chinese Taipei
1984	Ping Tung—Chinese Taipei
1985	Broward County—Broward County, Fla.
1986	Maracaibo—Maracaibo, Venezuela
1987	Taipei—Chinese Taipei
1988	Taipei—Chinese Taipei
1989	Taipei—Chinese Taipei
1990	Taipei—Chinese Taipei
1991	Taipei—Chinese Taipei
1992	Broward County—Broward County, Fla.
1993	Taipei—Chinese Taipei
1994	Taipei—Chinese Taipei
1995	Taipei—Chinese Taipei
1996	Taipei—Chinese Taipei
1997	Broward County—Broward County, Fla.
1998	District 13 California
1999	District 14, Orlando, Fla.
2000	Fraser Valley—British Columbia, Canada

APPENDIX 7. LITTLE LEAGUE SOFTBALL WORLD SERIES CHAMPIONS

1974	Wellswood—Tampa, Fla.		1987	Tampa Bay—Tampa, Fla.
1975	National—Medford, Ore.		1988	Greater Naples—Naples, Fla.
1976	Salinas—Salinas, Calif.		1989	Greater Naples—Naples, Fla.
1977	American—Salinas, Calif.		1990	Foothill—Glendale, Calif.
1978	Shippensburg—Shippensburg, Pa.		1991	Greater Naples—Naples, Fla.
1979	North Providence West—North Providence, R.I.		1992	Midway—Waco, Tex.
			1993	Midway—Waco, Tex.
1980	Glendale—Glendale, Calif.		1994	Midway—Waco, Tex.
1981	Gresham—Gresham, Ore.		1995	Midway—Waco, Tex.
1982	76er—Glendale, Calif.		1996	Countryside—Clearwater, Fla.
1983	Greater Naples—Naples, Fla.		1997	Midway—Waco, Tex.
1984	Albuquerque—Albuquerque, N.M.		1998	Midway—Waco, Tex.
1985	National—Brookfield, Ill.		1999	Midway—Waco, Tex.
1986	Tampa Bay—Tampa, Fla.		2000	Midway—Waco, Tex.

APPENDIX 8. JUNIOR LEAGUE SOFTBALL WORLD SERIES CHAMPIONS

1999 Midway—Woodway-Hewitt, Tex.

2000 Greater Naples—Naples, Fla.

APPENDIX 9. SENIOR LEAGUE SOFTBALL WORLD SERIES CHAMPIONS

1976	Wellswood—Tampa, Fla.		1989	Greater Naples—Naples, Fla.
1977	Wellswood—Tampa, Fla.		1990	Greater Naples—Naples, Fla.
1978	Wellswood—Tampa, Fla.		1991	Greater Naples—Naples, Fla.
1979	Gaylord—Gaylord, Mich.		1992	Greater Naples—Naples, Fla.
1980	Naples—Naples, Fla.		1993	Greater Naples—Naples, Fla.
1981	Shippensburg—Shippensburg, Pa.		1994	Greater Naples—Naples, Fla.
1982	Greater Naples—Naples, Fla.		1995	Greater Naples—Naples, Fla.
1983	Orange Park—Orange Park, Fla.		1996	Greater Naples—Naples, Fla.
1984	Naples—Naples, Fla.		1997	Parkview—Lancaster, Calif.
1985	Beaverdale—Des Moines, Iowa		1998	West Portage—Portage, Mich.
1986	Georgetown—Jennison, Mich.		1999	Stanton—Newport, Wilmington, Del.
1987	Quito—Campbell, Calif.		2000	Santa Cruz Valley—Eloy, Ariz.
1988	Tigard—Tigard, Ore.			

APPENDIX 10. BIG LEAGUE SOFTBALL WORLD SERIES CHAMPIONS

1982	Tampa, Fla.		1992	Orlando, Fla.
1983	Tampa, Fla.		1993	District 9 Washington
1984	Williamsport, Pa.		1994	Williamsport, Pa.
1985	Williamsport, Pa.		1995	District 13 Florida
1986	Tallmadge, Ohio		1996	Antelope Valley, Calif.
1987	District 4 Northern California		1997	Mechanicsville, Md.
1988	Portland, Maine		1998	District 7 Maryland
1989	Portland, Maine		1999	District 7 Maryland
1990	Williamsport, Pa.		2000	District 2 Michigan
1991	District 9 Texas			

APPENDIX 11. LITTLE LEAGUE BASEBALL WORLD SERIES PARTICIPANTS

* Denotes World Series Champion
# Denotes World Series Runner-Up

INTERNATIONAL PARTICIPANTS

Belgium

Shape	1981
Brussels	1984

Canada

National, Montreal	1952
National, Vancouver	1953
Valleyfield, Quebec	1958
Valleyfield, Quebec	1959
Parkdale Lions, Toronto	1960
Kiwanis East, Montreal	1961
Stoney Creek, Ontario	1962
Valleyfield, Quebec	1963
Valleyfield, Quebec	1964
Stoney Creek, Ontario	#1965
Central, Windsor	1966
East Trail, Trail, British Columbia	1967
Sherbrooke-Lennoxville, Quebec	1968
Valleyfield, Quebec	1969
Valleyfield, Quebec	1970
Brockville, Ontario	1971
South, Windsor	1972
Whalley, Surrey, British Columbia	1973
Esquimalt Victoria-West, British Columbia	1974
Trail, British Columbia	1976
Norcrest, Lethbridge, Alberta	1977
Whalley, Surrey, British Columbia	1978
Lennoxville, Sherbrooke, Quebec	1979

Trail, British Columbia	1980
Trail, British Columbia	1981
Rotary, Rouyn	1982
Sherbrooke Fluerimont, Sherbrooke, Quebec	1983
Conquitlan, British Columbia	1984
Glanbrook, Binbrook, Ontario	1985
Valleyfield, Quebec	1986
Glace Bay, Nova Scotia	1987
Glace Bay, Nova Scotia	1988
High Park, Toronto	1989
Trail, British Columbia	1990
Glace Bay, Nova Scotia	1991
Valleyfield, Quebec	1992
Lynn Valley, Vancouver	1993
Glace Bay, Nova Scotia	1994
High Park, Toronto	1995
Kennedy-Surrey, Surrey, British Columbia	1996
Whalley, Surrey, British Columbia	1997
Langley, British Columbia	1998
Gordon Head, Victoria, British Columbia	1999
High Park, Toronto, Ontario	2000

Dominican Republic

La Javilla, Santo Domingo	1978
Liquito Hernandez, Barahona	#1983
Rolando Paulino, Moca	1987
Luis Montas, San Cristobal	1991
Epy Guerrero, Santo Domingo	1992
Hatillo, San Cristobal	1995

Ramon Matias Mella, San Isidro	1996	

France

Poitiers Post, Vienne	1962

Germany

Berlin Command	1960
Pirmasens Post	1961
Wiesbaden	1964
Rhein Main	1966
Wiesbaden	1968
Wiesbaden	1969
Wiesbaden	1970
Bitburg, Bitburg Air Base	1973
Kaiserslautern	1976
Falcon, Ramstein Air Base	1990
Kaiserslautern	1992
Kaiserslautern	1993
Ramstein Air Base	1999

Greece

Athens, Athenai Airport	1974

Italy

Aviano, Aviano AB	1979

Japan

Kunitachi, Tokyo	1962
Tachikawa, Tokyo	1964
Arakawa, Tokyo	1965
Wakayama	1966
West Tokyo, Tokyo	*1967
Wakayama, Osaka	*1968
Chofu, Tokyo	*1976
Osaka Yodogawa, Osaka	1983
Seya, Yokohama	1997

Kashima, Ibaraki	#1998
Hirakata, Osaka	*1999
Musashi Fuchu, Tokyo	2000

Mariana Islands

Garapan City, Saipan	1993

Mexico

Industrial, Monterrey	*1957
Industrial, Monterrey	*1958
Industrial, Monterrey	1960
Industrial, Monterrey	1961
Del Norte, Monterrey	1962
Liga Pequena Obispado, Monterrey	1963
Liga Pequena Obispado, Monterrey	#1964
Liga Pequena Cuauhtemoc, San Nicholas, Monterrey	1966
Liga Pequena De Linares, A.C., Nuevo Leon	1967
Liga Pequena Mitras, A.C., Monterrey	1973
Unidad Modelo, Monterrey	1981
Mexicali/Baja California	#1985
Matamoros, Tamaulipas	1990
Linda Vista, Guadalupe	*1997
Linda Vista, Guadalupe	1998

Netherlands Antilles

Pabao, Willemstad, Curaçao	1980

Nicaragua

Chinandega	1968
Chinandega	1970

Panama

Willys R. Cook, Bethania	1984

Curundu	1988	Madrid	1971
David, Chiriqui	1993	Madrid	1972
Philippines		Torrejon AB, Madrid	1977
Zamboanga City	#1992	Torrejon AB, Madrid	1978
Puerto Rico		Torrejon AB, Madrid	1980
Caparra, San Juan	1959	Torrejon AB, Madrid	1982
Jorge Rosas, Mayaquez	1969	Torrejon AB, Madrid	1986
Cagus Gillette, Caguas	1971	*Taiwan*	
Almirante Gallery, San Juan	1972	Taipei	*1969
Canales, Puerto Nuevo	1976	Chayi	1970
Luis Llorens Torres, Santurce	1979	Tainan	*1971
Juan A. Bibiloni, Yabucoa	1999	Taipei	*1972
Saudi Arabia		Tainan City	*1973
Arabian Gulf, Al Khobar	1983	Kao Hsiung	*1974
Arabian Gulf, Al Khobar	1985	Li-Teh, Kao Hsiung	*1977
Aramco, Dhahran	1987	Pin-Kuang, Pin-Tung	*1978
Aramco, Dhahran	1988	Pu-Tzu Town, Chia-Yi	*1979
Aramco, Dhahran	1989	Long Kuong, Hua Lian	*1980
Arabian American, Dhahran	1991	Tai Ping, Tai Chung	*1981
Arabian American, Dhahran	1994	Pu-Tzu Town, Chia-Yi-Hsien	#1982
Arabian American, Dhahran	1995	Tainan Park	*1986
Arabian American, Dhahran	1996	Hua Lian	*1987
Arabian American, Dhahran	1997	Tai Ping, Tai Chung	*1988
Arabian American, Dhahran	1998	Kang-tu, Kao-Hsiung	#1989
Arabian American, Dhahran	2000	San-Hua, Tainan County	*1990
South Korea		Hsi Nan, Tai Chung	*1991
National, Seoul	*1984	Li-Jen, Tainan	1994
National, Seoul	*1985	Shan-Hua, Tainan	*1995
Spain		Fu-Hsing, Kao-Hsuing	*1996
Rota	1965	*Turkey*	
Rota	1967	Izmir	1963

Venezuela

Qulia, Maracaibo	1965
Coquivacoa, Maracaibo	1974
Coquivacoa, Maracaibo	1977
Coquivacoa, Maracaibo	1982
Coquivacoa, Maracaibo	1985
Coquivacoa, Maracaibo	1986
Coquivacoa, Maracaibo	1989
Coquivacoa, Maracaibo	*1994
Sierra Maestra, Maracaibo	*2000

UNITED STATES PARTICIPANTS

Alabama

Southside, Birmingham	*1953
Auburn	1955
Auburn	1956
National, Gadsden	1958
National, Gadsden	1959
South Brookley, Mobile	1964
Cottage Hill, Mobile	1990
National, Phenix City	#1999

Arizona

S. Mountain East Side, Phoenix	1965
Cactus, Tucson	#1973
International, Tucson	#1986

Arkansas

National, Little Rock	1952
National, Little Rock	1953
Burns Park, North Little Rock	1979

California

Jaycee, San Bernardino	1951
National, San Diego	1952
Lions Club, Colton	#1954
North Shore, San Diego	1955
Lions Club, Colton	1956
Northern, LaMesa	#1957
West Auburn, Auburn	#1959
East Lakewood	1960
Northern, El Cajon	*1961
Moreland, San Jose	*1962
National, Granada Hills	*1963
National, La Puente	1964
Airport, Sacramento	1966
Northridge City	1967
Bolsa, Garden Grove	1968
Briarwood, Santa Clara	#1969
Campbell	#1970
Red Bluff	#1974
American, Northridge	1975
Campbell	#1976
Western, El Cajon	#1977
San Ramon Valley, Danville	#1978
Campbell	#1979
National, Escondido	1981
Pacific, Sacramento	1983
Los Gatos	1984
Northwood, Irvine	#1987
Eastview, San Pedro	1989
Federal, Cypress	1990
San Ramon Valley, Danville	#1991
Long Beach, Long Beach	*1992
Long Beach, Long Beach	*1993

Northridge City, Northridge	#1994
Yorba Linda	1995
Moorpark	1996
South, Mission Viejo	#1997
Federal, Cypress	1998

Connecticut

Middleton	1948
Bridgeport	1949
Bridgeport	#1950
Stamford	*1951
National, Norwalk	1952
North End, Bridgeport	1957
Darien	1958
Stratford Original	#1963
Windsor Locks	*1965
Walter Smith, New Haven	1974
Forestville, Bristol	1976
Federal, Stamford	1981
American, Stamford	1983
McCabe-Waters, Bristol	1984
National, Trumbull	*1989

Florida

St. Petersburg	#1948
Pensacola	#1949
Pensacola	1950
National, Pensacola	1951
Orange, Lakeland	1954
West Tampa, Tampa	1967
West Tampa, Tampa	1969
Belmont Heights, Tampa	1973
Belmont Heights, Tampa	#1975

Belmont Heights, Tampa	#1980
Belmont Heights, Tampa	#1981
National, Sarasota	1982
National, Altamonte Springs	#1984
American, Sarasota	1986
Northside, Tampa	1989
National, Dunedin	1991
R.L. Turner, Panama City	1996
Manatee G.T. Bray, Bradenton	1997

Georgia

National, East Marietta	*1983

Hawaii

Pearl Harbor, Honolulu	1958
Windward, Oahu	1959
Pearl Harbor, Honolulu	1960
American, Hilo	1961
Wahiawa	1971
Community, Pearl City	1972
Pearl City	#1988

Idaho

South Central, Boise	1999

Illinois

Kankakee	1950
Thillen's, Chicago	1951
Joliet	1953
Melrose Park	1954
Kankakee	#1958
Kankakee	#1962
Jaycee, Kankakee	1966
North Roseland, Chicago	#1967
South Palatine	1978

Barrington	1981		*Maine*		
Jackie Robinson West, Chicago	1983		Suburban, Portland	1951	
Norridge	1986		East Augusta, Augusta	1971	
South Holland	1992		*Maryland*		

Indiana

Lafayette	1949		Hagerstown	1950	
Community Service, Whiting	1952		National, Hagerstown	1968	
American, Terre Haute	1961		Easton	1982	
George Rogers Clark, Jeffersonville	1965		Brunswick	1986	
American, Terre Haute	1968		*Massachusetts*		
South, Highland	1970		North, Newton	1953	
Anderson, Gary	#1971		Needham	1954	
Edison, Hammond	#1972		Winchester	1955	
Southport, Indianapolis	1984		Winchester	1956	
Chesterfield	1987		National, Andover	1988	
Dyer	1997		Middleboro	1994	
Brownsburg	1999		*Michigan*		

Iowa

Southeast, Davenport	1975		National, Hamtramck	1955	
Windsor, Des Moines	1976		National, Hamtramck	1956	
Grandview National, Des Moines	1980		Jaycee, Escanaba	1957	
East, Davenport	1989		National, Hamtramck	*1959	
National, Marshalltown	1996		Federal, Birmingham	1973	
East, Davenport	2000		Grosse Pointe Woods–Shores National, G. P. Woods	1979	

Kentucky

Gardenside, Lexington	1971		Pinery Park, Wyoming	1982	
South, Lexington	1978		Columbia, Brooklyn	1990	
			Georgetown, Jenison	1998	

Louisiana

Minnesota

Alexandria	1955		Central, Duluth	1963	
South, Lake Charles	1992		East Tonka, Minnetonka	1985	
			Brooklyn Center American	1994	
			Arden Hills	1995	

Mississippi	
Hub City, Hattiesburg	1977

New Hampshire	
Northside, Dover	1987
Bedford	1993
Goffstown	2000

New Jersey	
Hammonton	1947
Hammonton	1948
Hammonton	*1949
American, Hackensack	1952
Delaware, Merchantville	#1955
Delaware Township	#1956
Pitman	1962
American, West New York	#1966
American, Wayne	*1970
Lakewood	*1975
National, Ridgewood	1979
Nottingham, Hamilton Square	1992
East American, Toms River	1995
East American, Toms River	*1998
East American, Toms River	1999

New Mexico	
Lions Hondo, Roswell	*1956

New York	
Corning	1948
Corning	1949
Schenectady	#1953
National, Schenectady	*1954
National, Glen Falls	1955
Eastchester, Tuckahoe	1956

New York (cont.)	
National, Schenectady	1959
Mid-Island, Staten Island	*1964
New City	1972
Colonie	1973
Carman, Rotterdam	1977
American, Rockville Ctr.	1978
South Shore, Staten Island	1985
South Shore, Staten Island	1991

North Carolina	
Morresville	1952
Tar Heel, Greenville	1998

Ohio	
Canton	1949
Kiwanis, New Boston	1960
West, Elyria	1969
Tallmadge	1974
Youngstown	1977
W. Side American, Hamilton	1991
W. Side American, Hamilton	1993

Oklahoma	
National, Bartlesville	1964
Tulsa	1988

Oregon	
Rose City, Portland	1958

Pennsylvania	
West Shore, Harrisburg	1947
Jersey Shore	1947
Milton	1947
Montgomery	1947
Lock Haven	#1947
Lock Haven	*1948

Lock Haven	1949		American, Jackson	1974
Groundhog, Punxsutawney	1950		American, Morristown	1985
Potter-McKean	1951		American, Morristown	1987
Optimist, Monongahela	#1952		*Texas*	
Camp Hill	1953		National, Houston	*1950
Exchange Club, Masontown	1954		North Austin	#1951
Morrisville	*1955		Western, Galveston	1954
Exchange Club, Upper Darby	1956		NE Optimist, Fort Worth	#1960
American, Levittown	*1960		El Campo	#1961
American, Levittown	1961		Valley Verde, Del Rio	1962
Newtown-Edgemont	1967		National, North Houston	1963
Shippensburg	#1990		Northern, Waco	1965
Railway Park, Pottsville	1997		Westbury American, Houston	1966
Williamsport Area Teams, Brandon	1947		Northwest 45, Spring	1988
Maynard	*1947		Northwest 45, Spring	#1995
Montoursville	1947		Bellaire	#2000
Lincoln, Newberry	1947		*Virginia*	
Original	1947		Alexandria	1948
Sunday School	1947		Front Royal	1953
Loyalsock	1948		Hampton Wythe	1954
Newberry	1969		Tuckahoe, Richmond	#1968
Rhode Island			National, Vienna	1972
Westerly	1950		Tuckahoe, Richmond	1976
Darlington American, Pawtucket	1980		Tuckahoe, Richmond	1993
Western, Cranston	#1996		Central, Springfield	1994
South Carolina			*Washington*	
North Charleston	1949		Kirkland	1980
Clinton	1950		National, Kirkland	*1982
Tennessee			Hazel Dell, Vancouver	2000
National, Nashville	1970		*West Virginia*	
			Fairmont	1951

APPENDIX 12. PETER J. MCGOVERN LITTLE LEAGUE MUSEUM HALL OF EXCELLENCE

Since 1988, one or more Little League graduates who have demonstrated a commitment to excellence in their chosen profession and exemplify the values learned as youngsters in Little League Baseball are enshrined in the Peter J. McGovern Little League Museum Hall of Excellence. Those chosen for this special recognition are selected through a defined voting system by the Peter J. McGovern Little League Museum Advisory Board.

MEMBERS
(year of induction in parentheses)

KAREEM ABDUL-JABBAR (1992)
Member of the NBA Hall of Fame, played Little League Baseball in the Inwood Little League in New York City.

DAVE BARRY (1998)
Pulitzer Prize–winning humor columnist/author, played in the Armonk, N.Y., Little League.

DON BEAVER (1999)
North Carolina businessman and owner of several sports franchises, played in the 1952 Little League World Series for Mooresville, N.C.

BILL BRADLEY (1989)
Former U.S. Senator from New Jersey, Rhodes Scholar, and member of the NBA's Hall of Fame, played Little League Baseball in Crystal City, Mo.

LEONARD S. COLEMAN (1996)
President of the National League of Professional Baseball Clubs, played Little League in Montclair, N.J.

KEVIN COSTNER (2000)
Graduate of Saticoy Little League in Ventura, Calif., and Academy Award–winning actor/director.

TONY DUNGY (1998)
Head coach for the Tampa Bay Buccaneers and one of the most respected gentlemen in pro football, played in the Southeast Little League of Jackson, Minn.

VINCENT FORTANASCE (1994)
Board certified psychiatrist and neurologist as well as clinical professor at the University of Southern California School of Medicine, a graduate of the Elmont Little League of Queens, New York.

BILLY HUNTER (2000)
A graduate of the Delaware Township, N.J., Little League, led his team to the finals of the 1955 Little League Baseball World Series, played football at Syracuse and for the Miami Dolphins and Washington Redskins, and is now executive director of the NBA Players Association, the players' union.

HALE IRWIN (1993)
Scholar/athlete at the University of Colorado, one of the most successful members of the PGA; graduate of the Baxter Springs, Kans., Little League.

DALE MURPHY (1995)
A graduate of the Tulatin Little League, Portland, Ore., is one of the finest, most-respected major-league players of the last half of the twentieth century.

STORY MUSGRAVE (1994)
A NASA astronaut who has flown more than 17,000 hours, is a Boston-area Little League graduate.

DAN O'BRIEN (1997)
An Olympic decathlon gold-medalist, former world-record holder, and champion of adoption-related causes, played Little League in South Suburban Little League in Klamath Fall, Ore.

JIM PALMER (1994)
Three-time Cy Young Award–winning major-league pitcher, Baseball Hall of Famer, and analyst for ABC Sports, is a graduate of the Beverly Hills, Calif., Little League.

MICHAEL PLADUS (1999)
National Principal of the Year (Interboro High School, Prospect Park, Pa., 1999), graduated from the Shenandoah North, Pa., Little League.

DAN QUAYLE (1990)
Former U.S. Senator and Vice President of the United States, played baseball in the Hoosier Little League of Huntington, Ind., during the mid-1950s.

CAL RIPKEN JR. (1996)
Baseball's all-time ironman, played Little League Baseball at West Asheville, N.C., Little League.

NOLAN RYAN (1991)
Major League Baseball's all-time strikeout record holder and Baseball Hall of Famer, a graduate of the Alvin Little League in Alvin, Tex.

MIKE SCHMIDT (1991)
Baseball Hall of Fame third baseman, is a graduate of North Riverdale Little League in Dayton, Ohio.

TOM SEAVER (1988)
Major League Baseball Hall of Fame pitcher, is a graduate of the Spartan Little League of Fresno, Calif.

TOM SELLECK (1991)
Accomplished actor and entertainer, played in the Sherman Oaks, Calif., Little League.

BRIAN SIPE (1999)
Former quarterback for the Cleveland Browns, played in the Northern Little League, El Cajon, Calif., and in the 1961 Little League World Series.

ROBERT SLOAN (1996)
President of Baylor University in Waco, Tex., played at Western Little League, Abilene, Tex.

BRUCE SPRINGSTEEN (1997)
Award-winning singer/songwriter and social activist, played Little League Baseball in Freehold, N.J.

ROBERT STRATTA (2000)
A graduate of the North Roseland Little League in Chicago, pitched in the Little League World Series in 1967. He is now professor of surgery at the University of Tennessee—Memphis.

GEORGE WILL (1992)
Journalist, political analyst, and Pulitzer Prize–winning author, played Little League in Champaign, Ill.

APPENDIX 13. NOTABLE LITTLE LEAGUERS

MAJOR-LEAGUERS WHO PLAYED IN THE LITTLE LEAGUE WORLD SERIES

(year of participation in parentheses)

Wilson Alvarez (1982)

Jim Barbieri (1954)*

Derek Bell (1980–81)*

Larvell Blanks (1962)

Bill Connors (1954)

Charlie Hayes (1977)*

Ken Hubbs (1954)

Keith Lampard (1958)

Carney Lansford (1969)*

Vance Lovelace (1975)

Lloyd McClendon (1971)

Jim Pankovits (1968)

Marc Pisciotta (1983)

Boog Powell (1954)*

Gary Sheffield (1980)*

Carl Taylor (1954)

Hector Torres (1958)

Jason Varitek (1984)

Ed Vosberg (1973)**

Dan Wilson (1981)

Rick Wise (1958)*

* Denotes player who participated in Little League and Major League World Series.

** Denotes player who participated in Little League World Series, College World Series, and Major League World Series.

MEMBERS OF THE BASEBALL HALL OF FAME WHO PLAYED LITTLE LEAGUE BASEBALL

(year of induction in parentheses)

George Brett (1999)

Steve Carlton (1994)

Rollie Fingers (1992)

Jim "Catfish" Hunter (1987)

Jim Palmer (1990)

Nolan Ryan (1999)

Mike Schmidt (1995)

Tom Seaver (1992)

Don Sutton (1998)

Carl Yastrzemski (1989)

Robin Yount (1999)

OTHER WELL-KNOWNS WHO HAVE PLAYED LITTLE LEAGUE BASEBALL

Troy Aikman	NFL quarterback
George W. Bush	U.S. President
William Cohen	Former U.S. Secretary of Defense
Danny Devito	Professional actor/ director
Mike Ditka	NFL Hall of Fame tight end; former NFL Coach
Ray Ferraro	NHL player (played in 1976 Little League World Series)
Doug Flutie	NFL quarterback

Dennis Franz	Professional actor
Dirk Kempthorne	Governor of Idaho, former U.S. Senator
Huey Lewis	Professional singer/songwriter/entertainer
Stephane Matteau	NHL player (played in 1982 Little League World Series)
Mark McGwire	Major League Baseball's single-season home run king
Brent Musburger	Sports broadcaster
Laffit Pincay Jr.	National Horse Racing Hall of Fame jockey
Kurt Russell	Professional actor
Turk Schonert	Former NFL quarterback (played in 1968 Little League World Series)
Michael Smith	NASA shuttle pilot
Steve Spurrier	Heisman Trophy winner; college football coach
Al Trautwig	Sports broadcaster
Pierre Turgeon	NHL player (played in 1982 Little League World Series)

APPENDIX 14. LITTLE LEAGUE NATIONAL AWARDS

GEORGE AND BARBARA BUSH LITTLE LEAGUE PARENTS OF THE YEAR AWARD

The George and Barbara Bush Little League Parents of the Year Award, established in 1980, is presented annually to the parents of a major-league baseball player who were actively involved in their sons' Little League experience. The award is designed to be a symbolic recognition of the millions of mothers and fathers who each year respond to the call of parental duty and help provide a wholesome healthy arena for leadership training for the children of their respective communities. The award is named for former President George Bush and his wife, Barbara, who were volunteers during their children's early years in Texas and who continue to support Little League today.

	Recipients (parents of ...)
1981	Mr. & Mrs. Jack Schmidt (Mike Schmidt)
1982	Mr. & Mrs. Joseph Garvey (Steve Garvey)
1983	Mr. & Mrs. John Hernandez (Keith Hernandez)
1984	Mr. & Mrs. Max Palmer (Jim Palmer)
1985	Mr. & Mrs. James Carter (Gary Carter)
1986	Mr. & Mrs. Charles Murphy (Dale Murphy)
1987	Mr. & Mrs. Lynn Nolan Ryan Sr. (Nolan Ryan)
1988	Mr. & Mrs. Orel Hershiser Jr. (Orel Hershiser)
1989	Mr. & Mrs. Carl Yastrzemski (Carl Yastrzemski)
1990	Mr. & Mrs. Warren Scott (Mike Scott)
1991	Mr. & Mrs. Tony Drabek (Doug Drabek)
1992	Mr. & Mrs Frank Dravecky (Dave Dravecky)
1993	Mr. & Mrs. Frank Thomas (Frank Thomas)
1994	Mr. & Mrs. John Olerud (John Olerud)
1995	Mr. & Mrs. Leonard Greenwell (Mike Greenwell)
1996	Mr. & Mrs. Malcolm Mussina (Mike Mussina)
1997	Mr. & Mrs. Lee Caminiti (Ken Caminiti)
1998	Dr. & Mrs. John McGwire Mark McGwire)
1999	Mr. & Mrs. Norm Charlton (Norm Charlton)
2000	Mr. & Mrs. Charles Jeter (Derek Jeter)

LITTLE LEAGUE VOLUNTEER OF THE YEAR AWARD

The Little League Volunteer of the Year Award Program is recognized as the most important and visible of Little League Baseball's award programs. Designed to provide local leagues with the opportunity to honor a deserving individual with this prestigious distinction, the Little League Volunteer of the Year Award Program was established in 1989 as a vehicle for recognizing the efforts of nearly one million volunteers at the grass-roots level of Little League Baseball. The Little League Volunteer of the Year Award is presented during the week of the Little League World Series.

	Recipients
1989	Ed Janser, Terryville (Conn.) Little League
1990	Robert Beberg, Concord (Calif.) American Little League
1991	Floyd Hull, Federal Little League, Fort Lauderdale, Fla.
1992	George W. Groce, Kernersville (N.C.) Little League
1993	John Barrow, Holbrook (Ariz.) Little League
1994	Bob Crutchely, East Marietta (Ga.) National Little League
1995	Lynne Humphries, Lamar Little League, Richland, Tex.
1996	Marlin Culp, Osolo Little League, Elkhart, Ind.
1997	Wendy Covert, Saugerties (N.Y.) Little League
1998	Sam Fleishman, Fort Myers (Fla.) American Little League
1999	Vic Price, Great Falls (Va.) Little League
2000	Richard Hilton, East Marietta (Ga.) National Little League

LITTLE LEAGUE GOOD SPORT AWARD

The Little League Good Sport Award Program is designed to give local leagues the opportunity to recognize a Little Leaguer who has demonstrated superior qualities of sportsmanship, leadership, a commitment to teamwork, and a desire to excel. Of most importance, the criteria for selection of the Good Sport Award recipient is in no way based on the child's playing ability or personal statistics. This award program was established in 1989 to amplify the importance of Little League Baseball as a leadership training program utilizing baseball and softball as a vehicle for instilling in children these valuable principles. The Little League Good Sport of the Year Award is presented during the week of the Little League World Series.

	Recipients
1991	Rondy Spardella, Aldine Little League, Houston, Tex.
1992	Scott Ford, Walla Walla (Wash.) Little League
1993	Luis Rivera, Coatesville (Pa.) Little League
1994	Joey Pitchford, Pinole (Calif.) Little League
1995	Jose Aguire, Sunrise Little League, Canoga Park, Calif.
1996	Tracy Theriault, Sanford-Springvale Little League, Sanford, Maine
1997	Greg Turner, Northern Little League, San Angelo, Tex.
1998	Madison McDaniel, York County Little League, Yorktown, Va.
1999	Zachary Dwight, Woodland Hills Sunrise Little League, Calabasas, Calif.
2000	Caitlin Neeson, Southwestern Port St. Lucie (Fla.) Little League

LITTLE LEAGUE MOM OF THE YEAR AWARD

The Little League Baseball Mom of the Year Award was established in 1991 as a symbolic form of recognition and tribute to the millions of mothers in communities around the globe who contribute their time and effort to the Little League Baseball program. Each year Little Leaguers compose an essay that explains why their mothers should be the official Little League Mom of the Year. From that group, one Little Leaguer's mother is selected as the official Little League Baseball Mom of the Year. The Mom of the Year Award is presented during the week of the Little League World Series.

	Recipients
1991	Lisa Parker, Anderson (W.Va.) Little League
1992	Monique Evans, Riverside (Calif.) Little League
1993	Theresa Wiseman, Louisville (Ky.) Little League
1994	Donna Dahlen, Hanover (Pa.) Little League
1995	Dee Brankley, Onancock (Va.) Little League
1996	Julie Erskine, Storm Lake (Iowa) Little League
1997	Melissa Teeples, Sparta (Tenn.) American Little League
1998	Sherry Boyd, Panatine (Ill.) North Little League
1999	Sheelah Elliott, North Clark Little League, Yacolt, Wash.
2000	Brenda Hopper, Coventry (R.I.) Little League

LITTLE LEAGUE BASEBALL CHALLENGER AWARD

The Little League Baseball Challenger Award was established in 1998 as a way to recognize the loyal support of the many volunteers in the Challenger Division for physically and/or mentally disabled youngsters, which allows these individuals to experience the fun and fellowship of baseball regardless of limitations.

	Recipients
1998	Ed Beardsley, Edgewood Little League, Bristol, Conn.
1999	Jim Green, Jacksonville, Fla., District 11
2000	Jake Hardison, Virginia Beach, Va., District 8

BILL SHEA DISTINGUISHED LITTLE LEAGUE GRADUATE AWARD

Since 1959, Little League Baseball has developed and implemented a variety of award programs for the purposes of honoring the dedicated commitment of volunteers and recognizing graduates of the program who have attained respected public status. All the Little League Baseball award programs serve as vehicles to amplify the importance of adults who give freely of their time and energy, and as symbols of what a child can achieve by adhering to the values learned on a Little League field.

The Bill Shea Distinguished Little League Graduate Award was established in 1987 to serve a twofold purpose. First, and most important, the award is presented to a former Little Leaguer in major-league baseball who best exemplifies the spirit of Little League Baseball. Consideration for selection includes both the individual's ability and accomplishments and the individual's status as a positive role model.

Second, the award was established in honor of the many contributions made to Little League Baseball by Bill Shea, president of the Little League Foundation. Bill Shea is credited with bringing National League Baseball back to New York in the early 1960s while also working diligently for the advancement of Little League Baseball. Therefore, it is appropriate that a Little League award bearing his name be associated with Major League Baseball.

Recipients

1987	Bobby Valentine, Mickey Lione Little League, Stamford, Conn.
1988	Steve Garvey, Drew Park Little League, Tampa, Fla.
1989	Tom Seaver, Spartan Little League, Fresno, Calif.
1990	Jim Palmer, Beverly Hills (Calif.) Little League
1991	Dave Dravecky, South Youngstown Optimist Little League, Boardman, Ohio
1992	Steve Palermo, Oxford (Mass.) Little League
1993	Gary Carter, West Fullerton (Calif.) Little League
1994	Len Coleman, Montclair (N.J.) Little League
1995	Rick Monday, Sunset Little League, Santa Monica, Calif.
1996	No award
1997	Ken Griffey Sr., Donora (Pa.) Little League
1998	Don Sutton, Cantonment (Fla.) Little League
1999	Robin Yount, Woodland Hills (Calif.) Sunrise Little League
2000	George Brett, El Segundo (Calif.) American Little League

Index

Page numbers in *italics* refer to captions.

Abbott, Spence, 19
ABC television, *Wide World of Sports*, *16*, *124*, 124–25, 139
Abdul-Jabbar, Kareem, 180, *181*
accidents. *See* safety
Adams, Daniel Lucius, 6
Adkins, Monya Lee, 18
adult volunteers. *See* volunteers
African Americans
    all-black teams, 79, 166, *166*
    integrated teams, 78
Allen, Mel, 125
aluminum bats, 10, *110*, 111
American Association, 11
American Association for Health, Physical Education, and Recreation, 61
American Indian ball games, 4, 5, *5*
Americanism, promotion of, 64
American League, 11
American Legion baseball, 144, 145
Anderson Little League (Gary, Indiana), 166, *166*
Anti Spit-Tobacco Education Program, 193
Apalachee Indians, 5
ASAP (A Safety Awareness Program), 123, 193
Asia. *See* Japan; Pacific Region; Philippines; Taiwan
autographs, 50, *138*

Babcock, Barry, 123
Babe Ruth League, Inc., 120, 121, 122
Bad Kissengen Army Base team, 117
Bair, Bill, *30*, 46
Baker, Frank, 135
Baldwin, Guy, 58
Baldwin, Peg, 58, 59
Ball, Lucille, *132*
balls
    Little League, 18, 25, 56–57
    in sandlot baseball, 9

soft, 123
Barber, Red, 125
Barbieri, Jim, 71, *71*
Barr, James P., 186–87
baseball. *See also* major league baseball
    boys' teams, 8–11, 12–13
    criticism of organized boys' leagues, 61
    female players, 143–45
    first organized game, 4–7, 145
    Hall of Fame, 2, 16, 135
    history, 1–9
    in Japan, 65
    minor league, 11, 18, 19, 96
    popularized by military, 7, 62, 65, 136–38
    professional, 8, 11–12, 13
    rules, 6, 8
    school teams, 12
baseball fields. *See also* Carl E. Stotz Field; Lamade Stadium
    Bowman Field, 18, 19, *19*, 52, 96
    Demorest Field, 35–36, *36*, 37, *44*
    dimensions, 22
    lighting, 111
    Park Point (first Little League), 28, 35
    in parks, 13
    pitching distance increase, 109
bases, 29, *30*
bats
    aluminum, 10, *110*, 111
    with Little League name, *55*, 56–57
    in sandlot baseball, 9
    wood, *110*
Beardsley, Dave, 197–98, *198*
Beardsley, Ed, 197–98
Bebble, Anabelle, 27, 40
Bebble, Bert, *27*, 27–28, 40
Bebble, Eloise, 40
Bebble, George, 27–28, *27*, 34, 40, 41, 47
Bell, Derek, 176, *176*, *color photo section*
Bellandi, Al, 19
Belmont Heights Little League, Tampa, Florida, 176, *176*, 177, *color photo section*

Bench, Johnny, 125, 135
Berlin, West Germany, team, 127
Bernardi, Mike, 95, 132, 134–35, 168
Berndt, Irving "Bud," 58, *58*
Berra, Yogi, 104
Best, Ray, 22, *30*
Big League Baseball, 120, 173, 175
Big League Softball, 159
Bitburg Air Force Base (Germany) team, 168
Black Sox Scandal, 13
Blanford, Indiana, 144
Blattner, Buddy, 124
board of arbitration, 42
board of directors, Little League
    after incorporation, 69–70
    field representatives, 85, 88, 89
    legal battle with Stotz, 73–77, 80–85
    members, 40, 59, 84
    settlement with Stotz, 83, 85
Boggs, Wade, 176
Bosnia-Herzegovina, 195, *195*
Bowman Field, 18, 19, *19*, 52, 96
Bradley, Bill, 48, 84, *84*
Brandt, E. H., 58
Brett, George, 135, 184
Brewster, Dan, 50
Brooklyn Center, Minnesota, team, *151*
Brown, Louie, 34
Brown, Max M., 106
Brown, Robin C., 5
Brownell, Herbert, Jr., 64
Brown Memorial Park. *See also* Carl E. Stotz Field
    Bowman Field, 18, 19, *19*, 52, 96
    ownership, 106
Brucker, Victoria, *150*
Bunning, Jim, 19
burglars, 95
Burroughs, Sean, *color photo section*
Bush, Alvin R., 115, 150
Bush, George H. W., 84, 130
Bush, George W., 84, 126

Credits

Photographs courtesy of Little League Baseball, Incorporated: pages xii, xiv, xv, xvii, xviii, 2 (left), 5, 6, 7, 12, 14, 16, 17, 20 (left), 19 (right), 21, 23, 28, 29 (top left, top right & bottom right), 32, 34, 40, 42, 43, 45, 46 (right), 48, 50, 53, 54, 55, 56, 57, 58, 59, 60, 61, 63, 64, 66, 69, 70, 71, 78, 79, 81, 84, 86, 88, 89, 93, 94, 96, 97, 98, 99, 100, 101, 102, 104, 107, 108, 110, 111, 112, 113, 114, 115, 116, 117, 119, 121, 124, 125, 126, 128, 129, 130, 131, 132, 134, 135, 136, 137, 138, 139, 140, 142, 147, 149, 150, 151, 152, 153, 155 (right), 157, 158, 159, 160, 163, 165, 166, 167, 168, 169, 170, 171, 172, 176, 177, 178, 179, 181, 182, 184, 186 (bottom), 188, 189, 190, 191, 192, 193, 195, 196, 198, 200, and all color section photos.

Photographs courtesy of Karen Stotz Myers, from the Carl E. Stotz Collection: pages 18, 25, 27, 29 (bottom left), 30, 36, 37, 38, 43, 44, 46 (left), 51, 62, 68, 72, 186 (top), 187.

Photograph of Abner Doubleday on page 3 is courtesy of mrbaseball.com and Alexander Cartwright IV.

Photographs of *Saturday Evening Post* covers on pages 2 and 9 are courtesy of the *Saturday Evening Post.*

Photograph of 1941 Williamsport Grays on page 19 (left) is from the *Grit* and is courtesy of the *Williamsport Sun-Gazette.*

Photographs courtesy of the *Williamsport Sun-Gazette*: 19, 20 (right), and 174.

Photograph courtesy of the Putsee Vannucci Collection, Lycoming County Historical Society: page 19.

Photograph of Margaret Gisolo on page 144 is courtesy of Margaret Gisolo.

Photograph of Maria Pepe on page 146 is courtesy of Maria Pepe.

Photo of Kathryn Massar on page 155 is courtesy of Kathryn Massar.

Photograph courtesy of Little League Baseball, Incorporated, and Larson Design Group of Williamsport, Pennsylvania: page 194.